Master Spy

Bob picked up the phone. His father's voice blasted loud and clear into his ear. He skipped the pleasantries, just as he always did.

"What I want to know—why are you studying Russian?"

"Someday I'm going to catch Soviet spies."

"Horseshit. I sent you to college to become a doctor."

"Dad, what would you say if I told you I'd really like to be a cop? A truly high level cop like you."

"Don't even think about it."

———————

"Those looking for a brisk, page-turning dramatization of Hanssen's bizarre life and times will be amply rewarded . . . Schiller's book is likely to be as close as we'll ever get to the mind of the most heinous spy in FBI history."

P

ALSO BY LAWRENCE SCHILLER

American Tragedy
Perfect Murder, Perfect Town

IN COLLABORATION

LSD
by Richard Alpert, Ph.D., Sidney Cohen, M.D.,
and Lawrence Schiller

Ladies and Gentlemen, Lenny Bruce
by Albert Goldman from the
Journalism of Lawrence Schiller

LAWRENCE SCHILLER

MASTER SPY

The Life of Robert P. Hanssen

BASED UPON AN INVESTIGATION BY
NORMAN MAILER
AND
LAWRENCE SCHILLER
(Published in hardcover as *Into the Mirror*)

HarperTorch
An Imprint of HarperCollinsPublishers

This book was published in hardcover as *Into the Mirror* by HarperCollins.

Quotations from interviews by Lawrence Schiller and Norman Mailer are copyright © 2001 and 2002 by KLS Communications, Inc. Grateful acknowledgment is made to the following for permission to reprint previously published material and television broadcasts: ABC: Brief excerpt from ABC News on February 20, 2001. Used by permission of ABC News; Associated Press: Excerpt from March 4, 2001, copyright © 2001 by the Associated Press; printed by permission of The Associated Press; The *Washington Post:* Excerpt from March 3, 2001, copyright © 2001 by The *Washington Post; Time:* Excerpt from "The FBI Spy," Time, March 5, 2001 © 2001 Time Inc., reprinted by permission.

HARPERTORCH
An Imprint of HarperCollins*Publishers*
10 East 53rd Street
New York, New York 10022-5299

First HarperTorch paperback printing: November 2002
First HarperCollins hardcover printing: May 2002

HarperCollins ®, HarperTorch™, and ✦™ are trademarks of Harper-Collins Publishers Inc.

Printed in the United States of America

Visit HarperTorch on the World Wide Web at www.harpercollins.com

10 9 8 7 6 5 4 3 2 1

To KATHY AMERMAN,
my friend and wife,

And to my mother, JEAN,
for the loving years she's given all of her family.

———————————

Contents

Author's Note

The research for this narrative, which attempts to re-create the life of Robert Hanssen, began in March 2001, when I asked Norman Mailer to write a screenplay for a four-hour miniseries for CBS Television. I would produce and direct the motion picture, as I had done with *The Executioner's Song* and *American Tragedy,* for which Mailer also wrote the screenplays.

During the following nine months, Mailer and I interviewed members of Bonnie and Robert Hanssen's immediate family, his closest friends, past and present Special Agents of the FBI, former agents and officials of the KGB and SVR (organs of the Soviet Union and Russian governments), diplomats of the Soviet Union, past and present members of the Catholic Church and of Opus Dei, the personal Prelature of the Church, and others, who have asked not to be credited in this work. Those whom we spoke to gave us a window into Robert Hanssen's mind. His own writings over the years also provided a view, startling at times, particularly in his semipornographic writings.

I traveled to Germany and spent an entire day with Jack Hoschouer, who walked me through his long relationship with Robert Hanssen and his family, and corroborated what we had been told by family members and others. Later, Mailer met with Hoschouer in London. In Moscow, Viktor Cherkashin (Robert Hanssen's first Soviet handler) and Leonid Sherbashin (KGB, Moscow Center) gave us their first interviews on Hanssen and provided a unique perspective, as did one of several psychiatrists who saw Hanssen after his arrest.

Robert Hanssen and his wife, Bonnie, were not interviewed for this work because of a plea-bargain agreement they made with the Justice Department of the United States, which prohibited contacts with the media.

While Mailer was finishing the first draft of the screenplay in November 2001, I decided to write this book, using his draft as the foundation for my work, adding to it additional information from our interviews and from historical documents.

As a result, the work is novelistic in style. And much of its dialogue is derivative of Mailer's screenplay. In some ways, it resembles Mailer's *The Executioner's Song* and my *American Tragedy,* which I wrote with James Willworth.

My intention was not to document every moment or deed of Hanssen's life; rather, it was to build a psychological portrait of him from those events that reveal the complexities of the man and his unique character. It has been a search for the essence of his emotional and spiritual life—those elements of existence that drove him into his acts of betrayal.

His life, and his mind—by any degree—are so far removed from the ordinary that it is safe to say this story is unique, even extraordinary, in the range of its contradictions.

LAWRENCE SCHILLER
February 20, 2002

Introduction

On Monday, February 19, 2001, the day after the arrest of
Special Agent Robert Philip Hanssen, a shock, comparable in its intensity to the horror that would permeate all of
America on the morning of September 11, passed throughout the Federal Bureau of Investigation. Some indication
of the personal and public disarray inside the Bureau comes
through in the first news stories and press conferences:

ABC NEWS

FEBRUARY 20, 2001

To Russian intelligence, he was allegedly known as "Ramon," a longtime informant on U.S. secrets. But to resi-
dents in his quiet neighborhood in Vienna, Virginia, Robert
Hanssen, 56, was just "Bob," devout Christian and father
of six who could be seen at church every Sunday. For more
than 15 years, Hanssen allegedly spied for the Soviet Union
and Russia, passing on classified information for cash and
jewels. FBI officials say Hanssen was arrested Sunday night
after he deposited a package containing classified information in a park near his neighborhood. Overnight, he went
from being a low-key family man to only the third FBI
agent ever accused of spying.

His neighbors were stunned.

"It's a horrible thing," said Nancy Cullen, who said she has known the Hanssens for 10 years. "He just seemed like a regular person. Every Sunday—shuffling all those kids into the van, off to Mass."

Described as a father of six children and a devout Christian who belonged to a very conservative Catholic organization called Opus Dei—"Work of God"—he attended the same church as FBI director Louis Freeh.

FBI PRESS CONFERENCE

FEBRUARY 20, 2001

Following is the transcript of a news conference held by FBI director Louis Freeh regarding charges against FBI agent Robert Philip Hanssen.

DIRECTOR FREEH: Good afternoon, ladies and gentlemen. I'm Louis Freeh, the FBI director . . . Sunday night, as you heard, the FBI arrested Robert Philip Hanssen, who was charged with committing espionage.

Hanssen is a Special Agent of the FBI with a long career in counterintelligence.

The investigation that led to these charges is the direct result of the long-standing FBI-CIA efforts, ongoing since the Aldrich Ames case, to identify additional foreign penetrations of the United States intelligence community.

Since becoming director, over 7 1/2 years ago, I've ministered the FBI oath of office to over 4,600 Special Agents at the FBI. Each one of them—and I share with them the pride and sanctity of the words that they repeat—swear to support and defend the Constitution of the United States against all enemies, foreign and domestic, and to bear true faith and allegiance to the same.

Regrettably, I stand here today both saddened and outraged. The FBI agent who raised his hand and spoke those words over 25 years ago has been charged today with violating that oath in the most egregious and reprehensible manner possible. The FBI entrusted him with some of its most sensitive matter, and the U.S. government relied upon him for his service and integrity.

He has, as charged, abused and betrayed that trust. The crimes alleged are an affront not only to his fellow FBI employees, but also to the American people, not to mention the pain and suffering he has brought upon his family.

I take solace and satisfaction, however, that the FBI succeeded in this investigation with the help of all the people and entities that I've mentioned, and that, as an agency, we've lived up to our responsibility, no matter how painful that may be.

I'll take your questions now . . .

QUESTION: In all due respect, how can you call this a counterintelligence success when you had a spy working inside the FBI for over 15 years without being detected?

FREEH: . . . As an operation and as an investigation, it is an immense success. To conduct this investigation secretly, clandestinely, without any leaks and to do it to the point that we could catch, red-handed, an experienced intelligence officer laying down classified documents for his handlers . . . I think by any expert would be judged a huge success.

That does not, of course, answer the question as to why someone for 15 years can successfully operate. I've indicated a couple of the reasons in the documents why we think he was successful. As I said, the Russians, until they heard the morning reports, did not know his name, did not know where he worked. He is very, very carefully, throughout the affidavit, obsessed with his security. And he was very, very successful in masking and protecting his communications and his activities.

For 20 years, St. Catherine of Siena Catholic Church has attracted some of the area's most influential people to a secluded sanctuary in a grove of evergreen trees on Springvale Road in Great Falls. Doctors, lawyers, bureaucrats, technology executives, politicians, artists and intelligence operatives have found solace and unity in traditional Masses and in the deep-seated piety of the church's 4,000 members. They also have enjoyed the anonymity of worshiping in a quiet parish 20 miles from downtown Washington.

Or so it was until last week, when parishioner and FBI Special Agent Robert P. Hanssen was arrested on espionage charges. Suddenly, the church came under public scrutiny, and the names of its most famous members became widely known.

Supreme Court Justice Antonin Scalia and his wife attend regularly, as do Sen. Rick Santorum (R-PA.) and FBI Director Louis J. Freeh and their families . . .

The revelation about Hanssen has been an embarrassment for some of St. Catherine's parishioners. But foremost, it's a sad moment for the church, they say. Julian Heron, a parishioner who found a spiritual home on his first visit to the church, began crying when asked what effect Hanssen's arrest has had on the parish. He said that he didn't know Hanssen, but that hearing about the charges against him was an emotional blow, almost like the death of a family member.

"It's a tragedy for all of us," he said . . .

ASSOCIATED PRESS

MARCH 4, 2001

There has never been an espionage case quite like that of Bob Hanssen. From his first alleged contact with the KGB in 1985 until his arrest last week, Moscow's spy handlers, amazingly, never knew who he was. Despite their entreaties, Hanssen refused to meet with any of them, insisting on leaving the computer disks and documents in dead drops near his modest home in suburban northern Virginia, then collecting money and requests for new information after the men from Moscow had cleared out. But the information Hanssen is said to have provided Moscow was apparently so fabulous that the KGB and the SVR agreed to his terms. Not that they were thrilled about it. "I'll tell you this," says a senior official. "There was a lot of vodka spilled in Moscow trying to figure out who it was." And as gratifying as it must have been for Moscow's spymasters to have moles in both the CIA and the FBI, in the trapdoor world of smoke and mirrors, where paranoia is perhaps the paramount virtue, it also had to make them a little crazy. "It probably looked like a windfall," says Harry "Skip" Brandon, a retired FBI counterintelligence agent. "But they must have been turning themselves inside out trying to figure out if this was too good to be true." . . .

Some in the FBI, citing Hanssen's sallow complexion, dour mien, and somber black suits, called him "Dr. Death" and "The Mortician." That may have been just ribbing, commonplace in a macho culture like the FBI. But there may have been something else to it. "He was not a cigar-chomping, door-kicking FBI agent," said a former FBI official. In an agency where many leadership positions involve kicking down doors and placing agents in harm's way, such a deficiency could be a major career stopper . . .

TIME MAGAZINE

MARCH 3, 2001

It is possible, from the 100-page affidavit released by the FBI and interviews with his friends and colleagues, to begin to piece together clues to the puzzle, to gain the first insights into the twisted mind of a spy. He is described by those who knew him—who readily acknowledge that he was hard to truly know—as a brooding, controlling figure, fascinated by secrecy and obsessed by purity. He was, for much of his 56 years, a seeker of black-and-white certainty and higher truth who nonetheless plunged into the gray, morally compromised world of espionage.

Hanssen's own explanation to his Moscow handlers for his secret life, laid out in the bureau affidavit, was at once cryptic and grandiose: "I am either insanely brave or quite insane. I'd answer neither. I'd say, insanely loyal. Take your pick. There is insanity in all the answers."

MASTER
SPY

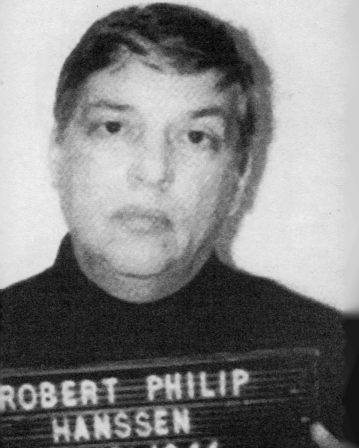
ROBERT PHILIP
HANSSEN
B 04-18-1944
A-WF-220648
BI WFO 02 18 01

PART ONE

Warriors and Wizards

1

1944–1950

Shortly after the arrest, Vivian Hanssen, the spy's mother, now eighty-eight years old, was interviewed in Venice, Florida, where she had been living for nearly thirty years.

"He has always been very honest and upright," she said. There was a pause that grew uncomfortably long before she added: "Bob's father, however, was strict with him. I was easy. But I suppose most families are like that."

From the date of her son's arrest, February 18, 2001, it is fifty-seven years back to 1944, when Robert was born. The father and mother lived at the time in a modest house that they owned, on a street with tall elms, in Norwood, near the northwestern corner of Chicago, and this family of three—mother, father, and son—was still living there in 1950, when Robert turned six. He was tall for his age, a thin, gangling boy, terribly nearsighted and forced to wear thick-rimmed glasses with heavy lenses.

On the occasion of this birthday, his mother was giving him a party at home. Robert sat alone while the other children, their mothers in the background, ran around the living room. Vivian, a pretty woman, who also had to wear eyeglasses, did her best to smile at everyone while encouraging Bob to get out of his chair.

A paper donkey was pinned to a corkboard on the wall, and it had a lot of tails stuck to it.

As Vivian tried to entice her son back into the game, Howard Hanssen, Bob's father, walked in. He was a well-built, good-looking man, and was dressed in his Chicago police sergeant's uniform—perfect, except for a big red lipstick smear on the collar of his shirt. With his gun on his hip and his way of looking at a person with narrowed eyes, as though he could read every bad thought in their heads, he terrified the kids. They stopped playing and froze. Seeing the paper donkey on the wall, Hanssen walked over, touched the tail pinned to its rear, and patted it.

"Well," he laughed. "One of you kids actually got it in the right place. Who was the winner? Was it you, Bob?"

The boy looked down and shook his head. Vivian slipped over behind him and put her hand on his shoulder.

"Well then, Bob. Where did you put the tail?" asked the father.

Bob knew what was coming. One of the kids would blurt it out. "There," the kid said, pointing. The others all giggled.

"Right in the kisser, eh?" said Howard. He turned to his son. "Tell you what, Bob. I guess you don't know doo-doo from spit!"

All the kids roared with laughter. Tears came into Bob's eyes, and into his mother's as well. Reflexively, Vivian lifted her hand from Bob's shoulder.

Howard left the room without another word to his son. Perhaps he was going to change his shirt. It smelled of perfume.

Later, after the party was over, Howard brought Bob back into the room where the paper donkey was still tacked to the wall.

"When you get into a contest," the father said, "win! That's it. Don't coast on mother-love, boy. There's a

4

tough, ugly, double-crossing world outside, and the only way to beat it is to win." He spoke as if Bob were on the verge of manhood.

"Yes, sir," Bob succeeded in saying without bursting into tears.

"Yes, sir, my eye! Say it like you mean what you say."

"Yes, sir," Bob repeated, but he couldn't hold it in. He started to sob.

Howard reached out for the blindfold that had been tossed aside after the pin-the-tail game was over and covered Bob's eyes with it. He lifted the boy, flipped him upside down, and grabbed him by the ankles before his head hit the ground. Then he began to whirl him around by his feet.

"You dizzy?" he asked, panting a little with the effort.

"Yes, sir," Bob managed to squeak out.

"All right." Howard set him on his feet and tightened the blindfold. "Now, go pin the tail."

When the boy staggered forward, he missed the donkey entirely. He could feel it. His pin had hit the wall, not even the cork. In a fright, the six-year-old took his blindfold off and began to tremble.

Howard was in a rage. "You don't learn, do you?" He picked up the boy by the ankles again and started whirling him around and around and around.

Robert was screaming. "Daddy, stop it! Please stop it! Please stop it!"

Vivian stood in the next room, bent over the kitchen sink. She was weeping, silently.

The more Robert screamed, the faster Howard whirled him around. "I'll keep on doing this until you stop that sniveling!"

The boy made an effort to stop, but it was weak, and the spinning went on until Howard's rage gave way to shortness of breath. Winded, Howard dropped his kid down on the living-room rug, upon which the boy immediately threw up. Howard's reaction was a reflex—it was as if some cheap punk he had just brought into the station was puking in the interrogation room. He put Robert's face into the vomit and then had to fight his impulse to scrub the boy's head back and forth. At that point, he stopped. He pulled the boy up to a standing position and forced his voice to be calm.

"I did this," said Howard, "because I want you to know how bad it feels when you lose. This is how it feels, Robert. Got it?"

Vivian came in timidly from the kitchen.

She was trembling. "You can't do what you're doing to the boy," she managed to say. "He's delicate." Her voice pinched off when she saw the look in her husband's eye, but she made herself speak up again. "Why do you have to be so hard on him? He's just a little boy."

"That's a question I can answer. It's because I don't want him to wind up like you."

"Yes, you want him to be like you and come home with lipstick on his shirt." She squeezed back a few tears before she began crying in earnest. Through her sobs, she tried to say, "You have to stop terrorizing that boy! He's all we've got!"

"Bless me," Howard said. "I'm married to the Chicago waterworks."

Vivian ran out of the room.

Howard turned to the boy. "Get a towel and clean up your puke."

Robert obeyed. While he wiped the rug, his father picked up the phone and began to talk.

"Put me down for a dime on Furlong Queen in the seventh," he said. "Yeah, I know I owe you two, but you'll get it by Friday." He laughed into the receiver.

Vivian crept back into the room and went over to Howard. She spoke softly so that Robert wouldn't hear.

"Respect what we have in him," she said to her husband. "He's so bright. Just don't ask everything of him. He's not as strong as you, and he never will be."

6

"Maybe, maybe not," Howard said. "But you tell me—what is the good of being a brilliant four-eyed cream puff?"

He walked out of the room, leaving Vivian remembering how it had been when they were first married and whether she had ever been in love with him. He had enjoyed going to the racetrack then, and she had liked going with him. When they were able to afford it on his cop's pay, they would travel to new and different tracks, even once to Canada. Those were the good times—fifteen years ago and more. She had really conceived Bob a little too late. By the time he arrived it was 1944, and they had already been childless for ten years, with Howard away in the service during the war. Like other soldiers, he had formed new habits. Maybe he'd been shy with women when they started, but now it was obvious he had a lot of confidence in that area—and that he'd lost respect for his wife.

Vivian must have been standing stock-still for more than a minute before she realized that her mother-in-law was in the room and had overheard her and Howard talking. Then she came up to Vivian and said with her special mean smile, "There's no use trying to stand up to my son. You're not strong enough."

"Don't tell me how to live with Howard when you don't even speak to your own husband."

"He's my *ex*-husband, Vivian. Getting divorced from that man was the happiest day of my life." She gave her daughter-in-law a look that said her next happiest day would be when Howard finally got rid of Vivian.

Meanwhile, Bob had slipped upstairs to his room. It was small, but it had Vivian's touch—neat, a nice color scheme. The boy stood in front of the washbasin and, with a wet cloth, wiped the vomit from his face and shirt. As he looked into the mirror, he began to sob and his face contorted. *"Stop crying!"* he ordered his image. *"Suck it up!"*

By supreme effort, he stopped. Now a new look came into his face. He had seen it before, when he studied himself closely in the mirror, without his glasses, his nose nearly touching the glass. He liked to call it the *bad* look. It showed up only when he wished he could kill his father. Then he did not feel weak. He felt stronger than anyone alive. But the feeling wasn't real. He could get it only by looking into the mirror.

At dinner that night, Howard, his mother, Vivian, and Bob sat at the table, eating in silence. As soon as Howard finished, he stood up from the table, put on his jacket, and left the house without a word. Bob got up then and went down to the basement to watch his grandfather turn the knobs on his shortwave radio. The grandfather lived in the basement while his ex-wife lived in the attic. An unusual arrangement, but it was 1950 and there was not enough money to support three separate households, no matter how unhappy they all were.

"Come look, Bob," said his grandfather. "I got a new gizmo for my radio this morning."

2

1954–1959

It went on like that, year after year. The taller Bob grew, the more awkward he became. By the time he was ten, he was spending a lot of hours in the basement with his grandfather working on the shortwave radio equipment.

"Bob, I'm proud of you," his grandfather told him on his birthday. "You're one bright kid. How many your age can say they already have their own radio call letters?"

"I love it, Grandpa. I feel like I can talk to strange planets."

"One day you will, Robert. You will."

"And I don't even have to go out of the house!"

Bob loved radio. He loved all machines, especially those that worked on electricity.

There was a look he had seen in the mirror when he wanted to kill his father. It was as pure as an electric shock. But things did not always go so badly with Howard these days. Sometimes Bob even had the secret thought that he loved his father more than he loved his mother.

Once, on one of those good days, Bob and Howard were standing on the street in front of a diner, looking up at the building above. It was one of the locations where the Chicago Police Department had its offices.

"Is that where you do the interrogations, Dad?"

9

"The third window on the left, eighth floor. Take a good look! If a guy we're interrogating tries to get stubborn on us, we sometimes have to use what we call *serious measures*."

"What are those, Dad?"

"Oh," said Howard casually, "that particular tactic we only do at night. Douse the lights, open the window, grab the guy by the ankles, and hang him out until he decides to talk."

"You do that?" Bob was so excited he thought he would wet his pants.

"It is one sure way to get a stubborn son of a bitch to tell the truth."

"Dad, do you mean it? Does that always work?"

Howard pointed down at the ground with two fingers. "Once in a while, we have an unfortunate accident. *Splat!*"

Bob was shocked and he was scared—had to pee for real now—but he also thought it was funny. *Splat!* Like the guy was a water balloon. He giggled.

"We say the suspect committed suicide." Howard roared with laughter. At the look of utter confidence on his father's face, Bob nodded heartily. He started laughing, too. He had to force himself to do it, but still—he knew it would make his father happy.

Howard steered him by the shoulder into the diner. Ordering coffee for himself and milk for the boy, he began to lay it out. Bob was intelligent enough, he had decided, to learn a few things early.

"Here's how it is," he said. "When I knew a man was guilty, I considered it an insult to my dignity if I didn't get a confession." At that moment, Howard sure looked full of dignity to Bob. His father's face was strong, like pictures he had seen in books of Vikings and of Civil War soldiers.

"You're a warrior, Dad," he said.

10

Howard nodded. He was actually enjoying the kid.

"Two kinds of people run the world, Robert—warriors and wizards." He nodded solemnly. "Warriors and wizards."

"I'm going to be a warrior," Bob said.

"That's the way to talk."

All the same, it was not often good between them. Sometimes it seemed as if Howard lived only to criticize. He was superb at it. Real mean. Obsessive when it came to his son. Maybe it reached its peak on the night Bob, at fourteen, gave a year-end speech to his school, something he had written himself.

"Democracy," he declared, standing at the podium, peering at the crowd through his glasses, "was an earth-shaking idea when it came along. Until that time, ordinary people didn't believe they could run a country by themselves. But democracy came along and said, 'Human beings are more good than bad. If people are able to express themselves, if there is liberty for all, then good will come out of things in society more often than bad.' That happened to be a very exciting idea for its time, and look at all we have done because it worked. Now we have a great democracy."

The audience gave loud applause. Everyone was very impressed. Her boy had the happiest smile that Vivian had ever seen on his face. He was in a great mood—until he realized that his father wasn't saying much. Once they got home, they just sat around in the living room, but it was so silent that Bob finally blurted out, "People came up and said it was the best speech they'd ever heard."

Vivian smiled slightly.

Howard sat there frowning.

"It was okay," he finally grunted. "Well presented. Well received."

"Was there anything wrong with it, sir?"

Howard glared at him. "Are you up to hearing what I have to say?"

"Yes, sir," Bob said.

"It was too sentimental."

Vivian opened her mouth to speak, then silenced herself.

Howard went on: "Democracy isn't what does it, kid. Society gets run from the top—get that straight. The way you talk, you could end up a wizard, hanging out with all the other wizards. That's what's happening to the country now. Every four-eyed twerp is getting to be a wizard."

Bob's hand involuntarily went up to his Coke-bottle glasses.

Howard still had his point to make. He looked scathingly at Robert's thin arms and said, "Overdevelopment of the mind is as sickening as underdevelopment of the body."

No, Howard was never satisfied. One night, a year later, Bob was in the basement, hanging out with his grandfather. There was a glass of whiskey in Grandpa's hand and a half-empty pint bottle sitting next to the radio. It was sad, Bob knew. Everyone—Vivian, Howard, and his grandmother—all agreed. His grandfather loved his whiskey neat, but he was going to die of it one of these days.

"I don't understand," Bob said, as his grandpa poured another half inch into the glass. "In the citywide science contest, I came in second. I was second in the whole *city*. Dad still complained. And then I was the valedictorian. Anybody can get up and beat their gums, Grandpa, but I gave a great speech. Everybody said so. Except him."

"Howard's as mean as cat piss," said Howard's father. "But you know . . . I was pretty hard on him when he was a boy. I always liked his older brother more. And, you know, that one turned out to be a drunk just like his

12

old man. You can blame some of Howard on this guy right here," he said, tapping his chest.

"But you're never mean to me," Bob said.

Grandpa gave an apologetic smile. "Sometimes, guys acquire a little wisdom before they croak."

Soon after, Grandpa fell asleep with the whiskey glass in his hand. The bottle was empty. Robert was used to that. He just curled up in his usual chair and read a James Bond paperback. He knew his grandfather didn't have long to live, and he wanted to be near him.

In fact, when Grandpa did pass away not long after, Bob took over the basement. He would study there or just sit by himself, feeling his grandfather's presence, which was still very strong.

A picture of him hung on the wall over the desk. At times Bob would talk to the picture.

"You have no idea how I miss you," he'd say. Then he would put down his textbook, stand up, stretch, and, after a while, do what he usually came here to do—that is, reach up to a small shelf in the joists and take out a box. It was packed with copies of *Playboy* magazine. Full of anticipation, he'd bring one into the tiny cellar bathroom and lock the door. When he was done, he would study his face in the mirror, the way he used to when he was a small boy. He then took out a notebook: *Fourth time today,* he wrote. *Hand-Sin. Hanssen is full of Hand-Sin. He is handsome and he is full of Hand-Sin.*

3

1959–1962

Upstairs, life didn't get better between Bob and his father. If it wasn't one thing, it was another. One time, a few friends Bob knew from high school happened to be with him in the living room as Howard came in from work. He often acted meaner when he was wearing his uniform. He cut right into the middle of their conversation. By the expression on his face, it was obvious that he didn't think much of Bob's friends.

"You boys play sports?" he asked.

"I play chess," one of them offered.

Howard made a small sound of derision. "Interested in girls yet?" he went on.

"Sure," the second boy said.

Unfortunately, the first one had to add, "We're interested in girls, Sergeant Hanssen, but I guess none of us go steady."

"Yeah? Ever have a date?"

"Not really, I guess."

Howard nodded, as if this were a conclusive piece of evidence. "Maybe Robert is a poor influence on you," he said.

Well, that was a little too much. The second teen, who was a little braver, said, "You're sort of an offbeat father, Sergeant Hanssen."

"I'm as regular as they come," Howard replied.

14

Bob looked at his friend who had dared to speak back to his father and saw him in a new light. Jack Hoschouer was his name. Bob had a feeling that in time to come the two of them could really get together.

He was right. He and Jack really got on. Bob felt as if this was the first friend he had ever truly liked to be around. And Jack seemed to feel the same way. They tried to sit together in every new class, and in chemistry they worked at the same lab table. They weren't exactly touchdown twins, but they did look a little alike, with both of them wearing very heavy eyeglasses. And their teamwork was good. Hoschouer usually did the pouring from one test tube into another while Hanssen made notes on a piece of paper on a clipboard. When a calculation was necessary, Bob would lay his clipboard down in order to get the answer on a slide rule. He was the only one in the class who used the instrument.

The teacher took notice and couldn't keep himself from saying, "I see old Slipstick Hanssen is working away."

The class laughed, but Bob kept going with his calculations as if nothing had been said. People did laugh at him sometimes, though he didn't know why. For what? His height? His glasses? Once the laughter quieted down, Hoschouer nudged Bob as if to say, *Forget them. Look at what I brought,* and offered him a peek at a new *Playboy* he had in his bookbag.

The girl on the cover was a typical Bunny: juicy breasts, rounded hips, and a smile on her face that said, *I'd like to meet you.* Bob almost had an orgasm looking at her, right in chemistry class! He didn't know if he was oversexed, but he certainly couldn't stop thinking about it, and when Jack grinned and whispered, "Wouldn't you like to slip your stick into her?" Bob did have an orgasm. It was involuntary, and he hated it, because he had to hide all the signs. Jack laughed, but experimentally, as if to see how Bob was reacting to the magazine. Bob pretended to be disapproving. It was the best way he knew to hide his feelings.

"Oh, come on," Bob said. "That's low-level stuff."

"Don't you think she's beautiful?"

"I don't think she should be posing like that."

"What about all the pictures you've shown me?"

"At least I didn't do it in school," Bob murmured, as if that should put an end to the argument.

In his senior year at Taft High School, Bob went to take a driving test for his license. While he waited inside his father's car, the driving examiner stood outside talking to Howard, who was wearing his new police lieutenant's uniform.

"Look, Mac," Howard said to the man. "I've got a disciplinary problem with my boy. He thinks he's a speed king."

It was true. Howard had let him drive once and saw something in Robert he had never seen before. The boy showed a wild streak behind the wheel. "Point is, don't let him pass the test."

As the men shook hands, Howard pressed a ten into the examiner's palm.

"I know what you mean, Lieutenant," the man said. "I have a problem with my boy, too."

Robert backed the car into the parking slot for the last part of the test. Did it perfectly.

The examiner put an X on the exam sheet. "Sorry, kiddo, you flunked."

Robert was surprised. "Why? I did everything you asked."

"Close, but no cigar."

On the way home, Howard let Bob have it. "This is the third time you flunked. I bet you were going too fast again."

"No, sir. I honestly don't think so." He was perplexed.

16

"Robert, you can only make progress by digesting your defeats."

"Yes, sir."

"Why did he flunk you?"

"I don't know, Dad—I just don't know." Bob shook his head. He looked about ready to cry.

"Looks like you have a hell of a lot of digesting to do." Howard couldn't help it. Once he got going, he couldn't put on the brakes. Being mean gave him a glow.

So it was off to college without a driver's license. Bob had been accepted at Knox, a fine small college about a hundred miles from Chicago, but when he got there, he was in a daze. He kept thinking of graduation at Taft. What a happy day it had been. Here at Knox, he felt a little out of it and didn't have any friends. But at Taft, after all the ceremonies were over, he and Jack Hoschouer had stood off to the side feeling like adults. The caps and gowns were certainly good for providing that feeling. Suddenly they realized they were going to have to say good-bye.

"I wish I had applied to Saint Olaf College, like you," Bob said. He realized too late that it was true. How terrific it would be to get to Minnesota and be that far away from home. Jack already had a job lined up there for this summer.

Jack only said, "Well, I'll be back next summer."

"It's just hit me," Bob said. "It's going to be ten months until we see each other."

"Yeah, I'll miss you," Jack said, then added, "I'll miss you a lot."

Bob felt emotional. They were best friends. At that moment he knew Jack liked him as much as he liked Jack. They were really a two-man team.

"I'm going to miss you like crazy," Bob blurted out. "You will always be my best friend. My best friend forever."

17

Jack was getting a little emotional, too.

"Best friends forever," he echoed. He said it before he even thought about it, but it did seem as if it was true. There was something about Hanssen. He was so deep. While Jack was certainly more popular in school, he didn't really feel equal to Bob. It was as if Jack was somehow more superficial. Original ideas were few and far between for him, while Bob's head was always dancing with something new.

Bob now said, "I'll sign my letters to you 'B2F.' Only you will know that it means 'Best Friends Forever'— secret code."

"'B2F.' Cool. Let's do it," Jack said. They would have hugged each other, but they were high school graduates now, so they just shook hands, pumping silently, solemnly.

4

1962–1964

At Knox, Bob knew from experience that he stood out from the other freshmen because of his being so tall. He didn't know that it was also due to the clean white shirt and dark pants he always wore and the plastic shirt-pocket protector holding three pens—not to mention his goofy walk and his thick glasses. He certainly felt a little uncomfortable all the time.

It was 1962. Most of the boys were wearing blue jeans and unkempt shirts, and the girls were in big skirts and saddle shoes, or straight skirts and sweater sets. Some guys might be neat but not starched, as Bob seemed to always be, and his efforts at conversation were less than spectacular.

"Hey, Bob," said a guy from his dorm. "What are you carrying in that box?"

"Oh, it's just laundry. I send it to my mother every week."

"Wow, that's great, man." But the kid walked off with a look on his face as if Bob had just said something tacky.

He would smile at girls on the way to class, and they would usually smile back but edge away from him on the path, just a little. Who was this tall dork with glasses so thick they made him look like a bug, and what was with that corny getup?

Bob called his father. He held the phone a good six

19

inches from his ear, as if the receiver might spurt flaming oil at a moment's notice.

"You want contact lenses. All right," said Howard. "I'll spring for them. But don't think you're not costing me an awful lot these days."

"Thank you, Dad, thank you." After he hung up, though, he felt like saying to the phone, *What's the big deal? You'll just go out and twist one more arm to pay for them.* Bob was in a rage, a totally useless rage. How many horses had Howard bet on? He always had the money for that.

Later that night, Bob joined some guys in one of the dorm rooms. The ashtrays were loaded with butts, but it was comfortable to sit on the facing cots, just five guys hanging around. Before long, Bob was talking up a streak. He was thinking of how good he'd look once the glasses were gone.

"My old man is fantastic," he told the others. "They say there's no cop as tough as him on the whole Chicago police force."

"Who's 'they'?" asked one of the guys.

"The men he works with. Every time I go to visit him at the station, the other cops tell me how great he is."

They all nodded. It was a little different from their family backgrounds.

"Must be interesting having a father who's a tough cop," another boy said.

"Sure it is. We live in Cicero, on a real slum street. My father wants it that way so he can keep his eye on the local hoodlums. You know what? Cicero—is the toughest town anywhere around Chicago. People can disappear there for saying the wrong thing. Any Negro who's crazy enough to go through Cicero, he's gone. We even have a lead-plated door on the front of our house to protect against bullets."

"Fantastic. How'd you feel living like that? You ever afraid?"

"You know, you get used to it," Robert said.

"You never feel any fear?"

"Comes and goes."

He felt like dynamite. The Hanssens' nice little house in Norwood felt a thousand miles away. No tall elms out the window—just bulletproof lead doors in Cicero. That was one real fantasy.

Some weeks later, Bob picked up the phone. His father's voice blasted loud and clear into his ear. He skipped the pleasantries, just as he always did.

"What I want to know—why are you studying Russian?"

"Someday I'm going to catch Soviet spies."

"Horseshit. I sent you to college to become a doctor."

"Dad, what would you say if I told you I'd really like to be a cop? A truly high-level cop like you."

"Don't even think about it."

"Dad, it's hard to get into medical school. They all say that even with very good grades you're more likely to end up in dental school."

"You don't want to be a dentist. You'll have to work a lot harder for your money."

"Doctor or dentist, you know I'm going to work hard."

Bob was uneasy after he hung up. He had been doing his best to lie, but his father was used to hearing liars talk. Howard had one hell of an ear for that. It was as if he knew that right now Bob didn't have the drive to study anything at all. And something in him rebelled when he tried to concentrate on science courses.

Feeling a need to talk about it, Bob went to his guidance counselor.

"Your high school grades were extraordinary," the man told him as he looked over Bob's records. "Do you have any idea what's wrong?"

"I don't know." He didn't. "I have trouble studying. I open a book and fall asleep."

"Maybe you need more exercise," the counselor suggested.

Bob had been hoping for some quick wisdom—some useful piece of brilliant advice—but all that came back was the same old song and dance he had always heard from teachers when they didn't know what else to say: get some exercise! He hated exercise. But he didn't seem like the person to admit it to.

"My roommate's always pushing me to learn to play basketball," he said.

"Could be a good idea." The counselor studied Bob's long fingers as he spoke. "Let's say you try that, and we'll watch the results."

Bob decided it was time to nod. "Yes, sir," he said.

The counselor smiled as if to say, *Got rid of this one with no trouble.*

That same afternoon, Bob and his roommate, Roger Buchman, were standing on a basketball court. Buchman kept bouncing the ball as he spoke, and the sound it made on the floor gave authority to his words.

"With your height, Bob, you sure could be a help to us in the intramural league. Only . . . I can see . . ."

"Yeah, I know," Bob said. "I have to pick up a few basics."

"Truthfully, did you ever play basketball before?"

He almost said yes. There was always a lie at the tip of his tongue. But he stopped himself.

"No," he said.

"I can teach you to dribble, help you with jump shots—the main thing, Bob, speaking frankly"—Buchman cleared his throat—"is that I have to show you how to run."

"I'm a little slow?"

Slow! He was like a turtle.

"Well," said Buchman, "I'm going to show you how

to lean forward and push off with the foot that's on the ground."

Yes, Hanssen had said it: basics. They went through the moves. It was obvious that Bob was even more in the dark than he had said.

Still, he practiced with Buchman—and without him. He cut classes to practice. He dribbled until he didn't lose the ball. He threw out his arms and legs on defense. He practiced jump shots and foul shots by the hour. He had heard the word: His height could make him an asset. After a month, Buchman was able to say with an honest expression and an all-but-sincere voice, "Bob, you are getting better."

Then came the first intramural game. Bob's side, being Dormitory, had no uniforms, just T-shirts and shorts. The opposition was a fraternity, Phi Sigma. They were wearing black T-shirts with PHI SIG printed in big white letters.

Buchman tried not to look at his pupil so that he didn't have to watch how far out of position Bob was, or how easy it was for a Phi Sig to dribble around him, but during a break, one of their teammates gave a verdict.

"Can't we get 'Big Stoop' off our team?" he asked.

"He's my roommate," Buchman said.

"Face it, Roger, we can do a lot better without him."

"I'll figure out something," Buchman said. He motioned for the squad to gather around. "All right, guys, we're only nine points behind. Let's close the gap."

Of course, the gap didn't close.

Later, in their room, Bob was really down.

"You know, Bob," Buchman explained. "It's just all those years you didn't play when you were a kid."

"I love basketball—I do, Roger."

"You'll get better. I know that. But listen, Bob—"

"I've studied up on the game. I know a lot about it by now."

"You do. You really grasp the logic and the theory in zone defense better than anyone else on the team."

"I tell you, Roger, I'd rather play basketball than eat. I'm not going to give up. I'm going to keep working at it." Hanssen's face was so full of passion that Roger was thrown off. He couldn't bring himself to crush Bob's enthusiasm.

"Well, that's great," said Buchman. He had only seven or eight players who showed up for the games. If they could get a lead in a couple of the upcoming contests, he could give Hanssen some minutes on the court. No point in devastating the guy if it meant that much to him.

Bob kept practicing. He neglected all else.

The following week was midterms. And there was Bob taking the Western Civilization I-A exam without having studied. The essay questions struck him as idiotic: "Discuss some of the forces behind the French Revolution." He was tempted to write, *Are you kidding? Rage, envy, discontent—say no more.* He hadn't done the reading. He faked it for a while, but he was pretty sure that he was mixing up the Estates General with the Committee for Public Safety. Around him were fifty students—caged in, sweating, and glancing up at the clock.

He put down his pen, rose, and turned in his paper.

"Are you sure you want to leave this early?" the professor asked. "You do have another hour."

"It's all right," Bob told him. "Frankly, I think the questions are kind of asinine."

He left without looking back and headed over to the gym, where he practiced left-handed layups one after another. The only points he had ever scored came in a game when he'd managed to be near the basket and had caught a high pass and popped it in. Afterward, the move twisted around in his mind to become a left-handed layup, so he kept practicing that shot. In the beginning it was important to become superior at least in one phase of the game. Still, improvement came slowly. After intermittent success, he had a stretch where he missed five in a row. He took the ball with both hands and slammed it to the floor, hard enough to drive it up almost to the rafters. He left the ball bouncing across the floor and walked out of the gym.

A week later, in the lunchroom, he saw a cute girl he liked and felt the usual catch in his throat from nervousness, but damnit, he was going to break his own ice. Now or never.

"Is this seat taken?" he asked.

"No." The girl inched her tray a bit to the side to make room for him. It took a moment for him to arrange his long legs under the table. "You're Bob, right?" she said.

"That's right, Bob Hanssen. And you're Cathy. We're in the same Western Civ class."

"I know." There was an awkward pause while Bob opened his napkin and salted his food. "You're a tall one," she said finally, sipping milk from a carton through a straw.

"Yeah," he told her. "Can't you guess? My sport is basketball."

She nodded. "I know," she said. "I saw the last game your dorm was in."

"Oh, that one . . . yeah."

"Yeah," she chimed in. "Weren't you on the bench the whole time?"

"As a matter of fact, I was . . . for a reason. You see, they asked me to coach."

"That's pretty good. That's pretty impressive," she said. Just then she saw a jock walking by and gave Bob a big smile.

"Will you excuse me? I've got to ask Joe a question about some kind of, you know, arrangement we may be making." She got up fast. "Bye-bye, Bob. Very interesting to talk to you."

Immediately, he was miserable. Now he knew he would never be able to touch her breasts, and he had had such a good time while they were talking, thinking of his hands feeling her up. It was no joke. He felt like vomiting. Instead, he took a stroll over to a file room in the annex of the administration building. It was empty, as he had expected. Lunchtime! He located a file drawer in the section that ran from *F* to *L,* opened it to "Hanssen," and took out his file. He removed a recently inserted paper that read "Western Civilization I-A Midterm Exam" and looked at the mark: 1.5. With his pen, he added a curving hat and a base to the 1. Now it looked like a respectable 2.5.

Then he examined a list of his old grades. It was a full spectrum: A+, A, A-, B+, B, B-, C+, C, C-. He skillfully changed all the C's to B-pluses with slightly curved backs. He did leave one C, but then deliberated and made it C-plus. His heart beating with the rapture of a daring deed well done, he walked out of the administration building.

5

1964

That summer, Bob finally got his driver's license. Without telling his father, he borrowed Jack Hoschouer's mother's car and took the test. The examiner was different from the one he'd had the last time, and he passed with no trouble. Bob might be a little awkward in his own body, but there was nothing wrong with his reflexes when it came to using a piece of machinery. In fact, the examiner complimented him.

"Kid, you're a good driver already. I have to say it—you passed with flying colors."

There was no stopping him when he went out for a drive with Jack afterward. Not until Hoschouer made him slow down.

"Hey, don't lose your license on the same day you get it!" Bob was really pushing Mrs. Hoschouer's car. It was a heap, not used to speed, and it soon gave signs of getting overheated.

Bob let it dawdle along. Still, he was excited. He had his license! He was laughing just thinking about the look on Howard's face when he found out.

Then a car cut in front of him, coming out of a side street. In it were two girls, not at all bad-looking.

Jack made the mistake of saying, "Hey, there's a pair." It was all Bob needed. When he waved at the girls, their car sped up. Either they were afraid of him or they were taunting him.

"Jack! I didn't know girls could drive that fast!" he said. Speeding up, he was soon on their bumper.

The girls were probably afraid, because they ran a red light.

Bob went through right after them.

"Stop!" Jack yelled. "Are you crazy?"

Bob smiled. He felt as if he understood his father for the first time. In him, he, too, had a hunter. He belted out a laugh, a loud sound almost like a yodel.

"Stop, Bob!" Jack yelled again. "There's going to be hell to pay if anything happens to my mother's car."

The girls went right through another red light, and Bob followed them, close behind. They were looking back at him, a little panicky. Hoschouer reached over and turned off the ignition, then pocketed the key. Bob had to coast to the curb, but he was still laughing wildly.

After the car was parked, Jack took over. Bob was still going a little nutty, dancing in the passenger seat and snapping his fingers to a song on the radio.

"I've got a license, I've got a license," he kept repeating until Jack said, "I know. Congratulations. That's wonderful. Now, calm down. I'm giving the youth sermon at church this Sunday, and I've got to rehearse. I went with you to your driving test, now it's your turn. You have to be my audience and tell me how I do."

Hoschouer climbed to the pulpit of the empty church and Bob settled into the fourth pew. Behind Jack was a very large, plain wooden cross on the wall. It had fluorescent tubes embedded in channels alongside it, and Hoschouer turned them on.

"I don't like those lights," Bob said. "They're hokey."

"I don't care what you don't like. Let me rehearse."

As Jack began reciting his speech, Bob couldn't stand his tone of voice. It was too pious, too sure of itself.

28

"Since this is youth Sunday in our church," Jack declared, "the question some of you may be asking yourselves is, Can kids be religious? I would say the answer is yes. Once they come to grips with the confusions that are built into the young nervous system. . . ."

By now, Bob was leaning way back and resting his feet on the pew in front of him. It annoyed Jack and broke his concentration.

Jack stopped his speech. "Put your feet down!" he said.

"Why? Nobody's here."

"Put your feet down, damnit! It really upsets me!"

"I didn't know they allowed swearing in a Methodist church, Jack."

"When you get it in your mind to do something, it's impossible to get you out of it. Get your feet down! It's disrespectful."

"I've always wanted to do this in church—be a little disrespectful, you know? It's science I respect, not religion."

But he slowly withdrew his feet, grinning as he did so. Then he stood up and bowed. He was still full of himself from passing the test and chasing the girls. And now he had even made the cool Jack Hoschouer lose his patience twice in one day! Not that Bob meant any harm. He admired Jack so much. Jack had a natural, pleasant manner with people. He was a little reserved but friendly—a good listener. Girls liked him a lot. Bob even got some of the benefits—occasionally a girl would go out with him if they were double-dating with Jack and his date. But he knew girls probably tolerated him because he was Jack's friend. You could tell the difference between them by what went into their high school yearbook. Lots of pictures of Jack in a number of different club activities, but only one photograph of Bob. Under it was his motto: "Science is the light of life." Not exactly thrilling to a lot of girls.

29

* * *

It wasn't until the spring of his junior year at Knox that Bob got the nerve to call Howard and tell him flat out that he wasn't going to apply to med school.

"My average just doesn't make it." He took a much-needed breath. "But I can study dentistry."

The pause on the phone line lasted a long time. Then Howard gave a loud sigh. "That is acceptable if you are telling the truth. But can you guarantee it? Are you going to get into dental school?"

"No way I'll miss."

"No way you'll miss. Good." Howard cleared his throat. "Now I have news for you. Your mom got you a job for this summer, some place she's working—Chicago State Mental Hospital. You'll be a psychiatric attendant, king of the loonies."

"That sounds okay. King of the loonies." Leave it to his old man. "But, Dad, why is Mom working?"

"What else is she going to do all day? Women her age should work. It's good for their plumbing."

Right after he hung up, Bob went over to the administration building. He had just a half hour before the doors were locked. Once again the file room was empty. Once again, he used his pen to change a few C-minuses to C-pluses and B-pluses and, for security's sake, a few B-minuses.

6

1966

Chicago State Mental Hospital was big and sprawling. It had so many buildings—and outbuildings and laboratories and dormitories for those attendants who slept on the grounds, and a huge cafeteria, and a big shabby lobby—that one just could not keep up with all the people who were working there. It would have been a lonely place for Bob, but Hoschouer had also gotten a job there, at Bob's urging, and Jack had already picked out the most eligible females—nurses, trainees, and attendants. Bob, as a result, had actually had a few fantasies about necking sessions with the girls Jack would provide for him. Or so he thought, on the basis of one conversation they had at the water fountain, where they stood around like two dudes in their spanking-new white uniforms.

"Concerning the female question," Jack was saying, "this is not the worst place to work. I met a delightful Asian girl yesterday. I don't know why, but I've got a big thing for Asian women."

"Nothing's on for me yet," Robert had to confess. "I thought you were going to steer something my way."

"I will. It takes time. But didn't your mother pick out a girl just for you? Didn't you tell me that?"

"Bonnie, she's called. I caught a glimpse of her walking down the hall. She looked okay. But, you know, you don't want a girl handpicked by your mother."

"I saw that one. Bonnie, huh? Bob, look again. She's stacked. You'd better move before I do."

Jack's remark was all it took. Bonnie's value was now obvious. Bob felt a pang at the thought of Jack moving in.

"Buddy," he said to Hoschouer, "a word to the wise is enough. She's mine."

Later, Bob managed to bump into Bonnie. He couldn't believe that he had even considered overlooking her. She was lovely. She had a beautiful figure. She looked like Natalie Wood.

Of course, Hanssen was trying so hard to be at ease that he was unnatural: "Bonnie, if I may inquire, how did you come to work here?"

She was breezy about it. "Family connections," she said. "My father's a psychiatrist."

Clumsy. He was so clumsy. "That's interesting, real interesting. My mother works here, too. She got me this job." He didn't even know why he'd said that. Probably to keep the conversation from dying. He looked at her solemnly, sincerely, then he laughed. She gave him a brief smile.

Soon, he was doing his best to keep an eye on her. He would spy on her from a distance. His hearing was good. He loved to listen to her voice. Also from a distance.

One time, he watched her putting lotion on the hands of a sick woman.

"Oh, my hands are so dry," the woman said.

"I know, dear," Bonnie told her. "They are dry, but this should moisten them. Let me massage your fingers." Bonnie's voice was so soothing.

She's beautiful and she's kind, Bob said to himself. She was like a heroine in one of the adventure novels he used to read when he was a kid. He watched Bonnie with another patient. Again he was unobserved.

"And then your mother died," Bonnie said to the old woman. "Oh, that is so sad. It must be a terrible feeling."

"Yes," said the patient. "You understand how I feel."

Bob nodded his head. He couldn't believe it. Maybe his mother *had* picked the right girl for him.

One day they took their coffee cups and sat down together at a table in the break room.

"So you used to do a lot of ham radio?" she asked.

"Oh yes," he said. "In high school, our club even used to go out with our radios and camp overnight and talk across to each other in different tents. Then we would get in touch with other hams by radio. We'd use our call letters for our names. Mine was WQDQ." He laughed at the memory. "You hear all kinds of things. Sometimes you catch a foreign guy with an accent who was saying things that were obviously in code." His voice speeded up. "And you have to wonder, are they going to blow something up? It's such a secretive, quiet thing you can do by yourself. Nobody sees you. Nobody knows who you really are. It's kind of deep."

"Do you see yourself as deep?" Bonnie asked.

He could see that she was serious about the question. Totally serious.

"No, I can't say I'm special," Bob said quickly, although he had wanted to agree with her. Of course he was deep.

"You're a liar. You *do* see yourself as special."

"No, you're the one who is special. And deep. And you are beautiful." He tried to say it with a winning smile.

Bonnie ignored the compliment. He couldn't tell if she heard that too often or didn't believe she was beautiful.

"Your mother thinks you might be interested in psychiatry," she answered.

"Maybe." He shrugged. "They say you make a good psychiatrist if you're a little off yourself." Now he gave his big laugh, the one that always got away from him. It was a whinny, just a little nutty.

"That's ridiculous," she said. "Do you have to have a toothache to be a good dentist?"

"Maybe."

"My father says many psychiatrists are opposed to religion."

"Are you religious?" he asked her.

"Well, my real first name is Bernadette, not Bonnie. So you can guess. My parents are very religious. Of course, my father does teach psychology as well."

"I'd like to meet him." But he said it too quickly. You had to be careful around her, he realized too late.

"Whoa, partner! I said I'd have a cup of coffee with you, not a family dinner!"

"You're quick," he told her before she could get any more annoyed with him. "Do you know how quick and keen you are?" he said without missing a beat. He had to watch himself. He couldn't rush her.

Pretty soon, however, a routine developed between them. Jack would take his mother's car, pick up Bonnie first and then Bob, who would be in the rear seat, leaning so far forward into the space between Jack and Bonnie that it was almost as if he was sitting between them.

One time on the drive to work, Bonnie made a remark that sounded a little strange. It came out of nowhere.

"Oh, I'm so glad," she said, "that my mom is crazy about my dad."

"Why?" Bob asked.

"Because if she wasn't madly in love with him, she would have been a nun."

Neither of them knew what to say. Finally Jack spoke up. "What about you, Bonnie? Did you ever think about becoming a nun?"

"I don't think I'm the sort that should," she answered. She looked awfully attractive at that moment.

"What's your reason for saying that?" Bob asked.

"Oh, I don't know." She paused. Then: "Yes, I do. I find boys kind of interesting."

"You do?"

"Kind of."

Ten minutes later, after Jack and Bob had left Bonnie and were walking down the hallway, Bob couldn't hold back. "Isn't she terrific?" he said.

"Definitely gorgeous. But kind of scatterbrained," Jack said.

"What do you mean by that?"

"Did you listen to her?" Jack tried to speak in her voice, "'I just find boys kind of interesting.'"

Bob was furious. "Shut up," he said to Jack.

"Hey," said Jack. "Watch it."

"No. You've never been more wrong in your life. She's not scatterbrained. She's very intelligent." Bob paused. Then he couldn't prevent himself from saying, "I just wish she liked me."

Still, she did pay some attention to him. He actually got to neck with her once after work while they were sitting on a park bench. Her body felt so alive, and her mouth was wonderful to him. He had kissed a few girls before, but this time was different. With his lips against Bonnie's, he felt as if he were kissing her soul. She had a fabulous soul, sweet as honeysuckle.

"I can't believe how crazy I am about you," Bob told her.

"Oh, you don't mean it at all," she said. "You're just trying to get me excited . . . in that way . . ."

"No, Bonnie. I want to marry you," he said. "You're the only woman for me, the only possible woman."

"This is too soon, Bob. I'm just not ready for anything of that sort. Not yet."

"No, I would always protect you. I just hope you like me. Do you like me?"

"I think you have the nicest smile," she told him. "That's why you caught me looking at you in the first place."

"So someday you will marry me." It wasn't a question. He said it as if it were a fact.

"Bob, please. We don't know anything about each other."

She held him off when he tried to kiss her again.

"Stop," she said. "I have to tell you something. You know, at this point in my life, I am dating more than one guy."

"That's all right," he said. But his stomach was turning inside out. He didn't know whether he was full of pain or full of excitement at the thought of another man having his hands on her.

"It doesn't bother you?" she asked.

"It doesn't change my determination to marry you. I dream of us having children together." He was surprised to hear those words come out of his mouth. He had never thought about children before. But he had the idea she would like that. Of course, he wasn't nearly as confident as he had tried to sound.

The next day, when he saw her in the hospital corridor, he made a point of smiling and blocking her path just enough so that she had to stop.

"How about a date tonight?" he asked.

He didn't like the look on her face today. She seemed very faraway.

"I can't, Bob. I have a date already."

"Is it somebody from the hospital?" He wondered if it was Jack. That thought was crazy. Nauseating, but thrilling at the same time.

She was annoyed that he was asking, but she told him, "No . . . it's someone who's going to pick me up after work."

"I hope you have a good time." Oh, what that one cost him!

"Thank you."

Bob stood in the shadow of a tree and watched Bonnie come down the steps of the hospital and stop at the curb. A car that must have been waiting drove up immediately, and her date jumped out, walked around to the other side, and opened the door for her. Before Bonnie had a chance to get in, Bob was there.

"I just wanted to say good-bye to you and say hello to your friend."

The friend was as short as Bonnie and had to look up at Bob.

"Hi," the guy said. His voice was a little weak, as if he was unsure of himself.

Bob smiled. Point made.

The next night, Bob was actually sitting on the steps of Bonnie's house when she drove up with another date.

"Hi," Bob said. "Believe it or not, I just happened to be taking a stroll and sat down here. Then I realized it was your house. No offense, Bonnie?"

"No, Bob, not at all, no, no."

She dashed by both men and went into her house.

He told Hoschouer all about his moves. "Jack, I've sat on her stoop the last three dates she's had. She must think I'm a little nuts."

Jack looked at him for a moment, then said, "Bob, in my experience, women don't really take to that kind of behavior."

"You're so successful with girls," Bob said suddenly. "I envy you, Jack. I really do."

"Hey, my friend, my expertise is exaggerated." Hoschouer was being honest, not modest. He'd had a few girlfriends, but for some reason everyone seemed to think he was a great ladies' man. That didn't exactly please him. If the truth were told—and part of Hoschouer's pride was that he would always tell himself the truth— way deep down, he still felt just a little in awe of women, kind of happier looking at nudes in *Playboy* than actually seeing a girl stark naked in front of him.

In the middle of their conversation, a little shoeshine boy, about twelve years old, somehow got in front of Bob with his shoe box and succeeded in bringing the two men to a halt. Bob was too engrossed in what they were talking about to put up with any interruption. He grabbed the boy by the elbows, turned him around, and kept right on walking.

"Jack, you've really got to give me a couple of tips on how to handle women. Especially Bonnie, I mean."

"Let her see you having coffee in the cafeteria with another woman."

In the cafeteria, Bob made a point of sitting at a table near the door. He was with a tall, blond girl. She was so tall that you could feel her height even when she was sitting down. Bob might have been the only guy in the place who was taller than she.

As Bonnie was leaving the lunchroom, she couldn't avoid passing by his table, and she certainly did stop.

"Bob, I want to tell you I'm going to Mexico for part of the summer." Her eyes were wide open as she looked at him. "I'm really excited about it. Acapulco is so beautiful, I've heard."

"I've heard it is, too. May I write to you?"

"Oh sure. Of course."

"I'm going to love sending letters to you."

Bonnie could tell that Bob was not really interested in that blond girl he was sitting with.

7

1966–1968

On a tropical evening, high up on an open-air terrace, Bonnie and a very attractive Mexican date were watching a cliff diver get ready to take his death-defying show-business dive into the narrow space below. Bonnie was excited. She was sipping a tequila punch as she admired the diver. He had to time his plunge to hit the seawater at exactly the moment when a wave had just come in; otherwise, he would dash himself to bits on the rocks below. She felt a thrilling, risky excitement in the atmosphere—sipping a sexy drink, sitting next to a sexy Mexican. Yet, to her real surprise, half of her—no, more than half of her—was thinking about a letter she had received from Bob that day.

Later, after the successful cliff dive, while she and the Mexican were dancing, it became awfully obvious that he was smiling at too many girls and that they were all smiling back. It was enough to make Bonnie feel more plain than beautiful and not at all desirable. By then, what with the tequila moving through her, Bob's letter was echoing in her head, her heart, and even in her belly.

Dear Bonnie,

Your family is so big and wonderful. I'm so happy you let me meet them. When I did, I thought: I've never seen this kind of warmth, this wonderful kind of interaction and unity that all of you people have. Such gaiety and life and diversion.

I had a different family life. I remember endless dinners with my grandmother and mother, who did not like each other at all. They just sat in silence at the table. I will say that my father is a strong, charming man, and wherever we went, I was always known as his son. Especially in social situations, so that side was often good, but that is the most warmth I can claim to receive from my people, whereas in your family, such witty bantering goes on between your father and mother. They are so alive, as opposed to the chilly silences I knew all through my childhood and adolescence. How I love it that everyone in your family argues and debates about everything. Such a vibrant group of people.

Forgive me, but I also couldn't help noticing when we worked together at the hospital that you felt such real empathy for the patients. You understood their suffering. I was amazed how a young woman as beautiful as you could care so much for these psychotic people.

It led me to understand that you will make an exceptional mother for any man's children who is ever fortunate enough to be wed to your beauty.

I know, even though you think it is too soon, that I will keep asking you and asking you to be my beloved bride, the woman I will adore for the rest of my life.

Throughout her vacation, Bonnie could not get that letter out of her mind, nor the ones that followed. Every time Bob wrote about how much he would love to have children, she would burst into tears high up in her hotel room with its little balcony looking out on the Pacific Ocean.

40

The day Bonnie went back to work, she spotted Bob playing basketball with some patients. She stood on the sideline and watched for a long time. He was so patient and tolerant with them, considering how uncoordinated they were.

The following day, when Bonnie was at the zoo with four or five patients, Bob appeared out of nowhere. She was surprised at how happy she was to see him and was about to tell him so, but he was already talking.

"I am shocked, absolutely shocked," he said, "that they let a young woman like you go on an outing with these mental patients, who they know are high-security. There's no one to protect you."

"Oh, Bob, they trust me. It's all right."

"It's ridiculous. I'm going to stay here. You might need some help before the day is over."

"Well, thank you. I did feel a little funny all on my own, I must admit."

This unexpected visit—his concern that he stay with her, that he protect her—meant as much to Bonnie, maybe even more, as the beautiful letters he had written to her in Mexico.

Yes, things had gotten serious enough between them that she had to tell her father about her feelings for Bob.

Her father, Leroy Wauck, was a powerful mix of opposites, and Bonnie was a little in awe of him. He was professorial yet virile, a devout Catholic who swore like a Marine but taught psychology at Loyola in Chicago. She saw him as a man of many parts, and he certainly did sometimes tease her a little too much for comfort.

"Well, Bonnie," he wanted to know, "I've been meaning to ask about Acapulco?"

"It was nice, Daddy, but I wanted to come back."

"Kind of soon, wasn't it?"

"A few days early. I just felt like I needed to come back here and not waste any more time. I'd like to tell you something." She took his hands. "I've been seeing a man here in Chicago, and it's gotten a little serious. You're the first person in the family to hear."

"You mean out of that whole crew of characters who've been ringing my doorbell for the last year you've finally made a choice?"

"Daddy, brace yourself. We're ready to get engaged."

"All right. Who the hell is he?"

"Bob Hanssen. You remember him—I invited him to the house one night for dinner."

"Yeah, I remember. The tall one. He spoke in such a low voice that I couldn't hear a damn word he said."

"Come on, Daddy. He's brilliant. I know you'll be able to talk to him a lot when you get to know him."

"Isn't he still in dental school?" She nodded. "So how will you pay the bills?" her father asked.

"Daddy, you have seven children, and I know the problems you have. You won't have to worry about us. Bob's an only child. His father will help us out until we can get on our feet."

"That sure is convenient. What does his father do?"

"He's a lieutenant on the city police force."

"A Chicago cop?" He whistled.

"Why did you whistle?"

"No reason. I'm just celebrating your engagement."

"Daddy, I promise you, Bob loves me. He's a sensitive man. We have wonderful talks."

"Well, we can always use a dentist in the family, what with the price of teeth these days!"

"Oh you," Bonnie chortled.

Bonnie and Bob sat on the couch in the Hanssens' basement, deep in one of their talks.

"I don't want to ever push you into doing something you don't want to, Bob. I promise you that," Bonnie said earnestly. "But my religion is the most important thing in my family's life. I mean, just think of it—they named me Bernadette, after the saint. You know, the one at Lourdes? The incorruptible saint? She was so holy that her body has never decomposed."

"I think that's fabulous. I'll always think of you as my incorruptible Bernadette, my little saint."

"Call me that and you'll be in big trouble."

"Okay. Bonnie, let me try to be serious. I am very much aware of the beauty and harmony that Catholicism brings to your family. The more I learn about it, the more I love it. I have to admit, it's more appealing in a lot of ways than the Lutheran Church."

"Are you saying that you would be willing to convert?"

That produced a long pause. "You know," Bob said finally, "I can't be sure. I don't know if I'm good enough."

"Oh, Bob, you're the kindest man I know. Of course you're good enough."

"I don't know if I could measure up. I'm just not sure yet."

There was one bump in the road he could never tell her about. How could he keep masturbating as many times as he did, day after day, and then go to Confession and tell a stranger about *that*?

She nodded. Even if she didn't know what was stopping Bob, she understood. There were always serious inner obstacles to conversion.

"It doesn't matter. I'll never rush you," she told him. "You'll come to the faith with a full heart when you're ready, because that's you. I know that. But, Bob, we have to raise our children as Catholics. If we have any, that is."

"No problem. No problem at all with that."

"Well, there is a problem, Bob. I haven't told you something." She took a deep breath. Tears came into her eyes. "You know, when I was sixteen . . ." she began hesitantly. It was hard to get the words out. "They had to operate on me. They removed one of my ovaries and part of the other one." She managed to look into his eyes. "I don't know if I'll be able to have children."

He had never loved her more. No wonder she was so faraway at times. He felt like crying himself.

"Bonnie, you'd be the world's best mother, and I'd love nothing more than to make babies with you, but if you can't have children, I'll still love you until the day I die."

"Do you know how different you are from other men?" she asked. "Before I met you, darling, I have to tell you—there was someone else that I seriously considered marrying, but he wanted sex. Of course, I couldn't agree to that before marriage. He actually told me it would be a good thing if we could find out—experimentally—if he could make me pregnant. I thought that was horrible. I could never look at him in the same way again. I stopped seeing him."

Bob held Bonnie. At that moment, it didn't matter whether they would have children or not. They would have each other.

8

1968

At the wedding party, there were about a hundred guests. Jack Hoschouer was there in his army lieutenant's uniform, accompanied by his Japanese-American newlywed wife. He had meant what he had said about Asian women. And now he would soon be on his way to Vietnam.

Bob stood in a corner talking to Leroy Wauck. It was hard for him to get through to his new father-in-law. The direct approach certainly didn't work, but he kept trying.

"I can't tell you how much your family means to me," Bob said.

Wauck held up a hand. "Wait until you've been around us awhile."

"No, let me say it: I know how deep the spirit of Catholicism is in your family. And I want to say, sir—and Bonnie and I have talked about this—that I also want to be a Catholic one day. But I'm just not ready yet. So, let me tell you how much I appreciate it that you allowed me to marry Bonnie."

Wauck nodded. "It's okay, Bob," he said. "Some people take years to convert. Some find the road to Damascus on a bus ride. Don't worry. This world is not as orderly as my dear religion."

"I love order. I worship it."

45

"Good luck!"

The wedding reception had its ups and downs. Right in front of Bob, Howard had ogled Bonnie, top to bottom, front and rear. Whether it was horseflesh or women, he just admired God-given curves. Couldn't help himself. But despite all his experience with broads, with whores, with good-time girls, he had never bothered to learn how to flirt. He kept his approach to the raw side. That got results with the women he knew. Now he was riled up that Bob—who didn't deserve it—had gotten himself a girl who looked like an Irish beauty, even if the roots were Polish or something other.

"Bonnie, now that you're married to my son, let me let you in on our family skeleton," he said.

Vivian, standing nearby, was in full flutter. Bad enough that she didn't know what her husband might say, but she could also see how uncomfortable Bonnie was. "Now, Howard . . . Please, Howard." She turned to Bonnie. "Don't pay him any mind. He always talks as if he's been drinking all night and he doesn't even touch the stuff."

"When you look at your bridegroom here," Howard continued as if Vivian hadn't said a word, "what do you see? A tall, handsome fellow—perfect, right? Well, watch out for appearances. Your bridegroom is a loser. A full-time, guaranteed loser. You should have gotten yourself engaged to the father."

"That's my dad's idea of humor at a wedding," Bob told Bonnie.

"More truth than jest," said Howard as Vivian somehow succeeded in steering him toward another good-looking woman.

There was also an odd episode with Jack Hoschouer. That was Bob's fault. He was still bouncing off walls from what his father had said.

"Congratulations, she sure is gorgeous," Jack said. "You don't know how envious I am that you got there first. I wouldn't have minded getting together with her."

"You wouldn't have minded?" asked Bob.

"I wouldn't have minded at all."

Suddenly, Bob said in an agitated whisper, "If you ever lay a finger on her . . . she's sacred to me, you jackal! Don't ever touch her!"

"Hey, hey," said Jack. "I was just kidding! Wow!" Then looking Bob in the eye, he added, "I would never, ever, do anything to hurt you, Bob. You know that. You're my buddy!" He meant it. You never blindsided a buddy. "B2F? Remember?" Jack reminded him. "B2F."

"Right. B2F." Bob's rage was almost like a plaster cast—crack it and it would fall off. Now he was nothing but mush inside. "I believe you, Jack," he said. "And I respect you for wearing that uniform. Here you are going over to Vietnam and you honor me by coming to my wedding. I'm sorry, Jack. I'm really sorry."

"This is getting too rich for my blood, buddy. Let me fill up my drink," Jack said.

Bob and Bonnie didn't go anywhere for a honeymoon. He couldn't take the time away from dental school, so they just stayed home and made love.

One morning after Bob had left, Bonnie stepped from the shower to dry herself off in the kitchen. Too late, she noticed that the shade was up and that right across the street a couple of construction workers were fixing a fire escape.

She saw them and tried to pull the shade down, but instead it flew up. When she reached for the cord, her towel fell. The workers stared straight at her for one frozen moment, then applauded and whistled as she flew out of the kitchen and slammed the door.

That night in bed, she told Bob about it.

"I felt like I was paralyzed," she said. "I couldn't move. It was awful! There they were, two hairy, dirty men looking at me and applauding!"

"They knew how lucky they were."

"Aren't you angry, Bob?"

"Of course I am," he said, quickly enough. "But it had nothing to do with you. It was an accident." He reached for her. He was feeling as excited to have her as he had ever felt, and that was saying an awful lot. They made love again and again and again that night, because each time he thought of those men looking at her, it got him aroused all over again. She seemed as turned on as he was, and each time she was right there with him. A small lamp with a red bulb glowed in the corner all night long.

"You're incredible. You're inexhaustible," she told him. "Who would ever have dreamed there's such energy in you? I had no idea how wonderful a honeymoon could be."

"You're the incredible one. I love you."

"And I love you," she said. "I love you so much."

In the morning, she was still glowing. "I can't believe how beautiful it is with you."

"You're heaven," he told her.

That evening, when he came home from school, Bonnie's face was set. An expressionless mask. Quite a contrast to the morning.

"Anything happen today?" He was uneasy. Something was wrong.

"Well, we just received the last of our wedding presents."

"Who from?"

"Jack."

"Jack sent something all the way from Vietnam?"

"Oh no. It was delivered right here from Chicago. Just a notice. It said that Lieutenant Hoschouer had ordered a gift subscription to *Playboy* for Mr. and Mrs. Hanssen."

The pause she maintained after saying this did Bob no good at all.

"A subscription for *us?*" she asked. "Bob, do you really look at stuff like *Playboy?*"

"Well . . . sort of. A little bit. From time to time."

"I can't stand the idea of this magazine coming to our house," she said.

"I didn't know you would feel that strongly." He could think of nothing better to say.

"What goes on when you make love to me?" she asked. "Are you thinking all the time of some filthy, rotten pictures you see in your mind? Would you rather be with a woman like that than with me?" She was yelling. She was usually so soft-spoken, but now he knew—she could really yell. "Get it straight, Bob—I am going to stop this subscription." Her voice was ugly. Strong and ugly. He had an idea of what her father might sound like in a rage. His sweet little Bonnie!

"Well . . . try to think about Jack's feelings." Too late, he immediately realized that it was the worst remark he could have made.

"That's the last thing I'll think about!" she shouted.

It was their first fight. He couldn't give up, though. He really wanted that subscription.

"Darling," he said in a reasonable tone of voice, "it's not a big deal. You don't always have to be more Catholic than the Pope."

She slapped him.

"Wow." He knew he was licked. "You don't have to worry," he told her. "I only think of you. You know you are the most gorgeous woman in the world for me—gorgeous, gorgeous, gorgeous." Actually, the sound of her voice had given him a headache.

9

1969–1970

A couple of days later, on Sunday afternoon, Bob was sleeping over his textbooks. Bonnie could see one big volume open to hideous pictures of teeth in various stages of decay and disease. She had just come home with bags of groceries. Now she nudged him.

"Is something the matter, darling?" She was feeling a little bad about the tongue-lashing she had given him about *Playboy*. "What's the matter, sweetheart?" she asked. His face looked so unhappy in his sleep.

"Oh!" he said, coming out of it. "I guess I was getting a little bored." It was the way he said *"bored."* The sound was so final.

"Bob, are you still sure you want to be a dentist?"

"Well, I guess so," he said. "My dad doesn't let me forget he's the one paying for all of it."

In school itself, the day was not boring so much as it was full of unexpected uneasiness and tension. His marks were excellent, but he still didn't like it. He always felt as if he was on the edge of a terrible misstep—as if he were in a dream.

There he was in his white smock, working on a poor old lady's mouth: "This will just take a moment," he told her. "I'll do my best to keep it from being painful." Actually, that was a lie. Even the needle from the Novocain injection was going to hurt her far-gone gums.

50

As he stared at the mouth, it began to morph. He blinked. It no longer looked like a mouth so much as a foul and diseased old vagina, wide open and smelly. Then his eyes allowed it all to coalesce back into an old lady's mouth with its sad, bad odor. He stepped away. He was drenched in sweat. They had to call another student to take over for him.

He didn't say anything to anybody, and a couple of hours later, he went back to work on other patients' teeth, but he was done with dental school. He knew it. When he would finally be in practice, what if he was working on a young beautiful girl someday and her mouth began to look like a beautiful, fragrant vagina? He could be in serious trouble. He cut his classroom labs for the next few days in order to take care of administrative details, and by the third day he had set it all up. On a pay phone in a hallway of the school, he called Bonnie.

"Hear me out," he told her. "You have to understand. I freaked out. So I said to myself, Do I want to spend the rest of my life with my fingers in somebody's wet, smelly mouth?"

"Bob, you can't do this. You only have one semester to go!"

"It doesn't matter. I can't go on."

"No, Bob, it does matter. What will you do? Your father will have to keep supporting us until you're earning money."

"Bonnie, dental school is done. It's all over. Even if I get my degree, I'll never practice. I'm going to get a degree in accounting instead. I've managed to transfer. A CPA makes a lot of money, too."

"You transferred without telling me?"

"I had to. There wasn't time to argue about it. And I love how the new upcoming tool in accounting will be computers."

"Computers? I don't even want to learn how to turn one on."

"Computers are an open-sesame to what comes next. Getting in early is going to guarantee our future."

"I can't follow you, Bob." She actually hung up on him. When he called her back, she did her best not to scream. How could he do all this without even mentioning it to her?

Next, he called his father.

"Now, let me get this straight," Howard said. "You just threw away all that dentistry training to go into accounting? One semester before you graduate?"

"Dad, I didn't just do it. I have a master plan."

"When don't you?"

"Dad, I'm going to use accounting to join the police force at a good beginning level. As I see it, they'll need me to audit the books of crooked firms."

"Now, you listen. I've been a cop all my life. I could have been an important man if I'd paid attention to education. But no, I was pigheaded. I had to be a cop. So all my working life I have had to worry, What do I do next week to augment my two-bit paycheck?"

"Dad, I see the police force as a stepping-stone."

"To what?"

"To bigger things."

"You are altogether ill-suited for the uniform. You're tall, but you don't have a clue how to handle yourself physically. Every little punk you run across will want to beat up on a tall guy like you."

"Maybe I disagree."

"Disagree. It's a free country. But you disgust me."

After that phone call, Bob didn't go home right away. Instead, he headed to a gun shop.

"I'd like to look at your Walther PPKs," Bob said.

The clerk removed one from a display case. It was beautiful—small, nicely balanced, lethal-looking. Eloquent.

"This is the James Bond gun," the clerk said.

"Exactly," said Bob, in a voice as assured as the secret agent's.

"A perfect choice. It's really smooth for undercover work." The clerk paused. "Excuse me—I guess I took it for granted that you're in undercover work."

"Keep that to yourself," Bob said.

"Given the length of your fingers and the size of your palm, controlling a PPK with one hand will be very easy for you."

Bob maneuvered the pistol. "Wrap it up," he said.

That afternoon, after hanging up with Bob, Bonnie learned how people can go crazy. There was a group of beatniks—or whatever they called themselves—who hung out in the parking lot of their apartment complex, and they had an old junk heap of a car. It was bad enough that they always left it in the spot reserved for Bonnie and Bob's car—and it was doubly bad that Bob did nothing about it (she had been coming to learn just how afraid he was of confrontation)—but now those beatniks would even hang out in their car and turn on a big portable radio to blast her ears, two stories up in her own apartment. And they wouldn't turn it down when she asked them to. Nor would they move their car. Yes, that afternoon she had learned how people can go crazy.

She had come home from her teaching job at the parochial school, which brought them a little extra money, and for once those beatniks were not idling around. But their car was right in her parking space again, and its windows were open. Then Bob called with his news. After that, she was just so angry she was ready for anything. She emptied the dirt out of a couple of clay pots—two plants were dying, anyway—put the soil in a garbage bag, filled a washpan with water, and went downstairs. She dumped the dirt onto the driver's seat, poured the water over it, and went back upstairs. She kept looking out the window every few minutes, just to check. By late afternoon, there they were, standing around the car, looking real dumb and shocked.

Bonnie threw open the window. "You don't have to wonder who did it to you," she yelled. "I did. And that's just the beginning. I swear that's just the beginning unless you move your car out of our space." She was surprised by her own voice. She didn't know how loud it could be.

Those beatniks moved the car before it got dark, just before Bob came home, and although she couldn't believe what she'd done, she was glad she had done it. It saved her from having a terrible fight with Bob over the gun when he told her about the purchase that night.

"What has this got to do with accounting?" she asked.

"Oh, Bonnie, a man has different sides." He nodded as if to give a lot of emphasis to what he had just said. "This is the exact weapon James Bond uses."

"I can't believe you went out and bought something this expensive just when you quit dental school. Tell the truth—what did it cost?"

"You won't believe it. Twenty-five bucks. On sale."

That placated Bonnie. "Well, I guess it's not that much after all. It might be good protection."

Undetected, he was busy scraping the $225 price tag off the handle of the Walther PPK.

Now that he had bought the gun, he felt ready for bigger things. If those beatniks ever came back to cause trouble because of what Bonnie had done to their car, well, he would have a reception for them.

He felt ready for action. There was one nurse at the dental school, maybe ten years older than him, who had eyes for him, and she was always inviting him to come over to her apartment after work. The woman half-pretended it was a joke, but her message made it obvious that it wasn't.

The nurse seemed to have nothing to do with the beatniks, except she did. Bob knew how Bonnie's voice had sounded when she yelled down at that gang. It would have sounded exactly like it did that time she yelled at him about the *Playboy* subscription. When he thought about it, he was really incensed about that. So one evening, after a long afternoon at Northwestern's graduate accounting school, he paid a visit to the nurse. He couldn't believe how fast they fell into bed and, even less, how quickly it was over. With Bonnie, he could go all night. With this woman, it was done on immediate delivery. And he felt a certain horror about it. He had to get out of her apartment at once.

She was pretty upset. "You can't leave now. You can't do this to me," she said.

Well, he could and he did. Her last words to him before he shut the door were, "You'll pay for this, you son of a bitch."

He did.

The woman called Bonnie before he even got home. She told Bonnie that she had really gotten it on with Bob, that Bob had told her that he loved her, and that he was grateful because the sex had been so fabulous.

No, he had to keep telling Bonnie, it was not true, the woman was lying. He had kissed her, yes, kissed her a few times and left, but never told her he loved her. No, he never wanted to see her again. He was temporarily insane to have gone there at all. He was sorry beyond words. He was discovering that it was much more difficult to get people to believe you when you were almost telling the truth than when you were lying flat out.

Bonnie didn't believe him at all. She was sure he'd had an incredible hour of passionate sex. How could he not? He was such a good lover.

It drove her right down into the emptiness she felt whenever she thought about the ovary she had lost at sixteen and the imperfect ovary that remained. Of course Bob looked at *Playboy* on the side. Of course he wanted other women. Of course he could not be trusted: she was not a whole woman.

About the time she felt ready to leave him, and in total despair for herself, they fell weeping into each other's arms.

"I'll never have anything to do with another woman," Bob swore. "I take a vow." He didn't know if he would keep such a vow, but he hoped he could.

Over the next few months, she forgave him. But not entirely. Something remained fragile. She could no longer trust him completely.

All the same, they did love having sex with each other. Nothing could stop that. But he had to slow down on some of his sexual ideas. It took a half year after the nurse episode for Bob to satisfy one desire he'd had ever since they were married. On a balmy evening as they were preparing for bed, while Bonnie was wrapped in a terrycloth robe after a shower and looking adorable, he made the overture.

"Would you think I was silly," he asked, "if I told you I wanted to commemorate what we have?" He said this most seriously and with a straight face.

"What do you mean?" she asked.

"Will you accept my thought as something very natural?"

"Will you tell me what this is all about?" Already, she had moved from anticipation to uneasiness.

"I would love to take some snapshots of you that would capture your beauty," he said, and before she could react, added, "Not Polaroids." She had once told him that she hated people who used Polaroids to take obscene pictures of each other. "These will be real photographs," he said, "taken with a good camera that I borrowed from a guy at the accounting office."

"Are these the kind of photographs I think they are?" she asked.

"Not exactly."

"Yes they are. I know what's in your mind, and I won't do it."

He had a look of real disappointment. "Oh," he said. "Please? You must."

"Must? How can you talk that way? It's ridiculous."

"Bonnie, I believe in God when I look at your body."

She turned away from him. "Honey, you're a nut," she said.

"These pictures will show how fabulous you are." His admiration for her was so evident, so dependable, that she softened, even allowed herself to play with the thought. She was curious. Could she possibly be as beautiful as he was always saying she was?

"Say I said yes. Who would you show these pictures to?" she asked.

"No one. I swear. They're for me. Myself alone."

"You swear by your love for me?" she asked. If he was telling the truth, it might be worth it.

"Yes. By my love for you."

Now she was tempted, no question. Still! . . .

"No," she said. "I can't do it. What if someone else saw them by accident? What if your father snooped around and saw them?"

"Nobody will ever see them except you and me. You know you want to do it."

"What makes you say that?"

"The light in your eye."

It was more than that. Bonnie was also thinking of the nurse he had gone to see that time. Maybe he had known he could do things like this with the nurse. Bonnie was ready to tell herself that she had to protect their marriage. There was no sin in the marriage bed.

"All right," she said. "I've always heard that to keep a husband, you've got to be a cook in the kitchen, a lady in the living room, and a whore in the bedroom."

57

"Where did you learn that?"

"A little pussycat told me." She opened her robe.

Afterward, Bob was putting away one of the photofloods he had clamped to a lamp.

"How are you going to print these?" she asked.

"At the photo shop on the ground floor of the office," he said. "I'll drop them off when I go in tomorrow morning, and I'll get them when I come out."

"You mean the people who work in that place are going to see them?"

"Honey, they don't even look at them. It's done by machine. They just run it through the developing tank."

"I can't believe I agreed to this." She saw there was no way to stop him now. It would be an endless argument, and there was no way to prove him wrong.

Still, she could hardly wait to see the pictures. Bob had said *"Ooh!"* and *"Ahh!"* so much while taking them, and afterward, he had been like a lion in bed. Maybe she *was* something after all.

The next day, when he picked up the photos at the shop, he couldn't keep from smiling a little when the guy behind the counter handed over the envelope and winked. There had been admiration in the wink.

10

1970–1972

Lieutenant Jack Hoschouer was sitting beside his driver as their jeep moved along a paved road in Vietnam. Going through a bag of mail, he opened a manila envelope from Bob. Pictures. He was expecting photos of Bonnie and Bob taken around the house. Bob had been sending him stuff like that for the last few months, but this batch was different. Here was Bonnie in a terrycloth robe. He flipped to the next one: Bonnie's bathrobe had dropped, only the belt held it around her waist. The photos progressed from there. This was a side of Bob he'd never seen before.

Hoschouer's field tent was lit by a gas lamp. A few big bugs were flitting around the table as he wrote a letter.

Dear Bob,

Here I am in a mud swamp in Vietnam wondering if I'm ever going to get laid again and there are these pictures of this beautiful naked woman you send me.

He reread the letter, and tore it up and started a new one.

Hey, Buddy,

Did you send me something you shouldn't have sent me? I think so.

Two weeks later, after another mail run, Jack was going through a new batch of letters and opened one from Bob:

I hope you enjoyed my little morale builder.

Back in Chicago, Bob was standing in front of the bathroom mirror. He dipped his finger in shaving cream, then wrote HAND-SIN on the glass. Then in a low voice, he began to speak to the mirror. The face that looked back at him was not his own but rather the reverse of his face. Right was left, and left was right. That convinced him he was not speaking to himself but to some aspect of himself—a guardian angel, maybe, or was it a demon? Whoever or whatever, he had begun to feel that any conversation he had with the mirror was an opportunity to tell the truth, or—sometimes better, sometimes worse—to hear the truth, because the mouth that was moving in the mirror was the reverse of his own mouth.

"*One day you say to yourself, 'Am I really in love?'*" he now told the mirror. "*Because in truth, I can say 'I love you' and not feel a thing. Yet the next day, I am full of amazing love with amazing Bonnie. I bet that faith— if I could find it—is exactly the same way. Even now I can feel I'm very near to the Lord one day, but on another He's remote. Sometimes I wonder: Am I devil- possessed? I am so in love with pornography. I guess pornography becomes its own kind of religion.*" He laughed his whinny of a laugh at the mirror. It was the goofball laugh that always came out of him when he felt full of contradictions so intense that they could blow him up.

Jack Hoschouer, back from Vietnam on a furlough, sat in his lieutenant's uniform—big as life, even bigger—in Bob and Bonnie's small living room. All the while he and Bob were talking—and Bob was on one of his talking streaks—there was Jack, looking way too much and way too often at Bonnie.

"You've got to see this film, *Investigation of a Citizen Above Suspicion*," Bob insisted. "The central figure deliberately leaves clues strewn around, suggesting that he's the perpetrator, but people say it can't be him—he's beyond suspicion because he's the police chief. That's fascinating. If you were going to commit crimes at that high a level, you'd have to be the police chief. But isn't it interesting? He feels compelled to implicate himself. It's as if the game is too easy for him."

Jack was still staring at Bonnie. His thoughts were far away. Realizing that Bob had stopped talking, he said with a start, "You know, I'm still jet-lagged—it feels so funny being back."

"You have a right to feel that way," Bob said. "You're a hero." He meant it. He added, "My buddy has become a hero." The sentiment in his voice was even more intense than his words.

"I'm no hero," Jack replied. "I just happened to kill a Viet Cong before he could kill me, for which I'm grateful. But most of the time we sat in one mud hole after another. The big excitement was to put clippings up on the bulletin board."

"Really, Jack? What kind of clippings?" Bonnie asked. It was obvious she had some idea of the answer.

"Now, don't get mad at me, Bonnie. *Playboy* clippings."

"You two are beyond belief," she said.

"Well, let's not exaggerate it all," Jack said mildly. But he couldn't help himself. He was still ogling Bonnie.

The visit was over and Bonnie was turning out the last of the lights.

"I don't care how much you trust Jack," she said. "I tell you, I never want to be alone with him."

"What are you talking about?" asked Bob.

"Your 'hero,' your best buddy, keeps undressing me with his eyes."

"Bonnie," he told her. "Jack has been out there fighting for our country. And tomorrow he's on his way to meet his wife in Hawaii. He's keyed up."

"I still say he was undressing me with his eyes."

"I can't blame him. I won't blame him."

Yet, Bob was up before dawn the next morning. His insomnia was ugly. He was on the verge of getting a severe migraine.

In the bathroom, he wrote HAND-SIN on the mirror. His head was already beginning to throb, but he was horny nonetheless. He was thinking about Jack's excitement while looking at Bonnie. He asked the mirror: *"Can a man abstain from masturbation?"* and he drew a line with his finger through the foam that said *Hand-Sin*. Then, damn if he didn't masturbate after all.

When he came out of the bathroom, Bonnie was writhing in bed.

"Bonnie, what's the matter?"

"My period started—just when I thought I might be pregnant. I know I was. But I've just lost it all."

He held her as she cried. "I promise you," he said with real urgency, "we're going to have children. Many children." Already he was the opposite of the man who had just been in the bathroom. Now he believed that the intensity of his emotion could by itself help to conceive a child.

62

She was inconsolable. "No," she told him, "I'm doomed to be barren."

"You're wrong. You're lovely. God loves you."

"No, I let you take those photographs. That was sinful, and now I'm being punished."

"Darling," he told her. "Please don't make me feel guilty about that. I've felt guilty all my life."

"Bob, I'm never going to take pictures like that again."

"Bonnie, God loves your beauty. He wouldn't have given you such beauty otherwise. Remember that."

In the next moment, she was altogether practical, thinking of the pictures. "Where are they now?"

Women are amazing, he decided. The only effective response to their intuitions was to lie and lie again.

"I cut them up and threw them away," he said. "I flushed them down the toilet."

Bonnie sat on the edge of the bed, her head bent in prayer.

"Lord, forgive me. Let a miracle take place. Let me be blessed with a child. I will pray to You for this to happen through the days, through the weeks, through the years. I take a vow. If I give birth to a child, I will join Opus Dei." She nearly shivered at the enormousness of that thought. She knew it was a real vow. Heaven help her! Joining Opus Dei was one step that changed your life forever.

11

1972–1975

A year later, her vow was to be tested. Bob was at his desk in a cubicle of the huge main office of the firm of Touche Ross, a young accountant sitting at one of the fifty desks, printout pages of analysis before him. When his phone rang, he was expecting to hear the voice of one of the executives.

"My water just broke," Bonnie told him.

"Wait right there. I'll pick you up at once."

"No, no," she said. "I'll meet you at the hospital."

Bob was on his feet, sweeping his papers together.

Two of Bonnie's sisters and one of her brothers were clustered around the hospital bed. They were elated, but Bob glowed as if a light had been turned on inside him. Bonnie leaned back against her pillows with a weary but wonderful sense of self-worth. She was slightly, but happily, hysterical.

"It's miraculous, most miraculous, miraculous," she kept saying. "A child, she's alive, she's beautiful."

"Let me show you the baby," Bob said to Bonnie's sisters and brother. "She's gorgeous and we've named her Jane."

"My doctor said I'm going to be written up in a medical book as a special case," said Bonnie. "Those fertility pills really worked!"

64

Back in the apartment, in the middle of the night, in a crib beside their bed, the baby started to cry. Bob got up, reached in for the infant, and walked back and forth with her.

"Honey, this child makes me feel like a giant. I'm going to do something exceptional in my life. I know I will."

"That's nice. I'm sleepy," said Bonnie.

"I love her even if she cries in the middle of the night," he said, and continued rocking the baby. "You'll see. Big changes are coming."

Two months later, Bob bought the Hanssen family home from his father, now that Howard was retiring to Florida, and moved in with Bonnie and their first child.

Then Bonnie found out about some other changes. He called her midmorning from his office cubicle. His instinct was very much at work. Big, startling, and unpleasant news was best communicated by phone. He couldn't take the chance of confronting her face-to-face.

"Darling," he said. "You'll never guess what I did."

"Did you ask for a raise?"

"Bigger than that, much bigger. I've been on this for a week. Today, I had my final meeting with a high official of the Chicago police force. The department has accepted me."

"What?"

"I filled out the forms some time ago. They are going to take me on to do investigations."

"No. . . ."

"Don't say no." He took a big gulp as she spoke. "It's all done. I've already done it."

He managed to get off the phone, somehow, but as soon as he stepped into their house, Bonnie handed him the receiver. Howard was on the line—the expense of long distance was already in his voice.

"You're a piece of work," came the verdict. "Just as

soon as my back is turned and I think I'm nicely retired in Florida, you decide to join the force. Thank you, Robert. You think you're going to be able to live on a cop's salary and stay honest? Or is your hand sticking out already for me to pony up a little more support?" Bob moved the receiver a few inches away from his ear as his father's voice took on even more sound and fury.

Bob was working in the same building where Howard had once pointed out to him, as a child, what could happen right outside an eighth-floor window.

Now he sat in a face-to-face meeting with a Captain Carew. That was a lot of brass to talk to.

"Robert," Carew said in a genial tone. "If you make half as good an officer as your father, we have acquired a real asset in you."

"I look forward to making my father feel the same way."

"May I ask why you waited this long to apply? Did you wait for Howard to retire?"

"How did you guess, sir?"

Carew began to laugh. "I figure you didn't want him around here to spoil it for you." Now he looked Bob right in the eye. "Your wife feel all right about this?"

Bob gave a small grin. "She said to me, 'You joined the police? I'm joining Opus Dei.'"

They both laughed.

"I promise you," Carew said, "nothing is more powerful than a woman who's decided to devote her life to God." He gave a wise and weary smile. "Yeah," he said, "Opus Dei is one big deal."

"Yes, sir," said Bob. "You have to feel as if in every daily act you are living as an apostle for Christ."

"Sounds as if you're ready to join yourself."

"No, sir," said Bob. "I'm not even good enough to be a Catholic."

*   *   *

66

Just about a year later, on the street outside the police building, Bob bumped into Roger Buchman, his old roommate from Knox.

"Bob, how's it going? You still get out on the basketball court?"

"No time for that now, Roger. I joined the Chicago police. I'm an undercover detective."

"Fantastic."

"Better than being a street cop. The work is interesting. Real interesting." Bob opened up his jacket to show his PPK in a shoulder holster.

"Say! That's okay. My old roommate!"

Bob buttoned his jacket with ceremony, then stuck out his hand.

"Roger, I'd love to talk, but I have to rush this morning."

His work space was no longer a cubicle. He had a real office, even if it was no more than a cubbyhole without windows. A large desk and a filing cabinet took up most of the room.

Bob sat at his desk, pushed a pile of papers over to the side, and began writing a letter: "*Jack, I confess the truth: I can't believe the low caliber of most policemen. After three years, it's been a bit of a disappointment.*"

He was still smarting from a recent conversation with Captain Carew. It had come a long time after their first powwow, and this one was not genial at all. Still, it had produced a good result:

"*Nonetheless,*" he continued in the letter to Jack, "*it crystallized the situation. I've applied to the FBI.*"

"All right, Bob," Carew had said. "Let's say this officer you've looked into did have his hand in the till. That, to me, is not necessarily the end of the world. I can tell you, he is not a bad guy. If we go forward with this, he is going to be seriously hurt."

67

"Captain Carew, I've been on this case for five months. I've taken every precaution not to make a mistake. I know he's well regarded. But, Captain, the facts are terrible. He's as rotten as rancid meat."

"The man has a family, Hanssen. He's been on the force for close to twenty years. If we proceed, he's going to lose his pension."

"He deserves to."

Carew was getting hot. "All right," he said. "Cool down. Honest cops want all other cops to be honest. You can go overboard with that. Life is complicated."

"I don't know if I see it that way."

"Well, why don't you try?" said Carew. "You have to understand, Hanssen, that the real issue is to maintain the morale of the organization." It was apparent that Carew had decided to sit on his temper. The soft approach was coming. "During the Red-scare years," he said, "your father did good, tough work getting evidence on Communists. He saw it as such a threat that, I will tell you, Bob, he wasn't above cutting a few corners. But then some lawsuits came up, filed by the lawyers of those Communists. They sent a motion to impound our files.

"Well, the files were in your father's office. Most mysteriously, there was a fire there. Your father was the one to put it out. Unfortunately, all the relevant files in that cabinet burned up.

"We did an internal investigation and what did we find? To no one's surprise in the department, it was decided that this was an accidental fire. To this day your father is highly respected around here for biting the bullet."

"I know. My father's basic idea is: Don't ask permission, do it."

"Good."

"I happen to agree with that."

"Good."

"But what bothers me is the stupidity around here. And the corruption. Not patriotic motives like the one you just referred to, but open corruption."

"Are you saying that you don't like police work, Robert?"

"Sir, I'd like to see it take place at a higher level."

Carew's lower lip extended as if to suggest that there was no need to chew on this one too long. "Bob, put in an application for the FBI. I'll send in the highest recommendation for you."

12

1976

And then, seven years after his marriage to Bonnie, there he was in Quantico, Virginia, not far from Washington, D.C., preparing for FBI training. In his dreams of being a Special Agent, searching for new and superior ways of fighting the Cold War on the home front, trapping and catching Soviet spies, he had never given much attention to the physical demands that would be put on him. With the exception of the few months he had devoted to basketball at Knox, he had never gone in for physical conditioning. Now, at Quantico, they ran him uphill and downhill, had him doing push-ups until his shoulders felt loose in their sockets, and, worse, martial arts. He was at about the bottom of the class for that. He didn't like getting hit, not at all, and he went through the bends trying to hit other people. It was embarrassing when he missed, which was almost all the time, and when he did land a blow, he felt ready to kill the guy. Wanted to, even if he couldn't catch him again. He felt real clumsy.

His pistol scores were exceptional, however. It was a skill he had honed over three years in the Chicago police force shooting gallery.

The art of the handgun was to marry the gun to your hand, and he was getting the highest scores in his new agents class. At times like this, he didn't mind being tall and having long arms. Shooting at a target was as easy as pointing his finger at it. He was also very good in any class that required the use of his mind. So he finally got through Quantico. If he hadn't passed physical training, he would have been given a handshake and a ticket back to Chicago.

When Bob arrived at Quantico he was given his badge, but now he was graduating from the academy at Quantico and receiving his credentials.

In a medium-size room, about a dozen men were being sworn in. Bob held up his hand and closed his eyes, as if to hear the words in all their clarity.

"I swear to support and defend the Constitution of the United States against all enemies, foreign and domestic, and to bear true faith and allegiance to the same."

These words were so moving to him that his eyes smarted from the effort of holding back all his emotion. He breathed deeply. He repeated: "I accept the obligation to consider the information coming into my knowledge as a sacred trust."

Later, in a smaller office on the same floor, Bob met one-on-one with a Supervisory Special Agent.

"We're big here on bravery, integrity, fidelity, honor," the man said. Bob repeated the last couple of words to himself, although his lips moved. "*Fidelity, honor.*'" His lips formed the words quietly.

"You seem to like those words," said the agent.

"*Semper fi,*" said Bob.

The agent looked at Bob's paper. "I don't see anything about that here, but you do talk like a former Marine."

"I wasn't in the Corps, but I have family ties." One more lie—what the hell.

"Yes," said the agent. "We have a lot of former Marines in the Bureau."

Finally, he was accepted as a Special Agent of the Federal Bureau of Investigation.

He was also ready to convert to Catholicism.

Earlier, at Quantico, after some misery with an incompatible roommate, a former Marine who made it evident he hadn't two bits' worth of respect, if that, for Hanssen, Bob had hooked up with a lean, good-looking Irishman named Peter Logan, who was courteous, decent, and as religious as they came—a real on-his-knees Catholic.

Logan was also intelligent, and they had long conversations about religion. Hanssen kept bringing the subject back to converting. Like others before him, he was at times more pious than many a priest.

"The Church has survived for so long," Hanssen would say, "and it is completely consistent. I like that. Consistency is the virtue I admire most."

"Why is that?" Peter asked.

"Well, every place I've worked, I find that the majority of people are not sufficiently dedicated to their jobs. There's a corruption of purpose in so many Americans now. I wonder if the Church is our only protection against that."

"As I see it," said Logan, "the thing to keep in mind is that there is really a holy, even a sanctified, mechanism to the Church." He nodded thoughtfully. "It's as if the early founders knew that most human beings are not ready to depend upon religious sincerity alone. So it was necessary to construct a set of divine instruments that we could attach ourselves to. You follow me?"

"I do," said Hanssen. "You must be talking about the sacraments."

"Exactly," said Peter Logan. "You see, Bob, it's one thing to be a Catholic. It's another to be a devout Catholic."

Bob Hanssen felt inflamed, or was it *illumined?* He understood. He felt, finally, the possibility of religious joy, the possibility of living with it.

"I love this idea," he said. "I get it now. I really do. The sacraments are working instruments of the Holy Spirit. I get it. That is the way we can attach ourselves to everything that is holy."

"Yes, it does give you a fair chance to cleanse yourself a little."

Bob longed for Bonnie at that moment. It was as if all the sex he had missed in these weeks of training had become part of the religious glory he could feel blazing in his heart.

Later, he called her. This was another announcement he was going to make over the phone. This time, however, it was because he couldn't bear to wait any longer to tell her.

"Darling, I know I've been getting ready for this all my life," he told her. "But now I am finally convinced. I'm going to convert."

She made a small, sweet sound of pleasure. "Maybe it was a good thing, joining the FBI. You said it would be."

"It's a blessing, my darling. I can't wait until training is over and we get together again."

"I didn't let myself realize it," she said, "but a little part of me was feeling so alone."

He was charged with emotion for her. "It feels so long until we can get together again," he said.

Bob had just finished making love to Bonnie for the second time in one night. She turned to him and asked:

"Darling, do other married couples have sex every day like we do, even after eight years of marriage?"

"I don't know," he answered with contentment. "I guess we're unusual that way."

Three hours later, in the bathroom, by a dim light, he stood alone with the mirror and his reflection.

"No *matter how much I make love to Bonnie,*" he said to the man in the glass, "*I still have to masturbate. Deep in the heart of the Church, maybe I will find an end to this oppression, this horror.*"

13

1976–1978

At the rear of a modest ranch house in Gary, Indiana, on the patio behind the garage, a barbecue party for FBI agents and their wives was wafting along on beer, briquette smoke, and meat. It was a small patio, and a good number of people were standing. The few who were seated, for the most part, were women.

Some of the men were feeling well oiled. A good deal of syndicate crime from St. Louis passed through the Gary office. The street work made for a lot of war stories.

"Okay, this is a good one," said a man whose build reflected how much work he did with weights. "We figured to borrow the suspect's car for a couple of hours and install a recorder with a switch under the seat on the passenger side. We figured I could tape what he's telling me whenever we're riding together. The idea was to save me from wearing a wire, because this was one fat fuck, and he was as suspicious as they come. He was always giving me a hug and patting down my back. Well, we succeeded with the installation. Put it in without a hitch."

"Did the material pay off?" asked one of the men listening.

"Get this: The installation wouldn't function properly. Every time this fatso opened his mouth, his ass would bounce up and down on the tape recorder. You should

75

have heard those sounds! *Whoomph, whoomph!*" He imitated the noises so well that the group broke out in raucous laughter.

In another corner of the patio, one of the Special Agents in Gary, a man much older than Bob, but almost as tall, was huddling with him.

"Once we got the okay for the wiretap, it was valid for ninety days. But that's where our problems began. We knew if we wanted to renew for another ninety, we'd have to start the application process in forty-five days, and you can't believe how that ups the paperwork, because they start getting nervous back in D.C. What are we up to, they want to know. Will the extra ninety justify itself in the budget?" The man kept droning on, but when Bob managed to get away, he couldn't find anyone else to talk to. He made the mistake of smiling at one middle-aged guy who had the look of a knuckle-dragger, and immediately he received a lecture.

"Buddy, you got a few posture problems. You have to learn to stand up a little straighter," the agent said. "When we break through a door, the sight of a guy as tall as you is going to freeze whoever's waiting on the other side. Learn to use your height. Use it, I tell you. It's nothing to be ashamed of."

Most of the agents were wearing shorts and polo shirts. A few had on FBI caps. Bob was dressed in his usual dark blue suit, white shirt, and tie, and he gave up on socializing soon enough, taking a seat by himself, perhaps ten feet away from Bonnie. She had been standing for most of the party, chatting away animatedly with a number of different people, when the wife of the ranking FBI agent decided to conduct a little informal interview with her. Perhaps it was the crucifix Bonnie was wearing.

"I hear you and your husband are from northwest Chicago," said the woman. She was middle-aged and starting to get plump, with big hair that was tinted a very pale violet. "What parish are you from?" she asked.

Bonnie told her: Mary, Seat of Wisdom.

"Is your husband from the same parish? Was that how you met?"

"Well, no. My husband grew up Lutheran. He only came into the Church after we were married."

"Was that his decision or was it because of you?"

"I wouldn't like to think it was only because of me," Bonnie said, a little taken aback by the woman's manner. Awfully blunt.

The ranking agent's wife put her hand on Bonnie's arm. "It doesn't always work when they convert, you know."

"Why not?" Bonnie asked in surprise. She would have liked to say, *What makes you think you know my husband when you never even laid eyes on me until today?*

"I can tell you're a tiny bit upset with me," the woman said, and then softened a bit. "My husband tells me I speak too frankly."

Bonnie was annoyed, but she was also a bit curious. "It's all right," she said. "I'd really like to hear what you have to say."

"You see, dear, some people who convert are looking to fill a need that the Church is not necessarily equipped to take care of."

"Well," Bonnie told the woman, "Bob has his needs like all of us, but he is the finest man I've ever known. He's a wonderful father."

The woman nodded. It was obvious she was unconvinced. "Good," she said. "I'm sure it will work out."

Bonnie smiled. "I'm sure it will."

With a group of wives closer to her own age, she had a more comfortable conversation about how to raise a family when there isn't really enough money coming in.

"Everything is so expensive these days," she complained. "Sometimes we get behind for the month, and then I feel like I'm treading water."

Bob was still sitting off by himself, looking slightly gloomy. *Why couldn't he,* thought Bonnie, *just stand up and make a little effort to join the conversation?*

"I can warn you," one of the women said. "Just pray your husband doesn't get stationed in New York. That is one city to put you in debt. It's so expensive, and there the salary is the same we get out here."

As they chatted, Bob reached into the attaché case he was keeping by his feet. It was made of Naugahyde and just a little scuffed. Why had he insisted on bringing it along? Now Bonnie saw him open it, take out a sandwich, and begin to eat. His timing was terrible. At the same moment, the hostess came by with a tray of hot appetizers.

"Won't you have some of *my* food?" she asked Bob. Bonnie could read the look on the hostess's face: *Where is this goofball from? The moon?* Her expression was loud and clear.

"Nervous stomach," Bob said. He looked embarrassed, and then confused. He started to take another bite of his sandwich, but then reached for one of the canapés. Bonnie looked daggers at him.

The conversation among the wives had taken a turn. Now it was on the frustrations of being an FBI man's spouse. "We've been at it twenty years," said one of the wives, "and in that time, maybe Frank has let me in on this much." She held up her thumb and forefinger an inch apart. "And that was only because the case was in the news."

Soon Bonnie felt as if she were in a dream. Here she was talking to one face, then another, and before she knew it, she was giving personal secrets away as if they didn't need to be kept to herself.

"Yes," she could hear herself saying, *"we have two children but would like to have more. We want a large family."*

78

"How many years have you been married?" someone asked.

"Getting on toward ten. The years race by. We've had a small problem or two—well, not so small." She could no longer contain herself. "Oh, I might as well tell you. I have had miscarriages." She was shocked to hear the words come out of her mouth. Why was she saying these things? Was she so starved for the company of girlfriends?

"That's awful," the woman said sympathetically.

Bonnie couldn't stop. Maybe it was the glass of wine she'd had, or maybe the novelty in Gary, Indiana, of this much socializing. She did like parties, even if Bob detested them. Whatever the reason, Bonnie had to tell this woman about her burden.

"I've had three miscarriages so far."

The women tried to be sympathetic. "Doesn't that scare you from trying for more children?"

"No. I won't allow it to. I let my body heal and then I'm ready to try again."

After the party, they drove back to the Hanssen family house, where they still lived. Bob was in his father's big easy chair, his feet up on a hassock, just as he did each day after the long commute.

Bonnie was still full of the party.

"I hope I didn't talk too much tonight," she said as she kissed him, a peck on the cheek. Then she had to add, "I guess I had to make up for you."

"You did?" Bob said, genuinely surprised.

"Darling, the idea of a party is for people to entertain each other and have a good time. You were just sitting there by yourself."

"Everyone was talking away. I don't see why I couldn't be quiet and do a little thinking." In fact, the lecture he'd received about his posture was eating at him. Had that knuckle-dragger been trying to tell him he was not enough of a stand-up agent?

79

"Honey," she said. "I don't want to be critical, but when people are really interested in what you have to say, your voice goes down to a whisper. I think you could talk to people a little more warmly. A little more openly."

"I see so much of those guys on the job that we're all talked out with each other." But Bob was thinking about his blunder with the sandwich. That was bothering him almost as much as the know-it-all arrogance of the knuckle-dragger.

"You could have said a few things to the women," Bonnie went on.

He smiled. "I didn't see one who was even remotely as beautiful as you. Why bother?"

"Oh, Bob, what am I going to do with you?" she moaned. "I would really like to have a social life."

What with his social awkwardness and her frustration, that was one night when they slept together without touching—a rare event.

When Bonnie heard that they would be moving, she was not happy. A year could go by, or two, and then they just reassigned you to another city, did it from above in Washington, as if you were chattel. No one ever asked you what you thought about it.

"What's the sense?" she asked Bob. "We're just beginning to get comfortable, and now they have us moving to New York. Of all places. Everybody says that is the most expensive town in America."

"It's FBI policy to move us," he tried to explain. "That's so we don't get complacent and spend our careers enjoying ourselves in places like Sarasota. There are twelve major cities, and we have to put in our time in at least one of them sooner or later."

"Our credit card debt is getting bigger every month," she said, her voice rising.

"Bonnie, don't start yelling. I can't take it!" He had actually snapped at her.

In response, Bonnie began shrieking. "I'll yell if I feel like it! We have real problems, and you're not listening!"

Bob turned and walked out of the room.

That night, as he lay in bed, his eyes closed, he could still see Bonnie's mouth screaming at him the way his father used to yell at him when he was a boy. New York was not going to be a picnic.

14

1979

Well, of course they couldn't afford to live in the city, but Bob couldn't help it. He and Bonnie saw a house in Westchester that she thought was lovely, and he agreed. It stood by itself, surrounded by trees, and it would be ideal for their children, Jane, Sue, and the new baby, Jack. In fact, three days after they signed the papers and moved in, Bob set up his camera on a tripod, released a ten-second time delay on the shutter, and he and Bonnie and the two girls clustered in front of the house for a photograph. In that first week, he must have taken three rolls of film. It was such a lovely little house. Living twenty miles out of the city had solved part of the problem of being assigned to New York.

It was just that the mortgage and related payments came close to eating half his after-tax salary. He had known it would be that way, but he just had to have this house. It suited his idea of how he and Bonnie and the girls should live.

He would find a way to take care of the bills. If nothing else, he would put up with his father's scorn and allow Howard to bail them out. Bob even felt a little gratified about making Howard so damn mad, even if the process was very disagreeable. He always felt as if he had been kicked in the liver after a financial session with Howard.

Meanwhile, the bills came in and his credit card debt zoomed.

One Saturday afternoon, Bonnie came back from the store to find Bob sitting in his easy chair, staring at the wall. It looked as if he had been studying it for quite some time.

"Bonnie," he said with the kind of throat clearing that confirmed her instinct. "I have something to tell you." She put the bag of groceries down and waited. Bob said, "I called my father and invited him to visit us."

"You did? Why?" But she knew. Certain questions did not have to be asked.

"Because he does take care of a few things when he visits," Bob said, "and we are now in debt."

"By how much?"

"You don't want to know."

"How much?"

"Ten thousand bucks."

"So soon? I can't believe it," she said. Her anger was not long in arriving, but she tried to reply quietly. "Bob, you spend money on insane things that we don't need." She paused for a moment to calm herself. "I don't want to see your father. I just don't feel ready to put up with him for a few days. Certainly not now." Three children were enough of a problem.

"The other alternative"—the words did not come easily to him—"is that we could go into bankruptcy."

Bonnie felt the pang in her stomach. "No, we can't do that," she said reflexively. Her upbringing so much as told her so. Bankruptcy was like contributing to the spread of evil. It left dark and ugly thoughts in others.

"Bonnie, I know I've let you down. I guess I'm not a good husband."

"You are a good husband. You are. It's just that you're a little impractical. And so am I." She sighed. Already she could feel the fear gnawing at her. "All right," she said. "We can't tell your father not to come. But you don't know what it's like when you're away at work and he's just sitting here looking at me. He still thinks he's a gift to every woman from six to sixty."

"Is he all right with the girls?"

She began to unpack the groceries. "I will say this for him. He likes the girls. He's all right with them. I'm the one who doesn't want to be alone with him. Bob, I don't want to complain, but he undresses me with his eyes. Just like Jack always does when he comes to visit." She tried to stop, but her list of grievances was growing. "Why doesn't Jack bring his wife more often when he comes to visit?" she asked.

"Honey, you know why. He's always been stationed in Europe, Germany, or someplace. He simply can't afford the plane ticket for his wife every time he's called back to the States."

"That's the only reason?"

"What else could it be?"

In the evening, Bob went to bed right after the children had been put to sleep. If Bonnie was feeling some sense of terror at his father's visit, so was Bob.

Already he could hear Howard's voice: *How can you kids get ten thousand bucks in debt so soon after I took care of the last damn batch of bills?*

All right, Dad, all right. In Bob's imagination, he was able to answer in a calm voice. *It just won't happen again. This is the last time . . . the last time . . . the last time.* The oncoming thunder of a migraine began to sound in his head. Ten minutes later, it felt as if it was rising from the depths of hell.

Jack paid them a visit before Howard did, and, to save on a hotel bill, slept on the couch in the living room. He was always good fun at early breakfast before Bob went off to work. But Bonnie just couldn't get comfortable around him, even if these days Jack was doing his best to be proper.

Bonnie, of course, couldn't help but go on and on about how expensive everything was. It was, at the least, a reliable conversational topic.

"To move from Indiana to New York and live on the same salary—in effect the FBI is asking us to make a sacrifice."

"You don't hear Jack complaining about the army," Bob said.

"Oh, I could," Jack said.

"That's my point." Bob was beaming. He was usually happy when Jack was there. "Let's not dwell on the bad. Something wonderful has also happened since we've come to New York. Jack, I came to realize it wasn't enough for me just to convert to Catholicism. I've been waiting to tell you. I've recently joined Opus Dei."

"Well," Jack responded, "that is a very big move."

"It is," Bob agreed. "It puts a great demand on you, and it's worth it. I've never seen more dedication among any group of human beings I've been involved with." He was still beaming. "I'd say this has been the best and most profound act I've ever taken." He paused and looked at Bonnie. "Except for marrying you."

"You said that just in time," said Bonnie, and they all laughed.

With traffic and all, it would take almost an hour for him to drive to work into the city and get parked. Bob stood up, gave Bonnie a big full kiss for Jack's benefit, shook his friend's hand, and left for the office.

Through the window, Bonnie and Jack watched him drive off. On this morning, to her surprise, she felt close to Jack, as if for once she agreed with Bob, who was always saying, "Jack is family."

"You know," she told him, "when Bob and I first came here, his work was kind of a downgrade for him. He so much wanted to be in counterintelligence." She had an inkling of why she felt friendly toward Jack right then. It felt good to be talking to someone who respected her husband. "Spy work has always fascinated him," she said, and nodded solemnly. "He's realized it's what he really wants to do. Just what he's been saying all his life: catch Soviet spies in the act. I understand that. I sometimes think the safety of this country depends on our ability to keep up with them. The spies."

"Hear, hear!" Jack said. He realized that he was still unable to keep himself from flirting with her.

"I'm serious," she said, and slapped his hand. "Listen to me. When we first came here, Bob was assigned to checking on securities-exchange malefactors. He said, 'It's demeaning to be dealing only with cheap, crooked clerks and SEC bureaucrats. I just might as well be back in Chicago.'"

"But Bob told me he's happy with his work," Jack said. "Happy now, at least."

"Yes, *now*, because he finally got himself moved into counterintelligence work. He switched positions with an agent who wanted to get out of it. Bob couldn't believe his luck. But most of the agents he knows would rather be in one of the crime squads. That's true even if they're on something as second-rate, Bob says, as white-collar crime."

"I have to say, Bob seems to be thriving," Jack said.

"Well, he is." Bonnie kept nodding as if she didn't quite believe her own words. "He thinks that one of these days they're going to give him a real operation to pull off." She paused. "That's the good news." All the animation drained out of her voice.

"And the bad news?"

"We're still very much in debt. I think we have to call on Bob's father again."

Jack nodded, and waited for her to continue.

"Last time was awful," Bonnie went on. "Howard literally scolded him in front of Jane and Sue. And he loved doing it. If he's going to give us money, he wants his pound of flesh."

"I can't believe that." Howard had always been reasonably civil around Jack. Good guy to good guy, uniform to uniform.

"Believe it!" Bonnie said. She told him how Howard had said to the kids, right in front of Bob, "Your dad isn't a cop. He's a bookkeeper."

"How did Bob react?"

"He just left the room, went upstairs, and lay down on the bed."

"He walked right out of the room?"

"Jack, that is how he deals with it. Another time, right in front of Jane, Howard pulled out a wad of bills and slapped them on the table. Then he said, 'Here's the money. You'll be looking for handouts all your life.'" She couldn't have looked more miserable. "Jane asked me later, 'Mommy, what's a handout?'"

"Jack, you have to get Bob to stand up to him," Bonnie said. After it came out of her mouth, she wondered if that was being disloyal to Bob. It wasn't, she decided. It was crucial.

Bob was at Confession early the next morning. The voice of the priest was a little whispery as it came through the grille.

"You are telling me that you and your friend exchange off-color pictures?"

"Yes, Father," Hanssen said.

"Are these pictures of children?"

"No, Father. Never."

"Are these pictures of men in a carnal relation?"

"Father, they are pictures of women. Nothing else."

"Unclothed women?"

"Yes, Father."

The priest cleared his throat. "What do you do with these pictures?"

"Father . . ." He faltered. "I don't really like to talk about it."

"Do you engage in unclean personal acts by yourself?"

"Yes, Father."

"Do you and your friend ever engage in unclean personal acts together?"

"No, Father. At times we do mail the photos to each other."

"Do you wish to end these practices?"

"Father, I pray morning and night to find the power to give up this inclination, which has such power over me."

Just as the trees shed their leaves for fall, Howard Hanssen arrived at Bob and Bonnie's house driving a rented Cadillac. He got out of the car with a couple of packages and set them down as soon as he walked through the door.

Inside, the two little girls and Little Jack ran up to him, and he lifted them in the air, hung them, one by one, upside down by their heels, flipped them right side up again, and roared with laughter.

Bonnie thought it was all a little too frantic, but she said nothing. After the children had stopped hanging on to him, he handed Bonnie a gift-wrapped box.

"All right, kids, out of here," he said. "I've got something special for your mother."

"Yes, Jane, Sue, go play now," Bonnie said. "Grandpa and I have to talk."

Howard was like a huge expectant hound watching her open the gift.

"Now that you're living near Sin City," he said, "I figure you're going to need this."

In the box was a bra with see-through cutouts and panties with a comparable hole in the crotch. The openings were outlined with gold thread.

"Care to admit to your old father-in-law that you like his gift?" Howard asked. Worst of all, his voice was thick. Full of excitement. Had he forgotten that she was pregnant again and was married to his son?

"Well," Bonnie began, but had to stop. Then she managed to continue in a monotone, "I must say . . . it's . . . special. Yes, it's special." Part of her shock was that Bob had already bought her similar lingerie.

"Don't be polite. When Bob comes home we can celebrate." He patted his wallet.

Bonnie pretended to ignore the gesture. Then she decided that she couldn't. Why must she continue to play this awful game with him?

"Howard," she said, and to her great relief, her voice did not quaver, "do you realize that every time you come here, you ridicule Bob?"

Howard smiled. "Just my way of talking. Tonight, you watch. When he sees this stuff on you, he'll blow a gasket."

"Howard, can't you see how pregnant I am?"

"You can stretch these panties."

"You're not responding to what I said before."

"Yeah," he said. "What?"

"I said that you ridicule him in front of the children."

"Bonnie, let him get to the point where he doesn't have to hide behind you, but can assert himself on his own."

"How can he assert himself when his father brings his wife these . . . gifts?" She was trying to keep control of herself, but it wasn't possible. "These are filthy, dirty, abhorred gifts."

"Hey," he said. "You don't like what I brought? Good, I'll give you the receipt. Trade them in for a gross of white cotton panties. Stretchable."

"That is enough! I've had enough!" Now she was screaming. "I've had ENOUGH! You are no longer welcome in this house unless you change! I will not expose my children to ridicule of their father!"

If Howard was chastened, it was barely evident.

"Bonnie, you'd better face it. You and Bob can't live without handouts from me."

"Oh, we will. I take a vow we will!"

"Come on, little Bonnie! If money had a handle, you wouldn't be able to find it. Bob may be a glorified accountant, but he treats the almighty dollar as if he's printing it himself."

He had succeeded in getting her totally enraged. At this moment, she felt herself to be absolutely his equal.

"All right, Howard. I may be married to a troubled man, but he's a fine human being, and you can't understand that! You do everything to diminish him. Why? Because he doesn't satisfy some swollen, egocentric, nauseating idea of what your son should be. Damnit"—this from Bonnie, who almost never swore—"damn you! Just get out of this house!"

"Okay, okay. I am now ready to leave," Howard said. He smiled—actually smiled, as if he had enjoyed her outburst. "When Bob finds out what you've done, he's going to vomit all over those panties. Tell him to look for the hole."

"Out! I don't care if I never see you again."

Howard walked toward the door, then turned around and laughed. "You're great, kiddo. You're the best workout I've had in a week."

"Get out."

He shut the door quietly behind himself.

That night, Bonnie said to Bob, "You will write to your father and tell him that if he continues to insult you in front of your children, he is not to visit here again."

The trouble was, she kept saying the same thing over and over, all night long.

"Bonnie, you have said that more than once. I hear you."

"I will say it again and again until you agree to write him that letter."

"You don't know what you're asking."

"It has to be done," Bonnie said.

Later, he sat down at his desk to do the letter. Bonnie

stood in the doorway, watching. After he had written a few lines, he said, "All right. It's finished. But you don't know what this will mean for us."

"Read it to me," Bonnie said.

"'Dear Dad, Bonnie has told me of her last conversation with you and I agree with everything she said. We don't want any more money from you. Your son, Robert.'"

He looked up at her as he sealed the envelope. Suddenly, he amazed her. He smiled. It was like sunlight after a string of rainy days.

"I guess, that if I were still a Protestant, I would feel like a born-again Christian," he said.

"What a funny thing to think," Bonnie said.

"Hey," Bob said. "I feel as though all my life has been leading up to just this moment." He handed her the letter. "Here. Put a stamp on it. Let's get it in the mail before we weaken."

15

1979

Bob sat in a crowded Midtown restaurant in New York City with FBI Special Agents Frankie Mack and Anthony Guardino.

"You know," Mack was saying, "I've had it up to here with hearing about how much it costs to live in New York. I think my wife is going nuts."

"Call me a flag-kisser," Anthony said, "but we are very loyal Americans. Here we are, always broke, knowing we could be rich. How? Easy. We're sitting at the mouth of a fucking gold mine."

"Yeah?" said Mack. "Where is the shovel?"

"It is so easy," Anthony said, "to make money off the Soviets. It could be huge."

"What kind of crazy shit is that?" asked Frankie Mack.

"I repeat—huge. It could be *huge*. Just get in contact with a KGB man or even a GRU man. Then slip the bum a couple of papers—nothing of consequence, nothing to do the Soviets any good, but we know they do get paid by their people to make contacts with us. They're so desperate; they'll pay real money for total crap. They'll tell themselves they see it as starters."

Hanssen spoke up suddenly. "Anthony, none of us is ever going to do that. They took us into the Bureau because they were certain they could trust us."

"Of course—exactly. That's why we don't do it," Mack said, and made a slicing motion across his throat. "Besides, it's life in prison."

"Worse than death." Anthony was animated. "Sixty years in the slammer." Then he gave a big laugh as if to make it crystal clear that this was just a lot of talk. He felt as if he had to. How could anybody be sure about Hanssen? He could be a brownie hound.

Mack wouldn't let it go, however. "None of this has foundation," he said. "There's no way to get that kind of money. Think about it. If you go out to meet the guy, right behind him come the cuffs. Don't you see? There's no Soviet you can trust."

They were always coming up with these hypothetical scenarios. It was a test of wits.

"I can't believe I'm listening to a conversation as stupid as this, and that you even persist in it," Bob said.

Anthony picked up on the look he was getting from Mack. "All right. It *is* stupid," he said. "We're just fucking around. No harm done."

"I agree, it's stupid." Mack forced himself to smile big. "Can you believe it? All three of us agreeing on something for once?"

After lunch, Bob was talking to nine agents. Among them were Anthony and Mack. Bob projected photographs of three men onto a screen. "All right," he said. "Bunky Fitzhugh has asked me to assist in this operation under his direction."

There was barely stifled mirth and derision in the room. It was no secret that Bunky no longer lived for the Bureau nearly so much as he lived for golf. Did he manage to put in even fifteen hours a week of real office time? Bob was the only one who didn't scorn Bunky. The supervisory agent had taken a shine to him, and Bob knew why: Bunky knew he could assign a lot of tricky jobs to Special

Agent Robert P. Hanssen and he was right. Up to now, Bob had delivered on every job Bunky had given him.

"I've collated all the surveillance reports on all the Soviet officials at AMTORG," Bob told the assembled agents, "and these three gentlemen come into high focus." He used his pointer to indicate each of the three in turn. "They are not only doing legitimate business here, but seventy-five percent probability, they are also serving GRU or KGB Intelligence. We now believe that they make their contacts with sympathetic Americans on Sundays. Why? Because the Bureau doesn't work on Sunday—simple as that."

A murmur came up from the men. Bob could even hear one of them groan, "Not a Sunday job!"

"Whether it makes us happy or not," Bob continued, "these people almost certainly meet their contacts or do their dead drops on Sunday. They have good reason to believe that we are at home, watching football. But this Sunday, you won't. Bunky's plan is for you to be in three groups, made up of three men each. Each group will work a continued close-focus surveillance on the particular AMTORG official I will assign to you.

"From studies made of the main building at AMTORG, it has been determined that the possibilities for surveillance on Sunday are reduced to these two exits."

Bob now projected a slide of the floor plan next to the photographs of the three AMTORG officials he had named.

"Grozhinsky," he said, "always comes out of this exit. Always." With the pointer, he touched the floor plan. "The other two always leave by the other exit. You'll be ready to follow them by vehicle, or if necessary on foot."

"I assume that if we catch them passing or receiving, we do not grab them," Mack said.

"Yes," Hanssen said with authority. "Bunky says that we have not been authorized to make a seizure. This operation is only to confirm our suspicions."

That Sunday, Bob was at his desk waiting for the three teams to report in. He stared at the phone, patiently. He was tense.

The phone rang. It was Bonnie.

"We can't talk now," Bob told her. "I'm on the watch for calls."

"Why are you working? I've been on pins and needles."

"Bonnie, please get off the line. I can't tell you." He hung up. The phone rang again.

"We lost the guy," Mack said.

"That's the second one lost. How did you manage that?" Bob said. "Bunky is going to be very mad."

"Bunky can't afford to be. He didn't give up his golf game, did he?"

"I don't want to listen to comments like that."

"Bob, take it easy. The truth is—and don't repeat this, 'cause it sours everything in the organization—do *not* repeat it . . ." Mack trailed off as he waited for a response.

"All right, I won't," Bob said.

"Two of my men didn't show up. One was sick—genuinely sick. The other one said, 'It's cockamamie to work on Sunday.' I couldn't manage the surveillance by myself. I lost my target."

"Then we're down to one team?"

"Don't count on the third gang."

"This is getting a little hard to believe," Bob finally said.

"Look, I've been in this a lot longer than you have. Let's have a drink and talk about this."

"When?" asked Bob.

"Right now."

"I don't drink very much," Bob replied.

"Fine. You can watch me drink. I enjoy getting a little loaded on Sunday afternoon."

* * *

They sat at a quiet Irish bar with just a few people in a couple of booths. Mack ordered a whiskey, Hanssen asked for a Coke.

"Bob, we're good people; we work hard most of the time, reasonably hard. It's a life. A lot of us—face it—are going nowhere. It's a job and I feel patriotic about the job, but patriotic can be spelled two ways—big *P* or little *p*. The fact of the matter is, we can get things done if we are allowed to do them in the way we're used to doing them. We don't try to be too ambitious on our own. We let the work help us as much as we help the work. You, on the other hand, have been suckered in by Bunky. You haven't had enough experience to be assigned by him to a job as big as this, but then you were the only guy he could count on. Because he's through and he knows it. Bunky is up for retirement in a year and he wanted to pull off one big one. That way, they might up his grade level at the end and entitle him to a bigger pension."

"So why did he pick me and not one of you?" Bob asked.

"Because we see through him. He knew he couldn't count on us."

"Then why wasn't he here on the ground with me?"

"That's what you have to worry about now. He will make the report—you can count on that. Since the operation didn't work, he will disassociate himself from it."

"And if it *had* worked, would he have taken the credit?"

"That," said Mack, "you can also count on. If it had worked." He took a good swig of his whiskey.

"When you get a blue-flamer like Bunky, even if he's all burned out, they still know all the moves on how to protect themselves."

"I still don't know what he was seeing in me."

"Okay," said Mack. "I'll tell you. He could spot the blue flame that is dying to come out of your ass. He can pick up on who's as ambitious as he used to be. Bob, you are too ambitious. Learn how little you can do, and who you can do it with."

It was very early the next morning when Bob got out of bed.

Bonnie stirred. "Are you all right?"

"I'm fine," he said. "I just have to think a few things out."

He headed down to the den and dialed Jack's number. He knew Jack would be asleep, but he had to call him, anyway.

"I'm sorry about the hour, Jack, but I just have to talk."

"Yeah," Jack said. "Okay, let me get my head open."

"I now understand," Bob stated, "what John Foster Dulles meant when he said, 'I'm going through an agonizing reappraisal.'"

"Oh sweet Christmas, what in hell are you talking about?"

"I'm practically choking with my sense of disgust."

"Disgust?"

"Yeah, at the inefficiencies and cynicism of my colleagues. They don't get it that the Bureau is there to protect America. To them, it's just a job."

Jack said, "Bob, get a hold of yourself. Face the unhappy news. Not everybody is going to be as gung ho as you."

"I have to say it," Bob went on. "In New York, our counterintelligence efforts against the Soviets are worse than weak. One could describe them as juvenile."

"You ask too much of your fellowman," Jack said. "In the army, we screw up by the numbers. Learn to accept that."

"I'm not willing to," Bob said. "Not when it concerns the Bureau."

"Have it your way. You always do."

"Jack, get it straight. I am in the full blast of a migraine now and I know what causes it. There are tremendous impulses in me. They flood everything."

"I can feel for you," Jack said, and knew that was not much of an answer for a guy who had a migraine.

"I appreciate that," Bob said. "Thank you, Jack. I do appreciate that you are listening to me. Tonight I realized that there are things in life that can drive you crazy."

Again, Jack could think of no words to help his friend in this bind.

Bob said, "Thank you. I am going to hang up now." The den was fading out before his eyes under the power of the migraine.

16

1979

He just could not get back to sleep. This once, he could guess the source of his migraine. It was clear enough. He was tremendously tempted to make a bold and terrifying move. The conversation he'd had with Anthony Guardino and Frankie Mack had gotten inside him, and he lived with it. He could solve his money problems with one strong initiative—he could sell a piece of information to the Soviets. The opportunity had come up.

The beauty of working at counterintelligence in a second-rate Bureau shop in Manhattan was that few of the agents on the premises understood how vital it was to protect important documents. Everything was on paper, and the Special Agents in counterintelligence, of which Bob was one, were trusted. The agents could get access to almost anything they wanted—even the *closed* files. Top-secret stuff. One document was true dynamite. Since Bob was assigned to the GRU squad, he knew that the Bureau had had a mole in the GRU since back in 1962! That's how successful the New York squad had been in the past. Now the guy was no less than a GRU general in New Delhi. His name was Dmitri Polyakov; code name: TOPHAT.

This piece of information would be worth fifty thousand to one hundred thousand dollars if he could deliver it through reliable sources. That, however, was just what

Bob did not have. His only useful connection to Soviet Intelligence, whether KGB or GRU, was a GRU officer assigned to the Soviet Mission to the United Nations. He would be insignificant in the espionage scheme of things going on in Washington. Because he was just a minor guy in New York, it might not be a good idea to ask for more than twenty grand. Sending vital information through a second-level messenger might only half-convince the GRU, but twenty thousand dollars might be a modest enough sum for the Soviets to take a flier.

Trying to think while in the grip of a migraine was like trying to hear someone whisper in a bowling alley. The same thoughts went around and around in Bob's head. Here was this nonentity in New York, this Alexei Karilovsky, this Soviet military officer, and Bob was the case agent for the GRU office. Karilovsky was not important enough to be under total scrutiny. No one was ever assigned to follow him—Bob had been instructed that it was enough to monitor him through routine wiretaps at the Soviet Mission to the U.N. And Bob knew his mail was not being looked at. It was that simple: Karilovsky was his man. Karilovsky was there to be used. Best of all, Bob was the only FBI Special Agent assigned to Karilovsky.

He decided to pull the trigger. He took a letter to the officer of a company run by the Soviet military intelligence, which stated, among other things, that the writer possessed valuable information on a high GRU officer once stationed in New York, a man who had been recruited by the FBI and subsequently had been handled by the CIA. For the sum of twenty thousand dollars, the name would be supplied.

Migraine or no migraine, Hanssen had thought it through. He gave the location of a dead drop and instructions on how to get in touch with him through encoded radio transmissions. It was the oldest of methods.

Bob also insisted that he would have contact only with Karilovsky.

He supplied the code name and the real name of the GRU general, and in return Karilovsky left the money for him at a specific location. If not for the tension of playing for the first time at such high stakes, it would have been no great matter.

They had not sent twenty thousand dollars, but fourteen thousand. Not what was requested, but it was just a little more than he needed to cover his debts.

Of course, it did not end there.

17

1979–1981

One morning, very pregnant by now with their fourth child, Bonnie carried towels from the washing machine in the kitchen up into the bathroom. On a little table was a pile of magazines, and as she set the towels down, she saw a copy of *Playboy* peeking out. In a fury, she picked it up and stalked right down to the basement, just in time to see Bob place his hand over a letter he was writing at his desk.

"Give me that piece of paper you just tried to hide," she demanded.

"There's no need to see it," he said quietly. "Really no need, Bonnie."

"I can't possibly trust you." She put a protective hand on her belly. "How can I trust you at a time like this? Bob, show me that piece of paper."

"Don't ask for it, Bonnie. It's an official FBI document."

"Bullshit," she said. It was the first time she had ever used that word.

For days she had been convinced that something was wrong. She couldn't fathom what it was; yet her dreams were disturbing. In one of them, she felt as if she had spent an entire night locked in a room where objects kept shifting their positions, sometimes by no more than an inch or two, but nothing remained exactly in place.

The moment she saw the copy of *Playboy,* however, she was convinced. Bob was having an affair with some woman. That was why he skipped Communion the last time they were in church. Indeed, for all of the eleven years they had been married, she had never been rid of the wound that awful nurse had managed to leave in her with one phone call. Bonnie had managed to trust Bob again, but—she had to admit the truth—she could not trust him completely. During every one of her pregnancies, she had suffered from jealousy, which grew and grew. The more her weight increased and her belly swelled, the more she feared that Bob would never find her attractive again.

This time the feeling that something was wrong was the most intense it had ever been. She felt no surprise at hearing herself say, "Give me that paper or I will believe you have gotten into something with another woman." She waved the *Playboy* as if it were evidence.

"Are we going around the track again on this stupid business?" Bob groaned. "*Playboy* has nothing to do with anything."

"Then what is that paper you are hiding?"

"It's an official document." His hand still covered it.

"It isn't. I saw you writing. It's a letter. Who is it to? Some new woman?"

"Bonnie, I haven't had anything to do with any woman but you since that one awful incident. I took a vow, if you remember. I have never broken that vow."

"Let me see the letter. Otherwise, I will still believe it is a woman."

She attempted to pull his hand off the paper. Finally, he did not resist her. If he didn't let her see it, his life would be drenched in misery for months to come. When she took the paper and held it under the light, she could see it was only the beginning of a letter, just a few words, and not even in his handwriting. He had printed every word in large block capitals.

"What does this mean? *'If you want more information that can be added to the first offering'*? What is this all about?"

Bob seized the piece of paper. With his long arm, he held it away from her. But Bonnie began to go after it in such a fury that he panicked. She could lose the child.

"Bonnie, stop! You're too pregnant for this." She kept trying to reach the paper. "All right," he said. "If you'll stop, I'll tell you what it is all about."

"Yes, I want to know."

"This is just a letter to a very dumb Russian."

"What? What are you talking about?"

"Honey," he said, and he put his hands on her shoulders, with as much tenderness as he could offer. "I have been doing all this for us. I managed to offer a piece of valueless information—true penny-ante stuff, total trash—to one of the Soviet organizations. And, believe it or not, they came back with enough money for us not to have to go to my father."

She shivered. "Oh, Bob, how can you tell me that? Now I even wish it was a woman."

"No, Bonnie, this is all right. I've been doing this for us."

"No, Bob, you took an oath of allegiance to our country. You know that and I know that." She took a deep breath. "We have to talk to our priest," she said.

"Darling, that could be an irrevocable step for us."

"It won't be. I don't believe it will be, but I can't live with this," she said. "How can I go to Confession if I'm allowing you to sell information to a group that wants to destroy America? It's a materialistic, godless force."

He was hit with the sickening terror that if he did not obey her, she would lose the child—even more, lose her love for him. Their marriage might be ruined forever. He gave in.

That night, Bob and Bonnie made an emergency call to their Opus Dei priest. His name was Robert P. Bucciarelli, which had always seemed like a good omen to Bonnie: he had the same first name and middle initial as her husband.

"You say," said Father Bucciarelli, "that you gave this information to some Russian Soviet group called the GRU. Explain it to me. Is that a branch of the KGB?"

"Oh no, Father," Hanssen said. "I would never go near the KGB. They're evil. They are the top-flight intelligence operation for the whole Soviet system. The GRU is just Soviet military intelligence. Very out-of-date. Stupid as they come."

"You are saying that this GRU is ineffectual?"

"Father, believe me, I wouldn't have gone near them otherwise."

The priest did not know what to make of the situation. "This is very serious," he said.

"Father, I only passed on information that they already possess." That was a lie.

"Even if true, it is still not an exculpation. You could be confirming data they did not trust until your piece of information came along."

"Father, it's absolutely harmless."

"Well, probably so—I certainly hope so—but under the circumstances, I think you had better surrender this information to your FBI authorities. They are the proper people to judge the seriousness of your act." Now it was Bonnie who gasped. She did not speak, but with her eyes, she beseeched the priest. Father Bucciarelli looked at both of them and shook his head. "Let me think about this overnight," he said.

It was like no other night they had ever spent together. They held each other in the darkness but could not find a word to say.

In the morning, Bob called in to the office and said he was too ill to come to work. He and Bonnie went back to see Father Bucciarelli.

As soon as they were seated, the priest told them, "I haven't slept all night. I kept thinking of your three children and how you will soon have a fourth. On reflection, I believe we must find a middle path. So tell me. Swear to me. Will you assert that these materials you gave to the GRU are, as you put it, trash? Exactly that, trash? They are of no value at all?"

"Father, I couldn't believe how gullible those Soviets were."

"Perhaps they presented themselves as fools in order to entice you further?"

"Definitely. Yes, I think they were offering me some easy money. They were probably trying to encourage me to approach them again. But I never will. How can I? My act was folly. To do it again would be treason."

"Could you take a vow to that effect?"

Hanssen nodded.

Then the priest said, "You understand, of course, that the money you recently obtained must be given to charity."

"Father, I only did this in the first place because I wished to avoid declaring bankruptcy. I did not want my wife subjected to that kind of humiliation. It goes so deep. The money I received has been spent to take care of our debts, all of them."

"Then we have a new concern. You still have to make up for the amount you spent by contributing an equal sum out of your present income to charity. May I suggest that you save enough each month to catch up in two years?"

"That's a perfect idea," Bonnie said.

Bob did not take his eyes off the priest's, which were focused upon his own face.

"Absolutely," Bob said. "I agree absolutely."

Bob and Bonnie were back at home, sitting on their couch, their hands clasped. Rarely had they felt closer.

Nonetheless, one question had to be resolved: Which charity was going to benefit?

"I was assuming we would give the money to Opus Dei," Bonnie said.

"Opus Dei is beautiful, and I can see why it's your first choice," Bob said. "Ever since I joined, I've felt energized with this wonderful basic idea that average people, average hardworking people, can find joy by living their daily lives as apostles for the Lord Jesus Christ. Just trying to be there as an apostle in every little daily act. It is really such a joyous conception. Hard to do, yet simple. Full of discipline and beautiful."

"Bob, that is a lovely thing you just said."

"Bonnie, I revere Opus Dei."

"Then why do you want to give the money to Mother Teresa?" Before he could answer, she added, "I do care about the work she does. But, Bob, Mother Teresa is not interested in trying to change and improve the world we inhabit. Opus Dei is."

"I agree with that," he said, "but I still want to give the money to Mother Teresa."

"Why, Bob? Why?"

"Because, Bonnie, she takes near-dead people off the streets of Calcutta, people who are dying of hunger and all kinds of terminal disease, and she brings them to her hospice. She doesn't have enough money to afford medicine for them. It hardly matters. In most cases, it's too late for medicine. But she and the sisters care for the people they take off the streets, care for them gently and tenderly until they pass away. And when people ask her why she goes to such lengths, she says that she doesn't want them to die with a curse in their heart against God."

Tears welled in Bonnie's eyes.

"Bob, there are times when you are the most spiritual person I know."

* * *

That night, Bob gazed at himself in the bathroom mirror.

"How can I afford," he whispered, *"to send five hundred dollars a month to Mother Teresa for two years?"*

By now, he wondered who spoke to whom during these moments before the reflecting glass. More and more, it was as if he were talking to a friend closer to him than even Jack Hoschouer. Sometimes the conversations were remarkable, sometimes no more than practical. Sometimes he had to wonder whether a war was going on between his soul and his demon. Sometimes he wondered who was who and which was which.

"Yes, I will keep my promise. I will send Mother Teresa five hundred dollars a month. I will do that anonymously. That must be done. So it's obvious. I must continue with the Soviets. For a little while. For no longer than the months it will take to be Prince Bountiful to the lady from Calcutta, that saint! And I swear that I will never do spying again. Yes, I swear from the center of my heart."

He grinned at himself. *"You are one bad boy, Robert,"* the lips in the mirror replied.

18

1981

He kept up the postal relationship with the GRU. He could tell that they were clearly concerned by the information he had sent. They asked for more verification, and he supplied them with the few additional details he was able to glean from the stacks of papers his squad was trusted with. He had to be very careful. But he had also come to the conclusion that the GRU would never believe his information.

It turned out pretty well. After three more exchanges, he had paid off the debt to Mother Teresa—for that was how he saw it—but the GRU had gotten tired of him.

By the end, Hanssen decided that he had not really been lying to Bonnie and to Father Bucciarelli. He was sure his information had been treated as trash.

What he didn't know was that based on his information the GRU had called TOPHAT back to Moscow. He was questioned about allegations of espionage, but conclusive evidence was not found to support the charges. As he was a general, he was reassigned to the GRU training academy and, two years later, was allowed to retire. However, in 1986 he was arrested for spying, then tried, and later executed in 1988.

In 1981 Bob was promoted to an accounting assignment at FBI Headquarters in Washington, D.C. Now he was a

Supervisory Special Agent in the Budget Unit. If ever the time had come to build his career with the FBI, and to settle into a real home, it was now. Maybe they could even put down roots. He loved the thought of having a large family grow up in northern Virginia, near Washington, D.C. Bonnie had known all her life how good it was to live with brothers and sisters, and Bob felt as if the ongoing emptiness of being an only child might finally give way to the sounds of a happy household.

PART TWO

Fourth Floor

1

1983

By their third year in Washington, the family had grown to four children. Jane was eleven, Sue was nine, Little Jack, born in 1977, was six, and Mark was three. Except for the way Bob towered over Bonnie as they walked together, the Hanssens looked like a typical family enjoying themselves in a highway motel's swimming pool on the way to Florida.

It was still early morning, but the kids were wet and full of excitement. It was the beginning of the third and last day of their trip south, and the family had the swimming pool all to themselves. Even their mother was splashing with them. Only Bob stood apart in his wet bathing trunks, his skin pale, his body tense.

"All right," he said. "Let's get out of the water. We have to leave soon."

"Bob, just relax," Bonnie said. "We'll be there by late afternoon."

"How can I relax?" he told her. "It's been four years since I've seen him." He had not even spoken to Howard two weeks ago. And then it was Howard who had called, inviting Bob and his family to drive down to Florida for a visit. Enough years had passed for Bob to say yes. They were certainly in enough of a cramped economic position to enjoy an inexpensive vacation as opposed to no vacation.

"Why is Grandpa's place called Venice?" Jane called up from the pool.

"That's not his place," Hanssen said. "That's the town he and Grandma live in."

"It's near Sarasota," Sue, always the knowing little nine-year-old, added, "and that's on the Gulf of Mexico."

"Yes. You are so smart," Jane replied.

The family was riding in their secondhand van, the kids in the back playing cards. Bob was driving and Bonnie was listening to the Beatles, who were definitely beginning to get on Bob's nerves.

"We've had that ruckus going in our ears for two hours," he said finally.

"I know, Bob, it's not your kind of music," Bonnie said, "but I grew up with them. I love the Beatles."

"Daddy, please," Jane called out from the back. "I love them, too."

"Okay, okay. I'll do my best to bear it." He was a ball of nerves by the time they passed the sign that read VENICE CITY LIMITS.

Howard Hanssen had bought a small one-story house, and he and Vivian were sitting on the porch when they arrived.

The girls jumped around Howard as he tossed Little Jack in the air and caught him. His hands were all over the children. Bonnie sat talking to Vivian on the sofa but did not miss a single one of Howard's moves.

Then Howard handed out presents. He made a great game of it, pretending each one was the last and that nothing was left for the next-youngest kid. He would shrug, he would cluck his tongue, he would say, "Golly, how did I forget you?" And then he would hunt in a corner and come up with another box while the kids were just wailing with laughter. Bob remained off to the side.

That evening, Jane was given the one small sofabed in

114

the corner of the living room, while Sue and Jack spread out in sleeping bags around the floor, and little Mark was given a waterproof pad. They giggled when the lights went out.

"Great! This is great!" Little Jack called out loudly. "I like sleeping on the floor!"

The next morning, Howard took a walk with the children and they pestered him with questions.

"Grandpa, are we going to the drugstore for candy?" Little Jack wanted to know.

"Only if you obey the rules," Howard said.

"What are the rules?" Jane asked.

Howard pointed to the pavement. "The first rule: Don't step on a crack. You'll break your mother's back."

"That's not true," Sue said in an authoritative voice.

"Don't be so sure. Are you really ready to take a chance?"

The children started walking in hobbled fashion, and Howard did, too. At all odd angles with their bodies, they still pranced down the street. After a little while, they all began to laugh.

Later in the day, Vivian was handing out dolls.

"Grandma, you really made these yourself?" Jane was impressed.

"I sewed them, yes, I did," Vivian said. "And here are twin piggy banks for you and Sue."

The girls squealed when they saw them. Vivian had painted the nicest flowers on them.

It was not until the end of a four-day visit, when the Hanssens were packing their van and the kids were ready to go, that Howard and Bob really began to talk to each other. Howard took him aside.

"I see you left reading material for me. It looks like religious stuff."

"Yes. I thought I'd lay it right next to your lounge chair." *Incredible,* Bob was thinking. The man still had the power to tighten him up. He was cringing inside waiting for the shot.

"You're not in any hopes I'll read it?" asked Howard.

"Who knows? Maybe someday," Bob said.

"Forget religion. It's for the worry-birds." But Howard looked at the ground and then put his hand on Bob's shoulder. "Son, I enjoyed this visit. You and Bonnie can be proud of your kids."

"Well, Dad, thank you for saying that." It actually choked him up a little.

The van kept rolling on the highway even after it got dark. The children were asleep, and Bob and Bonnie talked in low voices.

"You know," Bob said, "for the first time, I began to feel half-comfortable around him."

"He's much more impressed with you than he wants to allow."

"That's your doing, Bonnie. You made the change."

"But I have to tell you. He still worries me. That look in his eye when he's handling the children."

"No, I think he's mellowing out." Bob lowered his voice even more. "Bonnie, this visit did a great deal for me. I feel like a special piece of me that's always been suffering from something like malnutrition, really, something like spiritual malnutrition, is finally coming into its own."

"I don't understand how you talk. You've always been there for me."

Bob took one hand off the wheel to squeeze her hand in his.

2

1983

Bob showed his credentials and was admitted through the guard gate on Pennsylvania Avenue that leads to the Executive Office Building, part of the White House complex. He was going to the third-floor office of a man named Mike Shepard, who had been his immediate boss in Counterintelligence on the fourth floor at the Bureau's J. Edgar Hoover Building in D.C. Mike stood up to greet Bob when he came in. Shepard was a short, powerful, well-knit man, full of energy.

"Mike," said Bob, as they shook hands, "it's been too long. We really need you back on the fourth floor."

Shepard laughed. "I'll be returning in a few weeks. But I've got to say, working at the White House has been a real stimulating six months here."

"It can't be too soon for me. You're the only guy over there that I can talk to."

A look came into Shepard's face. It was obvious that Hanssen had come to have another heart-to-heart. Their friendship—such as it was—had based itself on this element. They could always get right to the point about what was bothering them, which Bob could hardly do with anyone else. Mike, therefore, got right into it.

"Okay, Bob," he said. "I can see that you are still the unhappiest man on the fourth floor. So, let me try to cheer you up. Some of the most effective people who ever lived had good reason to be dissatisfied for years. Why, just look at General Ulysses S. Grant when he was back there in Galena, Illinois, before the Civil War. He thought he was through. Nothing to do but work away in the hardware store." He made a point of laughing. Hanssen didn't always get these kinds of ironies. "The thing is, Bob, I could get tired of telling you that there are people in the Bureau who recognize your abilities."

"Maybe," Bob said. He almost added, *Maybe not.* Instead, he said, "It's going on eight years for me in the FBI, and sometimes I feel as if there's no traction under my feet."

"Bob, that's ridiculous. You already have reached the cream level—that wonderful cream level. I can tell you that I was never happier than when I was there. High enough on the ladder to get interesting assignments and yet not so high that you find yourself trapped in nothing but administrative work." Shepard tapped his chest. "All I ever do these days is oversee the work of talented guys like you."

"Well, thank you, Mike."

Shepard was, in fact, wondering how he could reach the man. Hanssen was damn talented, probably the brightest agent he had. All right, budget work was not enough for him, and yet even there Bob's work was hardly rudimentary. He had made it much more than serving up a spreadsheet. He was great at pulling together all the information and numbers on everything the Bureau had accomplished in a given area over the past year, and then equally good at projecting the needs for the following year. Shepard had had a lot of meetings with top people, and Hanssen was the one he liked to bring along. He could write excellent debriefing books to put under the director's hand when he had to testify on Capitol Hill, helped him to explain why they required ten or twenty million more dollars for this or that project. No one was better than Bob for preparing the most effective talking points.

He also cut quite a path when it came to dealing with engineers at a conference table. They would be looking for the money to design something new, and, all too often, Bob was the only one to spot the flaw in their concept. Not only technically, but strategically. Shepard remembered him saying once, "We don't need this. It won't amount to that much in the field."

"Why won't it?" the engineer across the table from him had asked.

"Because we don't have to have an improved device that will enable us to follow some Soviet who is ten blocks away. We already have the gadget you fellows designed that can follow him from nine blocks away. That's good enough for such purposes."

"Well, what are we looking for if not for this kind of continuing improvement?"

Bob could be awfully curt. "We don't need to know where that Soviet is now, it's where he's going to be ten minutes from now. It's not a technical problem but a lack of sufficient counterintelligence. Which is where these sequestered funds are going to go. That is my recommendation."

Shepard had to grin as he recalled the look on the technician's face. How the man had disliked Hanssen!

All the same, Bob was paying for the privilege of speaking his mind. His kind of intellectual arrogance ruffled Bureau egos. That particular technician had complained to his boss, who in turn had passed it on to Shepard, who could handle criticisms of Bob. All the same, it did not help to get Hanssen up to where he wanted to be.

"Okay, Bob," Shepard said to him now, "you are complaining that there's no traction under your feet. Well, maybe I have a couple of tough things to tell you." He held up a finger. "One—you've got to learn to dumb

119

down a little. Otherwise, you are going to alienate permanently some of the people who hang out around the top guys."

"Mike, I'm not sure I care. A lot of the guys around the director are just not as smart as they ought to be."

"All right, they aren't. You have to learn to suffer fools in high places," Shepard said.

"I don't agree. In the Bureau, it's our duty to be bright."

"Whoa!"

"No! Stupidity is a choice. Deep down, people choose to be stupid because it gives them power over other people. Ugly, negative power—the power to slow up people who are brighter than themselves. How dare these guys occupy high offices if they aren't obsessed with being good enough to fulfill their tasks?"

"Hey, Bob, when will you learn? If you can't sell yourself in the FBI, your ability to get up where you want to be and influence a few events is nil."

"Is that how people see me? That I can't sell myself?"

"Want me to serve it cold?"

"I'd like to find out."

"People respect you for your technological knowledge. Your insights. You are the resident computer genius. You help us out in a lot of ways that never get on paper. You got a lot of brownie points for that methodology you brought in this year, Bob. You really showed us how to classify our intelligence targets. I wish I had thought of it. Don't put all the KGB generals in one pile and all the colonels in another, you said. Classify them by priorities instead: What is the information they're after and what is their ability to get that information? One may have interesting nuclear info but little ability to get at the KGB files, so that's a lower priority for us than the KGB man who knows about it and also has access. Bob, you succeeded in revising our fundamental methodology on this matter. That is no small feat. Not in this Bureau. You are appreciated, man."

"I want to hear the negative side. How does the top echelon see me?"

All right, Shepard thought. *He is certainly asking for it.*

"Most blue-flamers perceive you as not having enough people skills."

"Maybe I'm a little tired of being judged by ex-knuckle-draggers whose only skill is the ability to make the director laugh."

"No one's asking you to become a knuckle-dragger and bust down doors. That's not your function."

"I can bust down doors with the best." What a lie! They both knew that. But, as Shepard could see, Bob was suffering from a highly developed case of ego-burn. No question. He was as ambitious as any blue-flamer.

"I'm infuriated, Bob. Are you ready to be realistic? Accept the fact. There are two kinds of people in our work. A warrior class. They go out and put on the handcuffs. They grab bad guys. Then there are us experts on the fourth floor. We study the hell out of everything and we can become very valuable. We're the researchers, the analysts. Learn to be content with that."

"My father used to use almost the same words. He called them warriors and wizards."

"Hey, I like that—warriors and wizards. That was your old man who said that?"

"Yes," said Bob. "Only, he was a warrior."

"Cheer up," said Mike. "Once I'm back on the fourth floor, there'll be some more challenging assignments for you."

"I'm taking that as a promise," Bob said, but it was spoken to himself as he walked down the hall. He was pretty worked up. Those stupid people at the top! Their idea of intelligence was to be able to summarize, make it easy for people above them, be able to put everything you knew in one lousy three-by-five index card.

Months later, in his living room, Bob was sitting in an armchair, his legs extended on a hassock, while Bonnie read by the light of a lamp on an end table next to the couch. She was looking over his alumni bulletin from Knox.

"Bob, this is amazing. You never tell me these things. I didn't know you were working over at the White House."

"Where did you get that idea?"

"Where else? In the alumni bulletin." She waved the magazine at him, then read aloud, "'Bob Hanssen now puts in his FBI hours at the Executive Office Building assigned to the White House.' Since when?"

Bob was uneasy. "Oh, from time to time I go over for consultation."

"With whom? Please tell me! It's exciting."

"Well, I went over to see Mike Shepard."

Bonnie was disappointed. That probably wouldn't be serious work. More like bull sessions. "Bob, is that really 'putting in hours' at the White House? You know, you don't have to try to impress people you haven't seen in twenty years. You're *you!*"

Hanssen gave his whinny of a laugh, embarrassed at being caught out.

3

1984

Mike Shepard was back in his office at the FBI building and ready to talk about a good assignment for Bob.

"The pressure is on to start using polygraphs for everyone in the Bureau," Shepard told Hanssen. "And that could certainly prove to be a mess for us here in Counterintelligence."

"For every Special Agent in Counterintelligence, I'd say."

"You can bet on that! Our job, damnit, is to keep thinking how people commit espionage. What's in the mind of the guy we're trying to catch? We have to learn to think like him, right? So the question is, is there a problem when you ask someone to take a polygraph? He might not be able to answer the question: Have you ever thought of committing espionage?" Shepard shrugged. "Look, I'm assigning you to the Polygraph Research Committee. You'll be working with blue-flamers. Just hard-drinking, tough, thick, decent."

"I guess I ought to say thank you."

"You will. You just research the issue and make a recommendation on what you think is best for the Bureau. Look into the effect of questions like: Did you ever go to strip joints when things were slow at the office? Or, Did you ever sleep with the girl with the big tits who sits across from you?"

"I'll find a way to translate all that," Hanssen said in his low voice.

"Okay, I'm kidding. No polygrapher is going to talk that way. Not here! But don't get too delicate. These blue-flamers are not in possession of a large vocabulary."

In a small conference room, Bob was talking to Mike's committee.

"The question we have to ask," he said, "is whether the polygraph will prove truly effective as a screening tool. There are, after all, two opposing kinds of bad results to avoid at all costs: false positives and false negatives."

One of the men he was talking to had white hair, another had dyed black hair, black as shoe polish.

"Would you explain that again?" asked one of the blue-flamers, the one with the white hair.

"It's the core of the problem. It's practically a built-in confusion. False positive means that we believe on the basis of the polygraph test—that is, the telltale spikes in response to a relevant question—that a Special Agent is lying when in fact he is not. All he's doing is having a nervous reaction. That can do irreparable harm to an honest agent who is not lying."

Bob was encouraged. The man with black hair actually looked sad at the thought; the guy with white hair nodded in sympathy.

"False negatives are worse," Bob went on. "A man who shows every sign of telling the truth can still be a liar. Obviously, any agent who is able to do espionage work in the first place could also be capable of lying his way through the test."

Black Hair spoke his mind. "I don't like any of this. Polygraphs, as I always understood it, are for criminals."

"Yes, sir. You could say there's a moral issue involved. Should we therefore be giving such tests to our own people?"

"I agree," White Hair said. "How do you ask good, hardworking FBI men to turn their private lives over to some geek who's never met them before?"

"Well," said Black Hair, "over at the CIA they give polygraphs all the time."

"That is certainly true," Bob cut in. "CIA people, by the nature of their work—and I don't want to cast aspersions—are more used to lying than we are."

"Well, isn't that the truth?" White Hair said. Black Hair chuckled.

"It's just so darn hard to talk to some stranger about your personal life," Hanssen commented.

"It has to be. The whole thing sounds too lopsided for us."

"Well, there is also talk that we train our own FBI men to give the test." Bob had debated whether to slip that one in, then decided it would help. He was right.

"I would never want to conduct such a test," said Black Hair. "It would make me feel dirty."

Later that week, Hanssen stuck his head into Mike's office and waited for Shepard to look up. After a moment, Mike felt his presence but nonetheless gave a start at the sight of Hanssen.

"Man, you're as silent as a monk when you come into a room," Mike said.

Hanssen had a smile. "I think it can be said that the Polygraph Research Committee will recommend that the Bureau *not* institute a polygraph program."

Shepard wagged one finger off his forehead in a quick salute.

4

1984

At twilight, the children were playing in the yard behind the house. There were enough trees at the end of the backyard to give the illusion that they were living at the edge of a forest. The boys played around a fort Bob had built for them out of scrap wood, and there was also a cage enclosure where they could feed a couple of rabbits. As they played, Little Jack, who was about five, fell down, skinned his knee, and let out a small moan. He tried not to cry.

Jack Hoschouer and Bob had been standing at the edge of the yard talking, and they now came over.

"Little Jack, be a man," Big Jack said. "It can't hurt that much."

The boy looked up at Jack's uniform and tried not to cry.

"It's okay, buddy, it's all right." Hanssen gently picked the boy up and put him on his feet. "Go inside. Mom will fix your knee."

"It doesn't hurt that much," Little Jack said.

"Good boy," said Big Jack.

"Daddy," Little Jack asked, "when you fall down, why does it hurt so much?"

"That's God's way of telling you to be more careful next time," Hanssen said.

"Is God always out there?"

126

"Always, Little Jack. He's out there waiting for us to love Him just as He loves us."

Hoschouer, who had no children, had been standing back a bit watching Bob with his son.

"So He is there?" the boy asked. "Everywhere?"

"Everywhere that there is love or pain, God is with you," Bob said.

The boy smiled. "That's nice." He paused. "I'm going in now to have Mom put a Band-Aid on."

After the boy left, Jack said, "Bob, you really do impart religion to your kids."

"There's nothing more important," Bob said.

Later that evening, the two men were sitting together on the back porch. Beyond the growth of trees, which the children viewed as a forest, was a paved road, and on the other side, perhaps fifty yards away, you could see the entrance to a small park. Beyond was a footbridge.

"You know," Hanssen said, "sometimes, when I'm here in the evening and look over there, I think that one of these days a KGB man is going to come by and make a drop right there. Right under the footbridge. And I, sitting here, will be ready for him." He laughed and tapped his breast. "I will have my trusty PPK in its holster, and I will step out quietly from this porch, cross the street, and collar that Soviet son of a gun."

Jack laughed. "Dream on."

"It's a joke, but, you know, it's no joke. At the Bureau we're obsessed with how sensitive some of our material is. That thought can be disturbing. How much is it really worth on the market, so to speak?"

"Well, such considerations do not reach critical mass," said Jack.

"Never. My Lord, never. You'd be doing it to your colleagues. Besides, who could really be tempted? It would become a dreadful act. Just think of the profound moral difference between us here in America and the Soviet Union," Bob said.

Since Jack held a top secret Army clearance, they sometimes touched on subjects like this in their conversations.

"Right," said Jack. "But, you know, one question I do want to ask you: From the overall picture we get at my end, which is probably not as good and clear as your stuff, the dirty little secret seems to be that we are so far ahead of the Soviets in every way that they really don't have a chance."

"That worries me, Jack. I think about it a lot. If the Soviets have no chance, then isn't it their best option to go in for a first nuclear strike and level the playing field a little?" Bob nodded at his own words. "I can tell you, I wake up many a night worrying that this house is only ten miles away from the White House. A nuclear weapon landing on that side of the Potomac might still take us out over here. And it could be worse. The Soviets are so inefficient they could easily hit here in Virginia by mistake."

"They could," Jack said.

"Sometimes I get into a crazy logic," said Bob. "I say to myself: If the Soviets did a little better, they wouldn't feel so desperate."

"Isn't that far-fetched?"

"Well, the Soviets are certainly desperate," Hanssen went on. "Pretty soon, we're going to know so much about good old Pavel or Ivan or whoever, that we'll probably be watching through the window when he gets out of line with his secretary."

"Ready to photograph Pavel in the act?" Jack laughed.

Hanssen whinnied. "When we do, I'll send you the pictures."

"That could be a nifty addition to the collection,"

Hoschouer said, and then stopped. There was an edgy pause. "Hey, buddy, it is real nice sitting here, but I'm getting restless. Why don't we take a stroll?"

Not talking at all, Jack and Bob walked in the park on the other side of the highway.

"I've been asking myself," Jack said at last. "Why do we keep exchanging pictures? We're big boys. Maybe we should stop."

"I agree," said Hanssen, but he halted long enough to snap a small twig off a bush. "Jack, I do agree," he said at last. "I'm pretty tired of going to Confession and admitting that I am still guilty of sexual indulgences when alone, which is how I describe jacking-off to my priest."

"What does he say?"

"He tells me to stop. He tells me to pray."

"Hey, friend, it's the craziest habit, isn't it?" Jack said, and gave a smile. He was doing his best to lighten the mood, but then he added, "I guess we're stuck in it. Stuck!"

"No, I'm ready to quit," said Hanssen.

"You sound determined."

"I am."

By early morning, however, with Jack asleep on the couch, Hanssen, in his underwear, approached quietly and woke him.

In a whisper, he said, "Bonnie is in the shower. Come take a look."

"I'm still asleep."

"No, come on, Jack, come on! Before she's done!"

"Bob, I'm still asleep."

"It's all right, buddy. Come on. Take a look."

He grabbed Jack by the arm and tried to pull him out of bed.

"This is not the place to start a fight," Jack said.

"You've got to see her. Nothing is as beautiful as her body when she's in the shower. After sixteen years of marriage, I still revere her body."

Jack followed him into the bedroom. The bathroom door was open, but the shower door was closed. She was obscured a little by the steam on the glass, but Jack did manage to catch some of the view.

Later, they didn't talk about it. Bob drove Jack to the airport, but they did not know how to begin to get into what had happened. After saying good-bye, Bob took his car through the rush-hour traffic down to his parking slot in the FBI garage.

5

1985

That morning in a large conference room at the Bureau, about fifty officials were present—prosecutors, Department of Justice people, supervisors, security and intelligence agents. Bob Hanssen was also there, with Mike Shepard. One of the top agents in the FBI was speaking.

"I want to thank all of you here, from the Department of Justice, FBI Headquarters, FBI Counterintelligence, for the job you've all done with fine cooperation in assembling this impressive mass of evidence against John Walker. If there are any people out there who might feel tempted to get into the same kind of trouble as Mr. Walker, now they will know what it is like when the FBI is given the signal to surge on a special like this. It will certainly keep them from attempting espionage in the first place. I would make a bet that John Walker is having these thoughts right now."

After the meeting, Hanssen made a point of accompanying Shepard to his office.

"It sure is awesome," Mike said, "what we can do when we get all the horses together."

"Awesome," Hanssen replied, and then actually looked Mike in the eye, which was not his habit with anyone. "I don't want to be out of line," he said, "but I do have to ask you something."

"A matter to which I can't respond?"

"I don't know," said Hanssen. "Maybe. I can certainly detect that something is going on in the Bureau that's kind of big. Nothing to do with Walker, but something big. I can feel it." He held up his hand. "Now, I can't make the claim that I have a reasonable need to know. But I am concerned. Because there is one facet I might have to deal with."

"I'm listening," Shepard said.

"One item is playing hell with my budget work."

"Look," Mike said with an easy smile. "Let me reconfirm that we think you are the single best accountant we've ever had the luck to get. So I will do my best to put up with your worries, but I'm not worried. You'll solve any ambiguities you'll encounter."

"Thank you," said Hanssen. "But don't see me just as an accountant." He smiled. In contrast to his typical expression, which often appeared dour, he did possess a big, warm smile, and obviously knew enough to use it often. "No," he added, "think of me rather as the honcho financial expert who has to explain away a sum of two hundred fifty million dollars in the proposed budget, a sum that's going to be spent in the next two years on a project that might as well be called 'Guess!' I don't know what the money is for. And I don't want to know. But I do think I've gotten onto it a little."

"That's quite a remark, Bob."

"Not really. It's like seeing a very large object in the fog. Under the costs for this project, more than a few bills have come in already for contract workers injured by methane fireballs. Well, methane fireballs are exactly what you would expect when a tunnel is being dug under swamp soil. And we have a lot of that right here in D.C. You and I also know we are in possession of technology that can detect signals from the keystrokes of Soviet ciphering machines provided we move our machines

132

in close enough. This adds up to tunnel work. I won't say I have no idea where that tunnel is going."

Shepard roared with laughter. Others in the Bureau might not agree, but he really enjoyed seeing Bob display his smarts. He leaned forward. "I, obviously, can't tell you whether you're right or wrong, but I will say this: When I was over at the White House, President Reagan signed the order to authorize this project, and wrote in the margin, 'Good idea. Don't get caught.'"

Right after this conversation, Bob was walking down the corridor with a Coke in his hand when a huge FBI agent with white hair, almost as tall as Bob and twice as wide, began to step along beside him. Hanssen was wearing the dark suit he always wore; it made him look especially thin. His white shirt was clean but unstarched. Walking next to the first big man was another agent, equally large, equally powerful.

"Hello, Digger," the first big man said.

"Digger?"

"You look like Digger O'Dell."

"Who is he?" Bob asked, and wished he hadn't.

"You don't watch television?"

"I make a point of not watching it."

"Well, if you ever break down, keep an eye out for the late-night reruns. In *The Great Gildersleeve,* Digger O'Dell is the friendly undertaker."

Hanssen did his best to give a big smile. "Thank you for the information."

"*Por nada,*" the man said.

Hanssen could hear it. As the other two walked away, they were chuckling.

In the bathroom that night, Bob was making low, growling sounds. Bonnie kept listening from the bedroom until she finally got up and rapped on the bathroom door.

"Bob, can you come out? You've been in there for ages."

The sounds ceased after a minute and the door opened. Bob looked red-faced.

"Honey, it's the same old story," he said.

"Good gracious, darling. Sometimes your constipation makes you sound like a musk ox in rut." She was trying to keep her face stern.

"How do you know the sounds musk oxen make?" He did his best to smile. Now she did laugh but almost at once shook her head.

"Bob, I guess it's really not that funny. I'm thinking of the children. We don't want to wake them up. Could you find a way to take care of it?"

6

.

1985

Maybe there was no way to take care of things like that. Bob did brighten up, however, when, a couple of days later, he took his FBI test at the Quantico indoors shooting range.

There, in a long vault of a room that resembled a parking garage, with its low ceiling and support columns on the floor, two dummy bodies were standing in position at several places.

The instructor was talking to him. "Ready for this shoot, Mr. Hanssen? You want to remember to point your gun in the appropriate direction."

Hanssen smiled. "I know. Nobody in Counterintelligence knows what to do with a handgun." The man had obviously not looked at his previous test scores.

"We'll see. Here's your scenario." The instructor pointed to two dummies about forty feet away. "You have chased these two bad guys into an underground parking garage. Now you've got to take them out. Beware! For all you know, there's another bad guy hiding behind that pillar." He pointed to a column that was twenty feet away. "When the bell goes off, go to it."

The bell rang. Hanssen fired two shots quickly. The two bad-guy dummies fell. He wheeled around to get a better angle on the column and, in passing one of the two fallen dummies, shot one of them again, this time in the head.

Then the instructor turned to two men waiting their turn. "Did you notice? When Mr. Hanssen passed the first target he hit, he pumped another shot in. Perfect! Just because you've dropped a guy, don't suppose he's dead. Shoot him again. Good technique. Great!"

Later, at FBI Headquarters, telling a couple of Soviet analysts in his section about the shoot at Quantico, Bob improved the story, mentioning modestly and in passing that he had succeeded in grazing a concrete pillar and nicked it in such a way that the bullet ricocheted behind another pillar and knocked down the third dummy. His audience nodded their heads politely, not saying a word, and then they walked out the door and down the hall. Hanssen shrugged.

Afterward, however, he heard his father's voice: *Yes, yes, Robert, you're pretty good at shooting dummies, but do you have the guts to hold a man by his heels, stick him out the window, and then let go?*

In fact, there were three real men he could kill. He would not have to pull a trigger, and it would not happen instantly. He did, however, know their names. They were three highly placed KGB officers who were working for the FBI. The question was whether to sell this information.

Not a week after visiting the firing range at Quantico, Bob suffered another migraine attack, complete with a pain so urgent that he understood how indicative it was of something he wanted to do, but did not dare to contemplate. He felt as if his head was going to explode if he pulled away from the desire.

What, then, was this desire? Back in 1979, he had known exactly: he had had to get enough money to pay off his debts or go bankrupt, and the GRU had been the answer.

This time, was it still money?

In the weeks that followed, he thought often about his situation. At the very least, it was money. He was looking at a new financial jam that could be much worse than the crisis in 1979. After the transition back from New York to Washington in 1981, he had bought their present house in Vienna, Virginia, a beautiful nine-room home on Whitecedar Court. It was definitely beyond their means, but he had wanted to make Bonnie happy, and he believed he had found the way to finance it.

But what a mess he was in now! His financial difficulties went all the way back to his father's retirement in 1972. Howard, in a generous mood, had sold his Norwood house to Bob—then at a reduced price. He and Bonnie had lived there, paying down the mortgage, until he joined the FBI in 1976, after which he commuted to Gary, Indiana. Thereafter, the real hazards of their economic situation began. Bob sold the place in Norwood at enough of a profit to be able to put down $10,000 on a house in Scarsdale, in Westchester, when the FBI moved him to the New York office. That house, at 150 Webster Road, had cost $43,500. Right after, real estate values exploded at an unbelievable rate around New York in the years between 1979 and 1981. When the family moved back to Washington in 1981, Bob was able to sell 150 Webster Road for $83,000. That left a nest egg—after real estate commissions, closing costs, and moving expenses—of about $45,000.

This nice little gain turned into new debt, however, since he proceeded to buy a better house, this nine-room beauty, on Whitecedar Court in Vienna. He paid $150,000 for it, which meant that all the profit from the sale of 150 Webster Road had to be used for the down payment. Interest payments were high in 1981—as high as 15 percent—and his property taxes had also gone up.

So he now had two mortgages totaling about $106,000, a conventional thirty-year first mortgage for $50,000, on which he paid close to $6,000 a year in principal and interest, and a second mortgage with a balloon of $56,000, on which he could pay interest only (another $6,360 a year). The principal—the entire $56,000—would be due as a lump sum in June of 1986.

Now, with five kids and another one on the way, and his annual salary at a little more than $58,000, including his overtime, he was spending close to half of his after-tax income on upkeep, property taxes, principal, and interest. Close to $20,000 a year went into the house. Add to that the cost of private schools for the children, his almost ungovernable desire to splurge on gifts for Bonnie and the kids, and programs for his computer. It was as if an old boyhood dream of purchasing every kind of new gadget to use with his shortwave radio—a dream he could never satisfy as an adolescent—had now reappeared in a variety of software upgrades for his computer. Each month, year after year, his debt grew.

Sometimes he felt as if spending money kept new migraine attacks at bay. That strategy seemed to be effective for a few months. But then his money problems sparked the old and familiar uneasiness he always felt before a new attack came on.

Despite all his urges to spend, and then spend more, he saw himself as thrifty. He would, for instance, never buy a new suit or shirt until he absolutely had to.

The more he pondered his financial straits, the more he realized that he was in the grip of something much more powerful than the "sexual indulgences when alone." That was always an available cop-out in Confession. This was larger.

On many a morning after a nearly sleepless night, he would feel frightened enough to hunch his long torso down under the covers and rest his head between Bonnie's comforting breasts.

He tried to face the facts of his situation. There was no way he would be able to pay off the principal on the balloon mortgage in the coming year. He simply did not have $56,000.

There were passing thoughts of going to his father for help, but his stomach told him in advance not to take on that shame. Or, for that matter, Bonnie's fury. Besides, there was another way out. He could apply for transfer to another city. That way, he could sell this house in Vienna, pay off the mortgages, and make a new profit. He thought they might get as much as $200,000.

The only city with openings available to someone with his skills and at his grade, however, was New York. Plus, Washington and New York were the only two cities with a lot of Soviets stationed in them. New York would not only accept him, but given how few FBI men wanted to be assigned there, the Bureau was ready to make him a Field Squad Supervisory Special Agent over one of their counterintelligence groups. That would be his point of argument with Bonnie. Yes, she hated New York and so did he, Bob was prepared to argue, but the move was essential for his career and their future well-being.

He applied for and accepted the transfer to New York. Then he proceeded to negotiate his way through Bonnie's disappointment at having to move again—her outbursts, her recrimination at how difficult this would be for the children, not to speak of the hideous memories of 150 Webster Road. Somehow, he navigated through the storm, and with tears in her eyes, she finally agreed to put the house on Whitecedar Court up for sale.

That was in August. Soon after, with no sale in sight, he was assigned to run a counterintelligence squad, named "Pocketwatch," in New York City. By September 23, he had to be ready to go to work there. They could find no immediate solution other than for Bonnie to remain in Virginia with the kids until they had a buyer for the house and the children had finished out the school semester. In New York, he could put up at the YMCA. As soon as their house sold, he would purchase a new home in Westchester.

The only trouble was that this could go on for several months, and it did. For several very long months. The occasional nibbles on purchasing the house in Vienna were nowhere near their asking price.

On top of that, Bob felt uncomfortable in his new office. It was situated in a Midtown building and he was in charge of about ten agents and a support group of five—a secretary, a couple of clerks, and two high-grade gofers. He did not have to work in a cubicle—he had a private office with a view of the Hudson—but still he was uneasy. He was not totally comfortable putting the authority of his position into practice.

He was having to learn much too quickly the fundamentals of managing both an office and a group of people who were strangers to him. He was lonely at the YMCA. He longed for Bonnie. He told her so on the phone. After seventeen years of marriage, he still missed her like crazy. On his first weekend in New York, he had even gone looking for a house to buy in Westchester. He was certainly not going to subject his family to any of the five boroughs of New York City.

Much to his dismay, he discovered the price of property in Westchester was high. Considering what was being offered, it was outrageously high.

He had to get on the track of some money. Only now, he was in New York and the man he wanted to contact—someone in the KGB—was in Washington.

*   *   *

On Tuesday, a week after his first Monday as a supervisor in the New York office, he managed to go back to Washington for a few days to organize future Bureau liaisons. On the drive down to D.C., while passing through Maryland, he mailed a letter he had composed the night before. It was addressed to the home of a Soviet who worked in the U.S.S.R. Embassy, a man named Degtyar, and would be postmarked Prince George County, Maryland, so it wouldn't be linked to him in any way.

Even as he dropped the letter in the box, he understood that there was more to his motives than this real and pressing need for money. He knew he had to get into a situation that presented real danger to him—a situation more dangerous than anything he had done before. It was as if his hand was being forced by this crazy uncontrollable desire to deal again with the Soviets.

The excitement he had felt—it was like being brave enough to make love to a girl in front of ten blue-flamers. He didn't know why this need to court danger had come up, but it felt as though it was starting to run his life. Was that why he had pulled Jack out of bed to see Bonnie in the shower?

7

1985

The letter addressed to Viktor Degtyar was delivered on October 4. Inside the outer envelope was a smaller sealed envelope, on which he had written:

MR. DEGTYAR, DO NOT OPEN. TAKE THIS ENVELOPE UNOPENED TO VIKTOR I. CHERKASHIN.

Inside the sealed envelope was the text of his letter:

DEAR MR. CHERKASHIN,

SOON, I WILL SEND A BOX OF DOCUMENTS TO YOU. THEY ARE FROM CERTAIN OF THE MOST SENSITIVE PROJECTS OF THE U.S. INTELLIGENCE COMMUNITY. ALL ARE ORIGINALS TO AID IN VERIFYING THEIR AUTHENTICITY. I BELIEVE THEY ARE SUFFICIENT TO JUSTIFY A $100,000 PAYMENT TO ME.

I MUST WARN OF CERTAIN RISKS TO MY SECURITY OF WHICH YOU MAY NOT BE AWARE. YOUR SERVICE HAS RECENTLY SUFFERED SOME SETBACKS. I WARN THAT MR. BORIS YUZHIN (LINE PR, SF), MR. SERGEY MOTORIN (LINE PR, WASH), AND MR. VALERIY MARTYNOV (LINE X, WASH), HAVE BEEN RECRUITED BY OUR "SPECIAL SERVICES."

DETAILS REGARDING PAYMENT AND FUTURE CON-
TACT WILL BE SENT TO YOU PERSONALLY. MY IDEN-
TITY AND ACTUAL POSITION IN THE COMMUNITY
MUST BE LEFT UNSTATED TO ENSURE MY SECURITY.

Degtyar, to whom he had mailed the letter, had a minor position in the KGB and was concealed under diplomatic cover. Hanssen had decided that Degtyar was not a
serious risk. He was not on the FBI's select list of KGB
men like Cherkashin, whose FBI file and assessments
Bob had access to as a Supervisory Special Agent.
Cherkashin was known to be the chief of the KGB Line
in Washington and therefore responsible for the Soviet
Embassy security, which included targeting the FBI and
CIA. He was, Bob concluded, the right man to handle
his case.

Yuzhin and Motorin had already been rotated back to
the Soviet Union. But to give away the name of Martynov made Bob hesitate.

In the end, he had decided it was necessary. Martynov
could be a danger to him as long as he worked in Washington. If to disclose him was to bring on his death—
well, Martynov, like himself, was a soldier in intelligence.
A soldier had to be ready to die. In fact, he wondered if
turning Martynov in might sooth his migraines. There
were cures that no doctor ever contemplated.

At the Soviet Embassy in Washington, D.C., a well-
dressed, modest-looking, middle-aged man entered the
building. This was Degtyar. He asked to see Cherkashin.

"I have no idea why the person who sent this chose
me," Degtyar said. "I am supposed to be known as a
diplomat."

Cherkashin merely nodded. He was a handsome man
in his late forties.

Degtyar continued: "I should have not been brought

143

into association with your work. It could prove embarrassing for all of us."

Now Cherkashin laughed. "Find me an American Embassy anywhere that is not crammed full of CIA men. We are much too pure. We work too hard at concealing our identities."

"It is a serious matter," Degtyar said. "Why did he send this letter to you by way of me?"

"Well, we don't necessarily know," Cherkashin said. "But if your new correspondent delivers what he promises, then he chose you precisely because he is high enough up in CIA or FBI Counterintelligence to know something that we don't know—which is that my mail is examined by the FBI and yours is not."

"What if he is not genuine? What if the FBI *is* studying my mail?"

"In that case, you will be embarrassed," said Cherkashin. "My advice is to stay calm. When our new friend mails his promised package to your house, just bring it in—*pronto*—as the Americans say." Cherkashin laughed at the look of unhappiness on Degtyar's face.

The package! Before he was even certain he was ready to sell secrets to the KGB, Bob had already decided how to do it. The first pass—the breaking of bread, so to speak, the first offering—had to be exceptional if they were going to give him anything close to the amount of money he would ask for. This meant he had to submit information that was not only valuable in content but convincing in appearance: he had to offer original documents.

Sometimes, only a few identical documents existed on a top-secret matter in the Bureau. Sometimes, depending on the number of people who had a need to know, there could be as many as twenty exact copies, each known as an original document.

Anyone in possession of that kind of paper, would,

without question, keep it in his safe. All the same, over the years, it had been Hanssen's experience that once the Bureau entrusted you with such a paper, it remained in your possession. Nobody was likely to ask for it. So he was ready to raid his own safe of several of his most valuable original papers as part of his package. His credibility to the KGB had to be assured.

On his first trip back to D.C. from New York, he collected what he needed. But he waited ten days before sending this collection to Degtyar. He wanted to make sure that no alarm bells were ringing.

When Degtyar received the package, he delivered it to Cherkashin. Indeed, an FBI camera installed in the window of a building across the street from the Soviet Embassy recorded this. Degtyar, who appeared daily at the Embassy, did not often come to work carrying a black canvas bag. That was, of course, just one more isolated piece of information to enter the FBI files containing surveillance reports on the entrance and exits of the visitors and daily occupants of the building.

8

1985

After studying the contents with considerable care,
Cherkashin disappeared for three days. He bypassed
Stanislav Androsov, his immediate superior in Washington, and flew to Moscow Center to meet with General
Anatoli Kireev, Chief of Directorate K, and examine the
documents together. The two men decided to have their
talk in a small safe-room.

Cherkashin spoke first. "Anatoli, let me warn you.
I'm prepared to embrace this new fellow. As yet, he is
without a name, but this information speaks for itself."

"Viktor, you are saying you give credence to a paper
that discloses the Americans have electronically pene-
trated one of our most secure diplomatic facilities in the
United States?"

"Yes," said Cherkashin. "He says there are no bugs to
be found, no wires. Yet, they can listen to everything that
transpires. He even gives the location of the device and
the methods utilized."

Anatoli tapped the papers. "They must have spent
tens of millions of dollars developing this technology."

"Americans spare no cost," Cherkashin replied.

"If true, this is the single largest contribution to our
intelligence here in many years. Do you really give it
credence?"

"Anatoli," said Cherkashin. "My job is not to say

146

nyet to each and every possibility that comes our way. By now, I can recognize that the best way to become a general in our organization is never to make a mistake. Just turn everything down, *nyet, nyet, nyet.* But I would like to think we are still here for a purpose. This new fellow, let us call him 'B' whoever he is, is obtaining his information from very high up in *their* woodwork."

"Or they are sending us a poison plant. On a very large scale. I, for one, don't like the feel of it. Not at all."

"Look—he corroborates what my mole, my CIA man Aldrich Ames, told us last June about Motorin and Martynov. How could their intelligence give up any people from *our* KGB who are working for *them?* It is as much against their ethics as it would be against ours."

"That is true. Very true. Unless, Viktor, they happen to know that *we* know these three are working for them."

"Anatoli, why are you so negative?"

"Dear friend, I have to be. The latest directives make me cautious."

"Perestroika! This new word. Yes! They tell us: Ease tension between our Soviet and the United States. No waves. Make no waves. Yes," said Viktor, "but Mr. Reagan wants waves. He is hardly in the spirit of perestroika."

Anatoli nodded. "I agree. It is not in the spirit at all. But what if American Intelligence is giving away this exceptionally valuable piece of information, this gilded sugarplum, because they have something better in mind, such as embarrassing Premier Gorbachev so badly with our own Soviet people that he has to give up his idea of perestroika? After all, to the American warmongers, perestroika will be a pain in the ass. Therefore, dear Viktor, I am not ready to say that this gift is genuine."

"Anatoli, look at the product. If this is a provocation, they would not dare to send original documents. Think of it! If it went wrong for them, some of their best people would have to walk the plank."

Anatoli shook his head. "If this adventure by the CIA or the FBI—we don't even know that much—is as big as it appears to be, then they might do anything to support their provocation." He held up his hand. "Anything, even to breaking basic rules of conduct."

Cherkashin raised a finger to the ceiling. "Anatoli, I say to you: Speak your doubts when you discuss this in Moscow Center, but I want to include my separate reaction."

"What if my superior agrees with me?" said Anatoli.

Cherkashin shrugged. "Then . . . finito! I have to accept what they say. I have, after all, been wrong a few times in my life."

"On that basis, I will deliver this with your recommendation and my doubts."

The next day, Cherkashin returned to Washington and the following day, strolling outside his residence, was photographed by the FBI.

In Moscow, the legendary Major-General Shebarshin was speaking to twenty students in a small lecture hall of the Lubyanka.

"One of our first principles," he told them, "is never to allow any agent cooperating with you to feel he is treacherous to his own country. Rather, get to know your man personally. Find out how he feels. Become apprised of his problems, his aspirations."

"Sir," a young KGB officer spoke up. "What if no meeting proves possible? What if you cannot learn his real identity?"

"Then you must ask yourself, are you dealing with a double agent? That is problem number one. Always. But if you decide this new agent is genuine, then you have to analyze his motives. Is it money? Or something more elusive."

"Isn't it usually money?" another student asked.

"No!" said Shebarshin. "Only in very rare cases do we deal with people who expect nothing but money. Search for more subtle motives. Maybe it is deep-seated sympathy for our cause. Or consider the opposite. Maybe, it is void of ideology. Maybe your potential client feels that his bosses do not appreciate his gifts. Look then for some overdeveloped romantic streak. Can it be that he wants to play a role in history?"

"If my agent hides his identity, to what extreme do I go to find out his name?"

"We do not put our man in jeopardy by trying too hard to find out. Live with uncertainty. Anonymous sources can be acceptable provided you receive a steady flow of first-rate information."

"Are you still telling us never to trust any agent completely?"

"Of course. Do not forget our old Russian saying: Another man's soul is darkness."

Later that day, Major-General Shebarshin was having a difficult time at the Kremlin. He had been summoned unexpectedly by a member of the Politburo, Igor Vladimirovich Kuparshin, and after the first, very few amenities, had been asked to deliver what Kuparshin was calling the Cherkashin Submission.

"Igor Vladimirovich, our KGB Intelligence is not open to other Soviet organs," Shebarshin proceeded to tell him. "We keep all new material secret."

"Are you saying that you are prepared to exclude our Politburo?"

"Not at all. I only say the process is not ready. This is the way we have always worked. In a few days, a week, two weeks, when our analysis is concluded, we will send it over immediately." Shebarshin was calm. He could cite three working decades of this tradition.

"I say: Times are changing," said Igor Vladimirovich.

"How can you be certain, for example, that you do not have leaks in your department?"

"I am not aware of any."

"It is conceivable that you are not aware enough."

"Igor Vladimirovich, do you wish to tell me you have actually been presented with material that we have not yet released? Or, with all respect, is it possible you are relying on rumors?"

Igor Vladimirovich held up a hand. "At the Politburo, we know this much. A communication from some new American agent has come in. He has given us names and is offering incredible original documents. We are told it is the most important transmission to KGB station Washington since the 1950s. Therefore, we need your opinion of this material." He paused. The pause lengthened. They were at odds.

To avoid an impasse, Igor Vladimirovich said, "If you must, speak in hypotheticals."

Shebarshin took more than a moment to decide. "Hypothetically," he said at last, "I will say that the information does reveal important matters. In a few days we will be ready and will present such material to you."

"What possibility is there that this information is false and has been prepared by U.S. Intelligence?"

"Our close-to-final conclusion is that American Intelligence would see the loss of this information as a genuine catastrophe to them."

"So they can only afford to deliver this information to us if they are actually planning a move that is exceptionally potent in the political or the military sphere? To gain something larger than what they are giving away?"

"One chance in one hundred. Maybe less. By our present estimate, the information is worth much more to us than anything they can gain from it."

Igor Vladimirovich was not convinced. "You say *one* chance in one hundred. This *one* gives me uneasiness."

"Igor Vladimirovich, what is your basis for such grave suspicion?"

"Perestroika. Perestroika itself. A most interesting policy. We say to America, 'Look, we are human beings. Just like you, we want a decent world. We want equable society for the entire globe.' But that makes no shift in American attitude. Ronald Reagan still calls us the 'Evil Empire.' He still tries to prepare all American people for war against our Soviet."

Shebarshin nodded. "We are not in disagreement concerning President Reagan's motives. At the KGB we have had one priority for four decades: Be ready to detect all signs that Americans are ready to launch their nuclear war against us. At present, we see no such signs. Reagan is talk, just talk."

"Some in our Politburo think it comes to more than talk. It pleases the American public to think that they are good and we are evil."

That night, Shebarshin went to the KGB chief's office off Dzerzhinsky Square. The chief stood up from his desk and crossed the room to greet him.

"So, now we know," he said, "what the Politburo wanted from us this morning. But what is Igor Vladimirovich up to? Is he hoping to embarrass Gorbachev?"

"Yes, I see such a campaign commencing," Shebarshin said. "I am certain that many in the Politburo want to get rid of the man."

"Tell me, Leonid, how do you feel about this?"

Shebarshin shrugged. "Gorbachev does not concern me," he said. "But I have some fear that no matter how it turns out, our KGB will suffer. A bad time approaches."

"That is future history," said the chief, "a notoriously perverse subject. I prefer immediate problems. What do you propose to do with this fellow who offers us technology but has no name?"

"I think we should give him half of what he asks for and decide on his authenticity by the measure of what he gives us next."

"I agree. Which process do we use to get the money to him?"

"I assure you," said Shebarshin, "he has taken care of that. He sent another letter to Cherkashin by way of Degtyar that names the park we are to go to and the footbridge under which we are to put the package. He will add six and we will subtract six from months, days, and hours. Vertical and horizontal tapes for signals on prearranged poles. Old and basic techniques of espionage. He as much as tells us not to sneer at his suggestions. He hints that the Americans are so fixed on our advanced technology that they pay no attention to the fundamentals anymore."

"I will not be surprised if he proves to be right."

9

1985

Earlier, during a trip back to Washington, Hanssen, while supervising a study on the use of mail covers, had reviewed papers on the current surveillance methods of the Bureau involving mail from New York to Alexandria, Virginia, where Degtyar was living, and had come to the conclusion that now it was relatively safe to send mail directly from New York.

On October 24, he sent the following message to Cherkashin:

DROP LOCATION: PLEASE LEAVE YOUR PACKAGE FOR ME UNDER THE CORNER (NEAREST THE STREET) OF THE WOODEN FOOTBRIDGE LOCATED JUST WEST OF THE ENTRANCE TO NOTTOWAY PARK. (ADC NORTHERN VIRGINIA STREET MAP, #14, D3)

PACKAGE PREPARATION: USE A GREEN OR BROWN PLASTIC TRASH BAG AND TRASH TO COVER A WATERPROOFED PACKAGE.

SIGNAL LOCATION: SIGNAL SITE WILL BE THE PICTORIAL "PEDESTRIAN CROSSING" SIGNPOST JUST WEST OF THE MAIN NOTTOWAY PARK ENTRANCE ON OLD COURTHOUSE ROAD. (THE SIGN IS THE ONE NEAREST THE BRIDGE JUST MENTIONED.)

SIGNALS: MY SIGNAL TO YOU: ONE VERTICAL MARK OF WHITE ADHESIVE TAPE MEANING I AM READY TO RECEIVE YOUR PACKAGE.

YOUR SIGNAL TO ME: ONE HORIZONTAL MARK OF WHITE ADHESIVE TAPE MEANING DROP FILLED.

MY SIGNAL TO YOU: ONE VERTICAL MARK OF WHITE ADHESIVE TAPE MEANING I HAVE RECEIVED YOUR PACKAGE.

(REMOVE OLD TAPE BEFORE LEAVING SIGNAL.)

Nottoway Park is in Fairfax County, in the Eastern District of Virginia, just a few miles from Hanssen's house in Vienna, where Bonnie and the children were still living.

On Saturday, November 2, 1985, the KGB loaded the Nottoway Park dead-drop site under the footbridge with a package wrapped in a plastic bag and sealed with waterproof tape. It contained $50,000 in cash.

That night, Bob celebrated by making love to Bonnie with as much skill and tenderness and force as he possessed.

Over the following week, he prepared another letter. Cherkashin received it by way of Degtyar on November 9. It was full of praise for Cherkashin's skills.

THANK YOU FOR THE $50,000. I ALSO APPRECIATE YOUR COURAGE AND PERSEVERANCE IN THE FACE OF GENERICALLY REPORTED BUREAUCRATIC OBSTA-CLES. I WOULD NOT HAVE CONTACTED YOU IF IT WERE NOT REPORTED THAT YOU WERE HELD IN ES-TEEM WITHIN YOUR ORGANIZATION, AN ORGANIZA-

154

TION I HAVE STUDIED FOR YEARS. I DID EXPECT SOME
COMMUNICATION PLAN IN YOUR RESPONSE. I
VIEWED THE POSTAL DELIVERY AS A NECESSARY RISK
AND DO NOT WISH TO TRUST AGAIN THAT CHANNEL
WITH VALUABLE MATERIAL. I DID THIS ONLY BE-
CAUSE I HAD TO, SO YOU WOULD TAKE MY OFFER SE-
RIOUSLY, THAT THERE BE NO MISUNDERSTANDING AS
TO MY LONG-TERM VALUE, AND TO OBTAIN APPRO-
PRIATE SECURITY FOR OUR RELATIONSHIP FROM THE
START.

Hanssen then suggested that they use the same site
again. "Same timing, same signals." He proposed September 9 as the date. By means of his suggested method
for calculation, this translated to March 3 of the following year, 1986. He added:

AS FAR AS THE FUNDS ARE CONCERNED, I HAVE LIT-
TLE NEED OR UTILITY FOR MORE THAN THE $100,000.
IT MERELY PROVIDES A DIFFICULTY SINCE I CAN NOT
SPEND IT, STORE IT OR INVEST IT EASILY WITHOUT
TRIPPING "DRUG MONEY" WARNING BELLS. PERHAPS
SOME DIAMONDS AS SECURITY TO MY CHILDREN
AND SOME GOOD WILL SO THAT WHEN THE TIME
COMES, YOU WILL ACCEPT MY SENIOR SERVICES AS A
GUEST LECTURER. EVENTUALLY, I WOULD APPRECI-
ATE AN ESCAPE PLAN. (NOTHING LASTS FOREVER.)

Since the KGB had enclosed a query with the $50,000
asking how he had been able to identify Yuzhin, Motorin, and Martynov as the U.S. Intelligence recruit-
ments, he added:

I CAN NOT PROVIDE DOCUMENTARY SUBSTANTIAT-
ING EVIDENCE WITHOUT AROUSING SUSPICION AT
THIS TIME. NEVERTHELESS, IT IS FROM MY OWN
KNOWLEDGE AS A MEMBER OF THE COMMUNITY EF-

FORT TO CAPITALIZE ON THE INFORMATION FROM WHICH I SPEAK. I HAVE SEEN VIDEO TAPES OF DEBRIEFINGS AND PHYSICALLY SAW THE LAST, THOUGH WE WERE NOT INTRODUCED. THE NAMES WERE PROVIDED TO ME AS PART OF MY DUTIES AS ONE OF THE FEW WHO NEEDED TO KNOW. YOU HAVE SOME AVENUES OF INQUIRY. SUBSTANTIAL FUNDS WERE PROVIDED IN EXCESS OF WHAT COULD HAVE BEEN SKIMMED FROM THEIR AGENTS. THE ACTIVE ONE HAS ALWAYS (IN THE PAST) USED A CONCEALMENT DEVICE—A BAG WITH BANK NOTES SEWN IN THE BASE DURING HOME LEAVES.

He was referring to Martynov as the "active one."

In fact, as the KGB soon discovered, Martynov, on his return to Moscow, did not conceal the money in a bag but in the lining of his coat. He would be arrested and executed in 1987. By then, Motorin had already been put to death and Yuzhin had been sent to prison.

10

1985

Given his familiarity with the KGB's methods, Hanssen had asked for $100,000 assuming that they would probably give him only one-third of that. He was pleased, therefore, when $50,000 was left. The amount emboldened him to look again for a house in Westchester.

All the same, he was full of anxiety in the next couple of weeks. New York, by itself, could always do that to him. But the ante had been raised: He had consigned three KGB men to years of imprisonment or a bullet to the back of the head—three men who had been working for the United States! If cosmic justice was ever a factor that came into play, wouldn't he have to be caught? And soon?

But from New York, he could not detect any signs of anything stirring in the Bureau. There had been some concern when Martynov was recalled to Moscow, but he had assured his FBI handler that it was an honor to be asked to escort home Vitaly Yurchenko. Certainly he was trusted, Martynov told them. Yurchenko, after all, was an international phenomenon—a KGB defector who was now defecting back to the Soviet Union. Of course, the KGB trusted him.

So his arrest on his return did cause some murmuring in a few offices on the fourth floor, although not as much as Bob had expected. It was assumed that the KGB had discovered something on their own. Bob learned that via the telephone and the grapevine. Yet for three nights in a row, he woke up drenched in sweat and startled to find himself at the YMCA. Late in November, he had a full anxiety attack when the sale of the house in Vienna was closed. It had sold for $175,000, a good $25,000 less than he had hoped for. With costs and commissions, he netted only $10,000. An additional $45,000 came back to him from the original down payment in 1981, so he was actually able to afford a place in Westchester without having to use the cash that came from the KGB. Still, the new house on Mead Street bothered him.

Located in Yorktown Heights and costing $165,000, it was nowhere equal in size, value, or comfort to their lovely home on Whitecedar Court. It was dingy and would be cramped now that they had six kids. Moreover, the street where it sat looked awfully dreary on the day they arrived and second-rate compared to their previous home in Virginia.

Bonnie couldn't contain herself. As they came up to the door and she got her first view, she had an outburst right in front of the children. Bob had gone all the way down to Vienna to pick them up and then had driven back to Westchester. After more than five hours in a car with five children and an infant, Bonnie had erupted.

It was even worse when they entered and she took in the rest of the place—the shabby interior and outdated plumbing fixtures. She couldn't help it. She started yelling at Bob in front of the kids, which she had rarely done before, and never like this. He stiffened. He was staggered. Yet there was nothing to do but put up with it. For a small and beautiful woman, her voice could be awfully ugly. A small part of him never forgave her for making that scene in front of the children.

Matters at the office in New York were not going well. Bob had a large operation to handle. There he was in a

Midtown commercial building, sitting in a suite of rooms, head of a bogus company that claimed to be doing consultation work, yet their IDs were false, and they had no legitimate customers. The building management might have grown suspicious, but if they did, nothing ever came of it—not with the premium rent they were receiving from the one FBI man who had been designated to deal with management. Even the cleaning women couldn't have a clear idea of what the company did. The outer office, with its five people on support staff, was open to the maids, but in the back was located what they called "The Vault." It was secured from electronic penetration—in case the Soviets learned who they were and wanted to throw a few microwaves at them. As if to underline the importance of the work done in these offices, one of the long walls in the Vault was filled with a half-dozen safes lined up next to one another.

Pocketwatch, part of the Bureau's Soviet division, was only one of a number of such offices. The Bureau had five divisions in New York City, across all five boroughs, and a thousand agents there. It was the FBI's largest field presence in any city of the U.S., even more than in Washington. Besides all the crime syndicates in New York, the United Nations was there—which meant the Soviets—and so there was a real need for counterintelligence.

From Bob's point of view, the Soviet division, of which his clandestine office space was just one part, was the most important element in the entire New York operation.

So, yes, there were things he liked about his move. Especially the size of the cases. What would have been a big operation in Gary, Indiana, was small change in New York, where everybody, it seemed, worked big cases. Pocketwatch was an important part of the very large electronic surveillance that the Bureau had set up to cover the Soviets in Manhattan; their targets included United Nations Soviets, the entire corps at the Soviet Consulate, and the many Soviet firms that worked out of AMTORG. Hanssen's part of the surveillance activities was conducted by ten Bureau agents, half of whom could, in varying degrees, read, understand, and even speak Russian, though they were Americans by birth. In some cases, the FBI did recruit foreign-born, naturalized Americans, but this work was just too sensitive to use them.

In spite of the importance of these operations, Hanssen was generally depressed. He was overseeing difficult and occasionally dangerous jobs, yet he was only the administrator. He could sit in judgment of those who were doing the work, but he did not go out on location himself. The agents under him were the ones taking the chances. They had the interesting assignments, the occasional break-ins, and they kept working up the profiles of those Russians who might be Soviet agents, as well as those who could conceivably end up spying for the Bureau. Did the man they were studying like strip clubs? Did he drink too much? If a target seemed promising and was taking a trip to another city, one of Hanssen's agents might be placed in the plane seat next to him. He oversaw the installation of wiretaps on many a suspicious company, and once he set up an operation where a pickpocket—a true thief with a criminal record—was used to plant a diamond with a note attached inside the jacket pocket of a promising KGB man. You could call that a bold attempt to recruit a man whose information might be truly valuable.

It didn't work. The Soviet Intelligence officer on whom they tried the trick must have reported it to his superiors, because soon afterward he was sent back to Russia, and, from what they could pick up, was still working for the KGB.

The intelligence work, then, did offer excitement on the daily job, but Hanssen was not out doing it himself, and he often found his authority to be humiliating. He didn't feel all that respected by his colleagues in the office. He didn't speak Russian, did not have to take chances on operations; he only filed reports. Then he filed more reports on the reports. He assigned tasks. He felt like a clerk.

A female agent assigned to Pocketwatch after the New Year bothered him the most. She made it clear when she arrived that she did not wish to be in counterintelligence. She preferred criminal work. Her name was Cathy Mellon, and she was one of the first four hundred women to be accepted by the FBI. After his retirement, J. Edgar Hoover's old rule that there was no need for women in the Bureau had also been retired.

Mellon was feisty. In her first interview, she told Bob she didn't know anything about foreign counterintelligence and that she didn't want to. She said she had been the first female police officer hired in Santa Fe, New Mexico, and was good with weapons. Being a single mother, she had worked nights and slept days while her two young girls were in school, and she had managed. She had even weathered the practical jokes of her fellow cops—one Christmas Eve they had stuck a poster of a stark-naked Santa Claus in her locker. But she had also succeeded in arresting a Mafia hit man, one of New York City's top ten fugitives, right there in Santa Fe. A rifle shot had even taken out the back window of her patrol car. Her partner was a sergeant who had been a professional football player, and he was not above getting into fistfights with perpetrators just for the pure joy of it. That worked for them as a team. She did the questioning pretty effectively, and he was one hell of a guy for backup.

Mellon had been interested in joining the FBI ever since she heard a lecture about the Bureau while in high school. Besides, the money was good. A Bureau salary came to almost three times as much as she was making in Santa Fe. Since she had full custody of her two girls and wanted to make a good life for them, she applied and was accepted. She passed all the firearms, physical, and mental tests with honors.

She told Bob she had liked working in New York up until now. They'd had her doing stuff comparable to what she did in New Mexico, staying on top of bikers and bank robberies, installing wiretaps on Mafia hangouts, even conducting a break-in that first year in New York. But now she had been reassigned. With no warning other than to be told she was transferred to an elite group—Counterintelligence. She didn't think there was anything very elite about it. Among the Bureau men she had worked with before, Counterintelligence was always put down. Criminal work was what was real. Those agents were her kind of guys. When agents from the Bank Robbery Squad sat around in a diner at lunch drinking scotch out of coffee mugs and telling war stories, laughing their heads off at the sheer wackiness of some of the Mafia perps and twerps they dealt with, she would be the only woman among them, and they treated her like an equal. She had her war stories, too.

Now, abruptly, she'd been transferred. The FBI was a military environment, she told herself—you have to do what you're told to do. But what a shock to meet her new boss.

He was a nerd, a true dork—tall, skinny, with a little potbelly already started, a clammy handshake, and no feel at all for how to talk to somebody. Not at all welcoming. Asked no questions about her family. She could tell at her first look that he would never use a curse word. There was nothing to hope for around him.

"Now, over here," he told her, "we like to give a little orientation for agents who have been in criminal work. That stuff can be interesting."

"It is," she interjected.

162

"Yes, for some. But we feel that the real challenging job is here in Counterintelligence, especially against the Soviets." He gave a little laugh, kind of an odd laugh. "It's highly secret stuff."

"Mr. Hanssen, why did they choose me?"

He looked at some papers on his desk. "No problem at all. When you were tested for entrance into the FBI, you took a language-aptitude test."

"I remember that. Yeah."

"On the basis of your test, you showed the highest ability to interpret foreign languages of just about anyone they'd ever tested."

"You're kidding."

"I am not. The results are right here." He tapped the folder.

"But I don't even *speak* one foreign language. I never studied any of that."

"Doesn't matter," he said. "This only measures your potential aptitude. For that, you had the highest score."

"Well that's fine, Mr. Hanssen, that's terrific, but isn't it kind of late in the day to get me started? I don't know one syllable of Russian."

"Oh, that's all right," he said. "We expect you to pick it up pretty quick."

"You do? How?"

"I'm going to put you on a set of tapes we possess of Soviet wiretaps. All you have to do now is listen to them. See what you can figure out. Down the road, we'll probably put you in a Russian class."

That was her introduction to Hanssen. She spent the next two months and a couple of hundred hours listening to these Russian wiretap tapes. She felt like a guinea pig. He kept asking whether she was making progress. No, she replied. That was about all she saw of him. She had to wonder if he was testing out some theory at her expense.

163

Bob had rarely met a woman who exhibited such contempt for him, and she had come into his office at a very bad time. Her presence kept insulting his image of himself. He could tell that she saw him as the exact opposite of macho and that irked him constantly, especially since he and Bonnie were still trying to get used to living on Mead Street, where the basic inefficiencies and downright tastelessness of the house kept getting to her.

That was one problem. A much bigger one was that he was feeling confusion and great uneasiness as he tried working with the KGB. A lot of little things had gone wrong—and some not so little.

11

1986–1987

The KGB had prepared to receive and load a dead drop for him on March 3, 1986. This proposed attempt had already involved a lot of mailing back and forth between a post office box in New York, held under a false identity, and Degtyar's address in Alexandria.

The KGB had loaded the previous dead drop with a series of queries and requests, but Bob could not leave Pocketwatch to go and pick up the new package. It would have been difficult for him to find an excuse to leave New York on that day, since he was organizing a job that had to be undertaken the same night in New York. In fact, something told him not to go. He congratulated himself for that instinct when he learned that a KGB line officer named Gundarov—who had defected to the United States two weeks earlier—was debriefed on March 4, one day after Bob was supposed to empty the dead drop. Bob also learned that the Bureau had shown Gundarov a photo of Viktor Cherkashin and had asked whether he knew him.

The jolt of adrenaline Bob felt on hearing this piece of information gave him a notion of how it might feel to be knocked down by a lightning bolt. He decided to have nothing to do with the KGB for quite a while. Then he found out that Cherkashin was one of more than one hundred KGB and GRU men Shepard was recommending the U.S. government expel. This kept Bob inactive even longer.

Outside the Embassy, Cherkashin had a casual drink with his local chief Stanislav Androsov. It took place in a crowded Washington bar chosen at random for its noise. There was another officer with Cherkashin and Androsov, one Aleksandr Kirillovitch Fefelov, who had been Cherkashin's subordinate and would deal with his cases.

In the bar, din or no din, the other two had to listen to Cherkashin rattle his fork against an empty glass whenever there was something confidential to discuss.

"You think that fork keeps our friends from hearing what we say?" asked Androsov. "Perhaps you still do not respect their technology."

"My method is crude, Stanislav, but crude methods can also be effective," said Cherkashin. "Besides! Since we didn't know where we would stop to drink, neither did they. So there is none of their equipment in place now. Not for a while at least."

"All right, before you depart from these teeming capitalist shores, can you please inform me—how much do we really know about your mystery man?" Stanislav was still not comfortable with the fact that Cherkashin had gone around him to discuss the matter directly with Moscow Center.

"Ninety-five percent probability he comes from Karpuski." Here, they all had to laugh. Karpuski was a throwaway name they had improvised tonight for the FBI. "He is attached to Karpuski's dog, who has a very wet nose." *Wet nose* was their term for Counterintelligence. As he said this, Cherkashin kept tapping his fork on the glass.

"How I hate this," said Stanislav. "We are going to have no face-to-face with this wet-nose dog of a fellow. Love but no kisses." They laughed because the drinks were good, but perhaps it was a subtle rebuke to Cherkashin.

"I wonder what your guy will do with last year's Christmas gifts?" said Fefelov.

"Oh, he will buy a new car, and then a boat," Cherkashin said, and kept *ting-tinging* on the glass. "Next, he will want an airplane. Ah, if only I could be in contact with him, I would say, 'Don't buy a second car. Don't attract attention.' But suppose he tells me, 'Am sorry. Already bought a boat.' What can I tell him then? I will say, 'Well, if you bought a boat, please invite some interesting people aboard. Learn something.' Next time, I will ask, 'Tell me about the boat?' He will say, 'Forget the boat. I bought a plane.'" They roared with laughter.

Now Cherkashin became serious. Almost reflectively, he tapped on the glass. "You know, I could have sworn he would be with us often and for a long time. Right off, he asks for an escape plan. Since then, we never hear another word. He misses a meeting. We even had to take back the second offering we put in place for him."

"Maybe word will come," said Fefelov, "after you are back in Moscow."

"If you hear, take good care of him. I could have sworn there was something about this guy that was special."

Around June 30, 1986, almost nine months after their last exchange, Degtyar received a typed letter at his residence in Alexandria. In part, it read:

I APOLOGIZE FOR THE DELAY SINCE OUR BREAK IN COMMUNICATIONS. I WANTED TO DETERMINE IF THERE WAS ANY CAUSE FOR CONCERN OVER SECURITY. I HAVE ONLY SEEN ONE ITEM WHICH HAS GIVEN ME PAUSE. WHEN THE FBI WAS FIRST GIVEN ACCESS TO VICTOR PETROVICH GUNDAREV, THEY ASKED . . . IF GUNDAREV KNEW VIKTOR CHERKASHIN. I THOUGHT THIS UNUSUAL. THE QUESTION CAME TO MIND, ARE

THEY SOMEHOW ABLE TO MONITOR FUNDS, I.E., TO KNOW THAT VIKTOR CHERKASHIN RECEIVED A LARGE AMOUNT OF MONEY FOR AN AGENT? I AM UNAWARE OF ANY SUCH ABILITY, BUT I MIGHT NOT KNOW THAT TYPE OF SOURCE REPORTING.

IF YOU WISH TO CONTINUE OUR DISCUSSIONS, PLEASE HAVE SOMEONE RUN AN ADVERTISEMENT IN THE WASHINGTON TIMES DURING THE WEEK OF 1/12/87 OR 1/19/87, FOR SALE, "DODGE DIPLOMAT, 1971, NEEDS ENGINE WORK, $1000." GIVE A PHONE NUMBER AND TIME OF DAY IN THE ADVERTISEMENT WHERE I CAN CALL. I WILL CALL AND LEAVE A PHONE NUMBER WHERE A RECORDED MESSAGE CAN BE LEFT FOR ME IN ONE HOUR. THE NUMBER WILL BE IN AREA CODE 212. I WILL NOT SPECIFY THAT AREA CODE ON THE LINE. I WILL RESPOND, "I'M SORRY, BUT THE MAN WITH THE CAR IS NOT HERE, CAN I GET YOUR NUMBER?"

The letter was signed "Ramon Garcia." Bob laughed to himself at how many hours the KGB would spend debating whether the "c-i-a" in *Garcia* was a hint that he worked for the agency or, to the contrary, was a ploy to throw them off the track.

They responded in the *Washington Times* with the ad he requested, and it ran from July 14, 1986, to July 18. The phone number they listed was (703) 451-9780, and they added: CALL NEXT MO., WED., FRI., 1 P.M. The number turned out to be to a public telephone in the parking lot of the Old Keene Mill Shopping Center in Fairfax County. On Monday, July 3, Bob called from New York. Fefelov took the call, followed the arranged rules, and told Bob that the site would be the same as the first drop, and in the same corner under the footbridge.

However, the KGB made an error. They left the package under the wrong corner of the bridge. Bob had managed to find a legitimate professional reason to travel from New York to Headquarters in D.C., but he did not find the drop that evening and went back to New York empty-handed.

He wrote a letter to Degtyar, communicated the unhappy news, and left word that he would call the same telephone number at the Old Keene Mill Shopping Center on August 18, 20, or 22.

Unknown to Bob, the KGB recorded the next phone call. Hanssen was holding one hand over the mouthpiece, attempting to muffle his voice. Fefelov said: "The car is still available for you, and as we have agreed last time, I have prepared all the papers and I left them on the same table. You didn't find them because I put them in another corner of the table."

Bob said, "I see." He was enraged. Cherkashin's street man was clunky. If anyone from the Bureau were listening in on the conversation, it would be obvious what they were talking about.

Fefelov said, "You shouldn't worry. Everything is okay. The papers are with me now."

"Good."

"It's not necessary to make any changes concerning the place and the time. Our company is reliable, and we are ready to give you a substantial discount, which will be enclosed in the papers. Now, about the date of our meeting, I suggest that our meeting will take place without delay on February thirteenth, one-three, one P.M. Okay, February thirteenth."

Now there was static on the telephone line. It was as if the interruption underlined how ridiculous his formula was for changing months, days, and hours by a coefficient of six. Ridiculous! They were having a conversation, here in August, about buying a car in February. In his excitement, Bob felt confused.

"February second," he said.

"Thirteenth. One-three," said Fefelov.

"One-three."

"Yes. Thirteenth. One P.M."

Bob flipped through a calendar while trying to figure out which day in August was involved and whether his schedule in New York would permit a trip to Virginia, on the suggested day. He grunted, "Let me see if I can do that. Hold on."

There was a pause while Bob heard himself whispering, "Six. . . six."

"Hello, okay?" said Fefelov.

Another pause. The date was for tomorrow! "That should be fine," said Bob, keeping his voice calm.

"Okay. We will confirm you, that *the* papers are waiting for you with *the* same horizontal tape in *the* same place as we did it *the* first time."

Was the man a total idiot? *Horizontal tape!* Why, this KGB man was so nervous.

"Very good," said Bob.

"After you receive *the* papers, you will send *the* letter confirming it. Okay?"

"Excellent."

"I hope you remember *the* address." Fefelov kept using *the* with great emphasis, since "the" did not exist, after all, in Russian. Bob had learned that on the first day of the Russian class he took back in college. "Husband speaks to wife" was how they spoke in their language.

"I believe it should be fine, and thank you very much," Bob said.

"Heh-heh. Not at all. Nice job. For both of us. Uh, have a nice evening, sir."

"Dos vidanya," said Bob.

"Bye-bye."

All right. The drop would be filled next morning at seven. He could go to D.C. later today, pick up the KGB's package in the morning, and be on his way back to New York, all in less than twenty-four hours, but why had he been such a show-off as to say *"Dos vidanya"*? It was probably on file at the FBI that he had studied Russian for that semester at Knox. He swore to himself he would never make another phone call to the KGB if he could help it.

On the morning of August 19, he mailed a letter to Degtyar with a north Virginia postmark. The message read simply: "Received $10,000, Ramon."

More than a year was to go by before the KGB would hear from him again. Given the hundred KGB men who had been expelled with Cherkashin in operation FAMISH, the KGB's operations in the United States were in too much disarray to contact them.

It was a peculiar time. Bob was now a Supervisory Special Agent in the Intelligence Division's Soviet Analytical Unit and wanted to be transferred back to D.C. Headquarters. He not only wanted to live again in a good suburb of northern Virginia like Vienna, but he also felt ready to get back in touch with the KGB. Living with opposed desires was *something else*. How few people besides himself could boast of such an ability?

In the meantime, he and Bonnie got on as well as they could in the cramped house on Mead Street. Bob commuted to work in the car and fudged expenses on tolls between Westchester and the city. Whenever he had to travel downtown to FBI Headquarters from the office in Midtown Manhattan, he would grab a handful of subway tokens from the fishbowl in the foyer that the FBI kept filled. It was an "honor" bowl, but he enjoyed having his pockets crammed full with tokens. The way he saw it, this was the Bureau's way of agreeing that their pay scale was too low for New York, so: "Here! Here's a perk!"

For that matter, he siphoned gas out of FBI cars into his sedan. Cathy Mellon concluded that the reason he was always ready to encourage the staff to go in for the same kind of skimming was that if they all did it, then no one would be in a position to blow the whistle. What a weird man, she decided. He had such an honorable look on his face even as he hinted that they could double or triple their monthly vouchers on commuting costs. Yes, if he got you dirty, how could you do anything to him?

All the same, these extra dollars he squirreled away were not enough to keep him from feeling poor in New York. He had to save that KGB money for the new house he would buy in Virginia.

Meanwhile he remained on the sidelines. That was the one constant in New York. His squad was not in the big leagues. They did not recruit KGB agents. Reading the papers that came across his desk, he was cognizant of the game that he never got to play. Cathy, who Bob had now shifted from listening to Russian tapes into more serious operations, was busy protecting a Recruitment in Place, referred to as an "RIP." She had to be on alert and ready to rescue him if he ever failed to come out of the Soviet Consulate when he was expected—a tricky set of decisions to make if you weren't sure that something had gone wrong. All the same, as if insensitive to how big a responsibility she had, Hanssen was not above giving her Simple-Simon lectures: "If the Soviets recruit any of our people," he would tell her, "we have a chance to pick that up with our surveillance. But what if some Bureau guy just decides to mail a package to some KGB official? That's our nightmare. That's why the Bureau has to recruit more and more KGB intelligence officers who can keep us informed on what material of ours is coming into their headquarters from Americans." It was as if he chose to ignore precisely what she was, in fact, already doing with her Soviet agent.

Just before he was transferred back to Washington Headquarters in August of 1987, he found out that Motorin and Martynov had been executed, the first in February, the latter in May, just two months ago.

He did not spend time thinking of either man down on his knees at the moment the back of his head was blown off by a KGB pistol. The image, however, did seep into Bob's dreams. He could not decide whether that was good or bad for those recurring headaches. He certainly did feel a strong impulse to get back to spying. If there was a judgment on his soul because of their deaths, then to hell with it. In for a penny, in for a pound.

12

1987–1988

Bob, Bonnie, and the children were happy to go back to Vienna. During this move, the timing for buying a house was better. They sold the place on Mead Street for $212,000, bringing in a gross profit of $47,000. After deducting $15,000 for closing costs, commissions, and transportation, they were left with $32,000. With the turnover, they could buy a better home. 9414 Talisman Drive, in Vienna, Virginia, was a split-level whose exterior was painted a chocolate brown. It had nine rooms, of which four were bedrooms; there were also two full baths, a fireplace, a half-finished basement, and central heating and air-conditioning, and it was fairly new. It had been built around 1978 when the area was developed. The house cost $205,000, but Bob put down $80,000, which consisted of the equity and profit from Mead Street. After the purchase, except for the hidden KGB money, he was left without any accountable cash again.

These financial difficulties aside, he did come back to FBI Headquarters in D.C. with a lot going for him. He was still at Grade 14, but then again one could get fixed at that level forever in the FBI, as there was nothing automatic about getting up to Grade 15. Only a small percentage of Special Agents ever rose that high. Although there was no increase in his salary, he was certainly working at a more prestigious level. His organizational skills had improved. Before he went to New York, he was already a Supervisory Special Agent in the Intelligence Division's Soviet Analytical Unit, but that title, if not his salary, was bumped up again one month later. Mike Shepard had come back from an around-the-world assignment, and on his return, a month and a day after Bob reported back to work in Washington, Shepard became Assistant Section Chief of the CI-3 Section in the Intelligence Division—a powerful position. In fact, Hanssen was the first person to walk into Shepard's office and greet him on his initial day back, and Shepard was certainly glad to see him.

Moreover, Bob was now becoming popular with agents and analysts who were having problems with their computers. That environment was in constant flux. The machines were always being upgraded and then they didn't always work very well with old printers. New printers had to be requisitioned, which took time and kicked off bureaucratic skirmishes. Or the network could be changed or upgraded and then nothing worked well. Bob became the man to see. He could tweak the settings of the machines so that they would function. That sometimes saved weeks, even months, of waiting for the computer technicians to come and make fixes that often didn't do any good. Bob was beginning to be viewed as a sort of computer Robin Hood.

By September 11, 1987, a week after Shepard had returned (and a little more than two years after Hanssen had sent his first letter to Cherkashin), Bob was in action again.

Ever since he had come back to Vienna, he had been feeling a pleasurable mixture of uneasiness and excitement. It was a little like his teenage years when he would get aroused at the thought of something different, even challenging, in each new *Playboy* picture.

One of the biggest reasons he had wanted to be back in Washington was the valuable material that would be at his disposal in D.C.

It didn't go all that smoothly, however. In their last communication, thirteen months earlier, the KGB had suggested using more sophisticated techniques. So Bob had contemplated the pros and cons of employing burst transmitters or meeting in selected sites, even in foreign cities. The more he considered it, however, the less he liked such procedures. The emphasis now in FBI Foreign Counterintelligence was not only to focus on the latest KGB advanced techniques, but to look for ways to overtake them technologically. The game was to turn each new KGB supertoy to the Bureau's advantage. Far better then, Bob decided, to go back to old-fashioned methods. Nobody in the Bureau would be looking for anything like that anymore.

Therefore, he rejected all the KGB proposals. In September, using the fake return address "R. Garcia, 125 Main St., Alexandria, Virginia," on a letter to B. N. Malkow, Degtyar's replacement, he wrote:

DEAR FRIENDS: NO, I HAVE DECIDED IT MUST BE ON MY ORIGINAL TERMS OR NOT AT ALL. I WILL NOT MEET ABROAD OR HERE. I WILL NOT MAINTAIN LISTS OF SITES OR MODIFIED EQUIPMENT. I WILL HELP YOU WHEN I CAN, AND IN TIME WE WILL DEVELOP METHODS OF EFFICIENT COMMUNICATION. UNLESS I SEE AN ABORT SIGNAL ON OUR POST FROM YOU BY 3/16, I WILL MAIL MY CONTACT A VALUABLE PACKAGE TIMED TO ARRIVE ON 3/18. I WILL AWAIT YOUR SIGNAL AND PACKAGE TO BE IN PLACE BEFORE 1:00 PM ON 3/22 OR ALTERNATELY THE FOLLOWING THREE WEEKS, SAME DAY AND TIME. IF MY TERMS ARE UNACCEPTABLE THEN PLACE NO SIGNALS AND WITHDRAW MY CONTACT. EXCELLENT WORK BY HIM HAS

ENSURED THIS CHANNEL IS SECURE FOR NOW. MY RE-
GARDS TO HIM AND TO THE PROFESSIONAL WAY YOU
HAVE HANDLED THIS MATTER.

SINCERELY, RAMON

He smiled knowingly at the compliment he had given.
They offered him false compliments; however, he could
return them in kind. Bullshit for bullshit! Using the formula he'd devised with the number "6," the dates in the
letter referred to September 10, 12, and 16.

Bob followed up immediately. On Monday, September 14, 1987, the KGB received in the mail a package
that contained top-secret National Security Council documents. The KGB responded the next day by loading the
"Park" dead-drop site they had used before with
$10,000. They also proposed two additional dead-drop
sites—one named "An," in Ellanor C. Lawrence Park in
Western Fairfax County, a bit out in the Eastern District
of Virginia, and another, "Den," even farther away. The
KGB proposed that the dead drop at "Park" or "An" be
loaded on September 26, 1987, and that the KGB would
respond by loading "Den": one site was for the drop; another was for the money pickup and future instructions.

He was furious. The KGB was underestimating his expertise and he would have to teach them how to proceed. Counterintelligence in the Bureau knew that the
KGB liked to set up drop sites twenty and thirty miles
away from their Embassy—the exurbs rather than the
suburbs of D.C. Accordingly, there was close FBI surveillance of the outer perimeter. Closer to home would
be safer.

By Wednesday, September 16, 1987, Hanssen had
cleared the "Park" dead-drop site and removed the signal. On September 26, 1987, the KGB recovered from
"Park" a package containing a handwritten letter.

MY FRIENDS:

THANK YOU FOR THE $10,000. I AM NOT A YOUNG MAN, AND THE COMMITMENTS ON MY TIME PREVENT USING DISTANT DROPS SUCH AS YOU SUGGEST. I KNOW IN THIS I AM MOVING YOU OUT OF YOUR SET MODES OF DOING BUSINESS, BUT MY EXPERIENCE TELLS ME THAT WE CAN BE ACTUALLY MORE SECURE IN EASIER MODES.

Depend upon it, he told himself, the KGB could be just as bureaucratic as the FBI. They, too, would persist in methods that were too advanced or too backward to fit a given situation.

On Sunday, November 15, 1987, the KGB alerted Hanssen that the dead drop at "An"—the faraway one, which he didn't want to use—would have a package. The KGB discovered, however, that Ramon did not clear it that day or the next. Two days later, on November 17, they were obliged to remove the package. On November 19, Thursday, a letter was received by Malkow, Ramon's new correspondent in Alexandria. It said:

UNABLE TO LOCATE "AN" BASED ON YOUR DESCRIPTION AT NIGHT. RECOGNIZE THAT I AM DRESSED IN BUSINESS SUIT AND CAN NOT SLOG AROUND IN INCH DEEP MUD. I SUGGEST WE USE AGAIN ORIGINAL SITE. I WILL SELECT SOME FEW SITES GOOD FOR ME AND PASS THEM TO YOU. RAMON

Even as he wrote the letter, he was thinking of how he had come out of the woods, his shoes caked in mud. He had had to stop by his car, take out a handkerchief, dip it in some stagnant water on the shoulder, and then, in the dim illumination of his parking lights, standing on one foot, clean one shoe, step into it, lift his other leg, clean the other shoe, and finally throw the handkerchief away before he could get into his car and drive off.

Fefelov had a new subordinate who did the drops, a young man, Boris. After he was shown Hanssen's last letter, he said, "You know, I could hate this guy! Nothing but trouble. Always complaining."

Fefelov held up his hands in reproach. "No, I would say he is different."

Boris threw up his hands as well. "I know," he said. "KGB style. Always think of the client first. Never reproach, never reproach."

"Boris, you always have to say, 'You're okay, man, you're special.'"

"He picks public parks!" said Boris. "That is full of risk for me. How does he know the police won't be on watch, right there ready for muggers? For rapists? If they stop Ramon, he's all right. He can show FBI credentials. If they stop me, disaster."

"No, Boris. You have tradecraft," Fefelov assured him. "You know how not to be followed."

Boris didn't agree. "I have made inquiries about Vienna. This Vienna in Virginia! FBI people live there. Retired CIA Intelligence people live there. Working CIA people also. Counterintelligence people. Military people. Such gentlemen will notice suspicious movement."

"Forget it, Boris. You must avoid surveillance. And don't forget to leave pepper on the drop."

Boris was offended. "Of course. I know how to keep dogs away. But does Ramon use pepper?"

"You told me yourself. You found the package last time. You came out sneezing."

"I hope he was sneezing, too. Fefelov, let us face it: He is a pain in the ass."

"He is still new," replied Fefelov. "He will get better. We will get better. But remember, Boris, he can still be one great fellow for us. Remember! His life is difficult. *He* is risking his life—not you!"

With this last remark, Fefelov stared at Boris. His eyes were cold and blue.

"Worst can happen for you—expulsion. You have to go back to Moscow—okay. You can go see your sweetheart. But Ramon will stay in jail for the rest of his life. So, I tell you: Satisfy his needs. Offer healing thoughts. Do it his way. Maybe I will put poetry in my letters to him."

"Ha, ha," said Boris. "Old KGB style. Ha, ha! But I tell you, a new world is coming. No need for poetry in this new world, no! Just lots of music!"

Bob's working conditions were now ideal for getting material to the KGB. The exchange operation that had taken place in Nottoway Park, near his home in Vienna—the original site—had listed material provided by KGB agent Vitaly Yurchenko shortly after his defection and before he decided in 1985 that he wished to go back to Moscow. Bob had also included an official technical document describing COINS-11, which was the most current version of the entire United States community's "On-line Intelligence System," a classified Community-wide intranet. In return, the KGB had given him $20,000 in cash and a letter from the KGB director telling him that he now had $100,000 deposited in a Moscow bank, which would earn as much as 7 percent interest. Hanssen shrugged. He was certain he would never see that money. It was a Soviet ploy, a fictitious deposit—but he liked the warmth in the tone of the letter.

He was ready to give them a lot more. The material was certainly there. Bob, now Deputy Chief of Soviet Counterintelligence Analysis, was working in a room with two other men on the fourth floor. Both of them, Walter Ballou and Jim King, were employed by the FBI as Intelligence Research Specialists. The three of them received all the cables that came in from New York, from the D.C. field office, from San Francisco, from Chicago—in all, from the twelve major U.S. areas. They were urgent, immediate, or routine: all classified and usually salmon pink in color.

Hanssen would review them and assign the follow-up to analysts working in little cubicles around the corner. He would spend a lot of time in his own room reviewing reports with his two colleagues and analyzing the information that had come in from the field. Periodically, he would go to top-level meetings for discussions of the more serious findings. It gave a turn to his humor to know that he was not only in a position to be one of the most damaging spies ever to come out of any country's woodwork, but that all this was happening while he was assigned to work in a room with two other men. He didn't even have a private office—just himself and two other men in one room without even a partition between them.

Of course, they were not always all there at the same time. They could be out walking the hall talking to people—amazing how many clues could be picked up about what was going on (and where to look for it) on a casual stroll up and back on the floor. And of course one or two or all three of them might be out at conferences of one sort or another. When he was alone, there were lots of opportunities for getting ahold of the right information.

He had a lot of material to give the KGB. During 1988, he mailed them seven diskettes. They were filled with continuing information on Stealth programs, FBI conversions of KGB personnel, technical surveillance systems, plus highly classified lists of FBI recruitment targets among various Soviet personnel. Besides the seven diskettes, he also made five drops. One package

181

was 530 pages, much of it top secret. There was a hoard of documents on the Bureau's human intelligence, concerning the Soviet military. In March 1988, he made three deliveries—one drop and two mailed diskettes. In July and September, he made two drops and two mailings. There was also a diskette mailed in April, another one in May, and a final drop in December. The last one was at a site called "Charlie," another footbridge in another park, and it took place on December 26, the day after Christmas.

13

1988

The more material Bob supplied to the KGB, the more he began to feel that his inner life was like a kaleidoscope. Sparkles of one mood slipped into another, all of them revolving in his mind. More and more these days he consulted the mirror.

"*I tell them I have children and that is true,*" he heard himself say to the glass. "*I also tell them I came across Kim Philby's book when I was fourteen—false. It wasn't even published until I was twenty-four. Lies and truth, truth and lies. Mix them nicely.*"

He smiled at the face that looked back at him. "*Evil has its own kingdom,*" he declared. "*In the land of evil, pornography is religion and lies are luminous. There is nothing banal about evil.*"

The mirror was everywhere, even on the fourth floor of the FBI building. One morning, walking down a corridor with several files under his arm, he went into the men's room, entered a stall, and, after propping the files against his knee, looked into the polished steel of its door.

"*Mike Shepard just gave me these materials,*" he whispered to the door. "*He wants me to ascertain if there is a mole inside the FBI. At this moment, by my knee, are summaries of all our reports from Soviet defectors. Once I have studied them, I will write a top-secret report and*

*put it in my next dead drop to the Soviets. Now I know
how a genius feels at the height of his powers."*

He would have enjoyed hearing Stanislav and Fefelov
talking to each other in the small, stuffy glass box about
eight feet by eight feet by eight feet that was suspended
on wires within a larger room at the Soviet Embassy,
only a couple of miles away from where he worked.

"I have to admit it, I think Ramon wrote this report
himself," Fefelov exclaimed. "I have changed my mind.
Ramon is a remarkable man. Not just a superagent, but
equal in our profession to Tolstoy, Goethe, Dickens,
Hemingway—a genius!"

"Excessive enthusiasm is not appropriate in our profession," Stanislav replied. "It is much too soon to talk
in this manner."

The pleasure of using the stall in the men's room increased. It was as if the polished-steel surface, while it
distorted his features, was nonetheless most available.
One time, however, speaking to himself, he became cau-
tionary. *"You are on all these committees,"* he said, *"you
have entrée to so much at CIA and NSA, you've been
grabbing documents everywhere. Are you showing off?
Are you doing too much? You are creating data points
all over the place. You could be traced by that eventually.
You are one of the few who has that much access. Why
give away so much? It's no longer for the money. I can't
even find a way to spend it. Now we live poor while I've
got money hidden everywhere. No, it is for the art of the
game. I have a natural desire to become the spy of the
century. Why not? I always knew that I was capable of
becoming extraordinary."*

One night at home, Bonnie walked in as Bob was screw-
ing two towel hooks into the top of the bathroom mirror.
   "Why are you putting those up?" she asked.

"They're useful for hanging my facecloths when I shave."

"Two? You only need one."

"I use two facecloths," he said. "I like to put astringent on one of them."

"All right, all right—but those hooks look so wrong there," she said as she left the bathroom.

As soon as the door was locked, he draped a red cloth over the hooks. That gave the mirror more presence, made it look a little more like a miniature chapel.

"I am happy only when I am working at my best for both sides at once," Hanssen said to the glass. "Let the cops get better and the crooks get better. Thereby, you have an interesting society. Fewer fools. Is it too much to hope for that?"

If he didn't sense how close to the door Bonnie was in the next room, he would have growled. He had never been feeling more animal in his life.

In the following week, Bob hired a carpenter to install a very expensive front door in their house.

"Can we afford this?" asked Bonnie.

"We have to," Bob said. "This is the door to a splendid family who will grow up here."

Tears came into Bonnie's eyes. "If I didn't know you meant every word of it, I would say that's too rich for my blood," she said. At times like this, the elegance of his sentiments moved her, deeply and meaningfully.

These days, he was free of the migraine attacks, but he had new tensions to deal with. He was horny all the time. Sometimes he would masturbate twice in a day and then make love to Bonnie that night. Other times, he had to look for a different kind of release. Occasionally, when he was alone in the car, he would scream, utter deep grunts, and then murmur to himself for a while as he came down on the quiet side, ready to ponder his next move.

One night, in the middle of April, coming home from

a dead drop, driving much too fast on an empty four-lane road, he began to growl and shout in all the freedom of being alone in his car. He became so immersed in the operatic feelings within him that he did not pay attention to a wild driver speeding up on him in the right lane. Damn if the guy didn't then proceed to make a quick left turn in front of him. Didn't pull it off. They collided. It was a T-bone smackup and clearly the other driver's fault, but it was Bob who was injured.

That was how he came to know Walter Ballou better. Walter was the analyst who shared the office with him and Jim King. Since he also lived in Vienna, he would, for the period that Bob was incapacitated, pick him up on the way to work.

Hanssen would sit shotgun with his arm and elbow in a cast, while in the backseat were his daughters Jane and Sue on their way to school, wearing their uniforms—saddle shoes, kneesocks, and plaid wool skirts. Jane was sixteen and Sue was fourteen, and, of course, the girls kept whispering to each other.

"Your accident wouldn't have happened," said Walter one morning, "if you'd had a sports car. It's a lot nimbler in emergencies." Walter was as tall as Bob but so heavy that he had a bit of a waddle when he walked. He hardly seemed like the sort of fellow to be that knowing about sports cars.

"I won't argue," said Bob.

But Jane and Sue had heard, and they got excited.

"Oh, Daddy, get a sports car!" Sue squealed.

"It'd be wonderful. We could learn to drive in a sports car," Jane added. "We could even take our test in a sports car."

"Don't count on it. They're expensive," Hanssen said.

"Oh, Daddy, don't say no."

"Drop it," said their father. It was one of the few times Ballou heard him speak to them in a curt tone.

The girls' school was convenient to the men's route to work, and Ballou thought it was awfully neat-looking. But then it ought to have been. Oakcrest was a parochial school for the children of Opus Dei members.

Both girls got out, and as they did, turned to Walter.

"Thank you, Dr. Ballou," Jane said.

"Thank you, Dr. Ballou," Sue said.

They waved politely, almost perfunctorily, as the car drove off.

A few minutes down the road, Ballou and Hanssen got into a bit of a religious discussion. The radio happened to be tuned in to NPR, and a woman, obviously a liberal pundit, could be heard: ". . . and it is crucial," she was saying, "that we never forget the social contract, which, as we know, is the foundation of morality."

Hanssen reached forward with his good arm and switched off the radio. "Enough of that."

"Okay," Walter said. "I guess I have given you veto rights over my radio."

"Walter, that woman is a fool. Morality has nothing to do with this so-called social contract. We are only moral when we feel God within us. That's when you know that everything you do does count."

"Bob, I have to say, that sounds kind of narcissistic to me. Who are we to be the arbiters? I think you have to question the validity of thoughts like that."

"It's not narcissistic. Not at all. God wants us to love and serve Him."

"Bob, how can you know what God wants?"

Hanssen smiled. "You can feel it in your heart. I tell you, sometimes you know exactly what God wants."

"Bob, I don't pretend to be any more than a cafeteria Catholic, but I will tell you this: Saint John Vianney once said that most people commit a majority of their sins in church—they take Communion when they shouldn't. Usually, they have fudged on Confession."

"What an odd remark. Do you have anybody in mind?"

"No one like you," said Walter.

In the middle of the night, Bob woke up thinking that one over. He had come to an agreeable understanding with himself about going to Confession. In Opus Dei, you were required to go at least once a week, but of course, he was not about to tell his priest anything about what he was doing with the Soviets—not after that little episode in 1979. They might give him absolution once or twice if he swore to cease such activity, but he knew he didn't feel ready to stop. And if he continued spying, they would refuse to give him absolution—at the least!—and Bonnie, of course, would know almost at once that he was not taking Communion.

He was able to work it out for himself: Spying for the Soviets was not a mortal but a venial sin, he decided. The Soviets were such a messed-up system (except for the KGB, who were only half messed-up) that they were no longer a threat to America. They were hardly in a position to use what he gave them. Since they were just about washed up, his acts in that direction were venial. *He* could judge them to be venial.

When it came to sex, however, he was ready to confess. Over and over again. He could be forgiven for masturbation, because it was "an ungovernable impulse." The Church must have decided a thousand years ago that if it could not give absolution for repeated sexual sins and vices, there would be few practicing Catholics left. So they accepted "ungovernable impulses."

"You must pray, my son," he heard often enough.

"Oh, Father, I will pray."

Indeed, he did. Coming out of the box, he would pray on his knees, pray before the eyes of everyone.

On this night when he awoke, he wondered if his spying was also an ungovernable impulse. Even if it was, he knew the Church would not agree. That was pretty clear to him. A venial sin. He made it back to sleep.

These days, with all the action, each week before a drop was a little different. It depended on the interval between them. Usually, he liked to have a week to recover and savor the money he picked up, then another week, at least, to prepare material and check his security. He had his ways. Often, on the weekend before a drop, he would feel particularly excited. He liked to do a drop or a pickup on Monday night. Guys on surveillance for the Bureau would probably be watching *Monday Night Football,* believing the KGB was also glued to the tube.

One Sunday night, Bonnie was wearing a silk bathrobe and he was in his shorts.

"You're so beautiful," he told her. "No woman your age can possibly be as beautiful. We have to take pictures of you."

"Does it mean that much to you?" she asked.

"It does. Oh, it does," he said. "I don't want your beauty to be unrecorded. That would be such a loss."

"Bob, if it pleases you that much . . ." She took a long pause, but in the end she said, "I want so much to please you. . . ." Yet she remained suspicious of him—he could tell. Twenty years had gone by, but she still remembered the female voice on the phone that afternoon when he had stolen off to make love to that middle-aged bitch of a nurse.

"I adore you," he said. "I will always adore you. I'm mad for you. I love your desire to please me."

He reached for a loaded Polaroid camera on the bureau.

Slowly, Bonnie opened her robe. The Polaroid flashed.

A couple of weeks later, on the Fourth of July, they were having a party in their backyard, and it was going nicely. Each of the younger kids was given a Roman candle to hold, and either Bob or Bonnie escorted them around the yard while the candle sizzled and sparked. Even Lisa, who was only two, was taken around the yard, although Bonnie of course held the candle for her.

An hour later, Jack and Bob were sitting on the patio. The remains of the fireworks had been gathered neatly in a trash basket a few yards away. As they sat in silence, the crickets could be heard in the nearby woods, and occasionally a birdcall.

Bob broke the silence. "Those Polaroids of Bonnie—incredible, aren't they?"

"Damn good," Jack said.

"She only agreed to pose because I didn't have to take the film roll to a photo shop."

"Isn't this the first time in years?" Jack asked.

"It has been years. But she agreed. I think she must want to expose herself." He gave his laugh. "Secretly. She even keeps it as a secret from herself." Now Bob held up a finger before speaking as if to indicate the importance of what he was about to say. "Remember a few years ago," he said, "when I insisted that you look at Bonnie in the shower?"

Jack's instinct was to hold him back. "Kind of an in-between thing. I could hardly see her."

"Well, I've come up with a winner. You know the balcony outside our bedroom? That little deck is the easiest thing to get to. There's a small ladder in the garage. Once you get up there, you can see right into our bedroom."

"Good Lord! Even thinking about that makes me uncomfortable."

"No, it's okay. I could lift the shade just an inch or two." Bob paused. "Jack, wouldn't you like to see Bonnie and me making love?"

190

"Don't talk like that. I'm human. It scares me. I don't know that I want to go from fantasy to reality. That might be too much."

"Why don't we try it? Try it once at least."

"I don't know. It could hurt our relationship."

"It's okay," Hanssen told him. "I know how I feel, Jack. I am ready to give you full permission to see me and my wife in the act."

"I'm not sure I can follow this. Why?" But Jack's voice was neither steady nor disapproving. He was at a real loss. He had never been able to come to grips with this side of his relationship to Bob. It was too crazy. A year could go by, and they might hardly refer to anything sexual. The visits just felt comfortable, as relaxing as visits between old friends should be. Then this other factor would suddenly flare up. But now, this suggestion! This was almost off his register. Yet, God knows, he was startled at how excited it made him.

"Bonnie is so beautiful," Bob said. "I want you to appreciate how blessed I am."

That night, Jack carried a ladder from the garage to the back wall of the house. Then he climbed up to the balcony, bent over, and peered in through the promised space between the shade and the window sash. By the side of the bed, a small lamp with a soft light lit the scene. Had Bob ever enjoyed making love this much before? He didn't think so. Jack, he told himself, might be more of an athlete, but could he ever demonstrate this kind of sexual prowess? No, Jack would have to be exceptionally impressed.

The next morning, the two men drove into Washington. For most of the way they did not speak. Finally, Bob could not maintain the silence.

"How do you feel?" he asked.

"Buddy, it's your wife. I don't want to talk about it."

"You didn't enjoy it?"

There was a tone of such disbelief in his voice that Jack had to respond. "All right," he said. "I did. I did enjoy it."

"Like to see something of that sort again?"

They sat in silence, listening to the quiet hum of the tires.

"All right, yes," Jack said at last. "I guess I'm saying yes. When do we do it again?"

"Tonight. What I really want to know is the angle you would like to see it from."

"The angle? "

"Who would you like to see on top?"

"Nobody's ever had a conversation like this."

Bob whinnied. These days he was making that crazy laugh an awful lot. It was as if the whole world was out of kilter, and he could sure enjoy that. "Come on, Jack. What's wrong with giving you the menu?"

They drove on. It was agreed that Bonnie would be on top.

Two nights later, after Jack had left, Bob was talking to Jane and Sue in the living room.

"Daddy, do you really believe the Soviet Union is going to collapse?" Sue asked.

"It has to. It is run by godless Communists," Hanssen replied.

"Don't you have a lot to do with fighting them?" Jane asked.

He waited to answer as he always did before saying anything at home about his work. It gave a confidential tone to what he offered.

"Well," he remarked, "I can tell you that Counterintelligence is there to block the efforts of Soviet Intelligence. I like to think we do the best job we can—sometimes under trying circumstances."

"This is so good," Sue said. "My assignment for tomorrow is to write an essay on why America is opposed to Communism. I know why, I think, but the subject is so large. Where do you start?"

"Approach it this way: We know the Soviet Union is run by godless Communists. We also know that you have to have God in your life. If He is not a driving force behind every thought and impulse, then sooner or later you are bound to fail as a human being. The same is true for a nation that dismisses God."

"That's so great, Dad! It makes so much sense," Sue said. "It's so clean."

"You're super, Dad," Jane added.

14

1989

One morning in Shepard's office, Mike said, "You know, someday I would like to write a book called *The Other Victims*."

They had been chatting for a while about office details, and the statement seemed to come out of nowhere. "Who are they?" Hanssen asked.

"Everyone who writes about espionage concentrates on the spy," said Shepard. His lips were pursed, as if he were gathering in the thought. "But who is there to ask what the consequences are to the family of the spy?"

Hanssen gave a profound nod. "Oh, Mike," he said. "If you ever write that book, we can stop espionage." Then he gave his odd laugh.

"Bob, are you all right? You look like you're in pain," Mike said.

"It just came on me suddenly. It's nothing. A kidney spasm."

That afternoon, when Shepard stepped by Bob's office, he found Hanssen on the floor writhing in pain. Near him, on the floor, was Walter Ballou, also in pain, also writhing. Indeed, their pain was so acute that they did not see Mike at first, and when they did, they dispensed with office etiquette.

"Good Lord! What on earth is going on?" Mike Shepard asked.

"I think we're passing kidney stones," Hanssen replied.

"Together? Both of you at once?"

"Yeah," said Walter.

"You both got it at the same time?"

"That's what happens when you work together." Ballou managed to laugh at his own remark.

"I won't tell anyone," Shepard said.

Now they all laughed—Shepard at his own joke, and the other two just for the pleasure of laughing while in agony.

Bob passed the kidney stone later that day, and twenty-four hours later, on January 31, 1989, he made a special drop. The KGB man, who was making his daily check of the telephone pole that they used to send signals to each other, observed that red tape had been used instead of white. That signified an emergency.

Boris was alerted by Fefelov. "It will be very hard for me to go out today," Boris said. "I am seriously behind on a couple of matters."

"So now you will be more seriously behind. Just do it. He has given us an emergency signal. Do it, and respect the dry-cleaning."

Boris nodded. Dry-cleaning! It meant he had to drive around Washington and the Maryland and Virginia suburbs for four hours—four hours—in order to make sure that he was not being followed. Only then could he go to the drop site.

Boris was able, at last, to park near the footbridge. It was still daylight, but the area looked deserted, so he got out, strolled about, saw that the coast was clear, and stooped to pick up a package lying between the bank and the timbers.

An hour later, Stanislav Androsov and Fefelov were in the glass box reading Hanssen's message. It said:

AN IMPORTANT TOP SECRET DOCUMENT IS EN-CLOSED. MAY I REQUEST THAT THIS DOCUMENT, ONCE COPIED, BE RETURNED, FOR ITS ABSENCE FROM MY FILES COULD, ON SOME FUTURE OCCA-SION, CAUSE ME DIFFICULTY. SEND TO MOSCOW CEN-TER RIGHT AWAY.

Fefelov smacked his fist on the table. "Right away? He is bypassing us. Who does he think he is?"

"Do what he says," Stanislav Androsov told him. "Send it to the Center today."

The next drop was made by the KGB, and when Hanssen picked it up, he discovered that they had sent him a diamond, which he had requested a few months earlier, as part of a payment. Just why he wanted a precious stone he couldn't say. It was frivolous. He couldn't cash it in quickly during an emergency. But possessing a gem appealed to him. It was the kind of compact little treasure James Bond might have enjoyed. And it would be good to have if he ever got stranded in a foreign land.

THE CHAIRMAN OF OUR ORGANIZATION IN MOSCOW SENDS HIS CONGRATULATIONS TO YOU FOR THE LAT-EST MATERIAL SENT TO THE CENTER. WE THANK YOU FOR YOUR LAST EXCEPTIONALLY INTERESTING DOCU-MENT WHICH WE NOW RETURN WITH $18,000 CASH AND A DIAMOND VALUED AT $11,700 DOLLARS. FOR-GIVE US FOR ASKING, BUT HAVE YOU TAKEN APPROPRI-ATE SECURITY PRECAUTIONS FOR THE POSSESSION OF SUCH?

To which Hanssen replied:

FRET NOT. I WILL SAY IF NECESSARY THAT THE DIA-
MOND CAME FROM MY GRANDMOTHER. NEEDLESS
TO SAY, SHE IS LONG DEAD. RAMON

The next note from the KGB informed Hanssen about
awards given to Cherkashin and Androsov.

ENCLOSED IS $55,000 IN CASH AND INSTRUCTIONS ON
HOW TO INFORM US WHICH MATERIALS SHOULD BE
OPENED BY US IN WASHINGTON AND WHICH SHOULD
GO TO MOSCOW CENTER. THE CHAIRMAN OF THE
KGB AGAIN CONVEYS HIS REGARDS.

Hanssen was riding a crest. He felt full of magic, like
a wave on a great day that starts in heaven and comes up
behind a surfer.

ENCLOSED ARE SEVERAL DOCUMENTS INCLUDING A
DEPARTMENT OF COUNTERINTELLIGENCE NATIONAL
INTELLIGENCE ESTIMATE ENTITLED "THE SOVIET
SYSTEM IN CRISES: PROSPECTS FOR THE NEXT TWO
YEARS." IT HAS NOT YET BEEN RELEASED. AS YOU
WILL SEE, IT IS DATED NOVEMBER, 1989. THE REASON:
I CAN TAKE A BOW FOR THE AUTHORSHIP OF THIS
DOCUMENT.

I THANK YOU FOR THE CHRISTMAS GREETINGS AND
THE $38,000 IN CASH YOU LEFT FOR ME ON THE EX-
CHANGE.

15

1989–1990

The year 1989 had been almost as active as 1988. From the emergency signal on January 31 through to Christmas night, Bob had made seven drops and had mailed one diskette. In 1988 he had used "Park" site three times and then moved on to "Bob" and "Charlie." In 1989 he used "Bob" three times, "Charlie" twice, "Doris" once, and "Ellis" once. All the sites were under footbridges in small parks within a few miles of his home.

On March 20, Hanssen made two packages composed of 539 documents of classified information and one diskette. It all added up to a top-secret program of the Measurement and Signature Intelligence Committee on its objectives and capabilities—a highly detailed critical study. In May he compromised the FBI investigation of Felix Bloch, a State Department official who had been meeting with a Soviet illegal based in Austria. He also sent them a document entitled "National Intelligence Program 90–91 TOP SECRET." In August he gave them the details of a highly compartmentalized program designed to ensure the continuity of the U.S. government in the event of a major nuclear attack by the Soviets. The program also included the means of defense, and the means of retaliation, in the wake of such a move. An extraordinary document. There was more. In September he finally alerted the KGB to the tunnel project. Because

198

of the exceptional information he had given them with his first offering in 1985, that detailed description of the penetration by the U.S. government into most rooms, closets, and crevices of the Soviet Embassy, American surveillance of the Embassy had been thwarted. Meanwhile, the Soviets had continued building their new Embassy up on Mount Alto. In response, the U.S. had continued developing the tunnel beneath—that developed operation would enable them to penetrate conversations in the new building. Bob had discovered the commencement of that operation back in 1984 in his conversation with Shepard about methane fireballs, but now, he decided, was the time to inform the KGB. Five weeks later, after this formidable news had been studied at Moscow Center, the KGB sent him $55,000. By now, he had received a total of $265,000 over the years.

For Christmas night, 1989, Bob left a full package at the dead drop called "Bob." An alphabetical coincidence! Orderly whenever possible, the KGB called their drop sites "An," "Bob," "Charlie," "Doris," "Ellis," etc.

The package contained details of U.S. penetration into another Soviet establishment, and a detailed study entitled "The Soviet System in Crisis—Prospects for the Next Two Years." Also disclosed were three more highly protected FBI sources within the KGB, as well as information the Bureau had received from four defectors. In return, the KGB left a package for Bob containing $38,000, together with two diskettes. One asked for more information on a number of classified technical projects, but the other diskette consisted only of Christmas greetings from the KGB. After all, it was appropriate. He was supplying them with unbelievable gifts on Christmas night.

Jack Hoschouer happened to be in town, to complete his military-attaché training, and had come over on Christmas morning, to be with the family. Most of the gifts under the tree had already been opened by the time he got there and were by now strewn over the sofa or, in the case of the younger kids, the toys were already being played with on the floor. The older girls had their boxes neatly piled up, and Jack was soon trying on a spectacular leather jacket that Bob had bought for him.

"Now something for you and your family," Jack said.

He reached behind the couch. He had deposited a large package there as soon as he had come in, and now he pulled it out. Under the wrapping was an American flag that, unfolded, came to five feet by eight feet.

Bob exclaimed: "This is exceptional."

"Well, it is, kind of," Jack admitted.

Bonnie examined it and marveled at the craftsmanship. "Every stripe on this flag is sewn together. And each star matches the star on the other side. It's truly fine work."

"Superb work," Bob said.

When they hoisted up the flag on the pole outside, Bob looked at it with tears in his eyes.

Jack had to smile. "Hey, fellow, you look overwhelmed."

"Stop it," Hanssen said. "I'm too close to crying."

At seven in the evening, after Jack had left and the Christmas presents were neatly stacked, all the wrappings, boxes, and ribbons were stuffed into plastic bags that the kids would take out to the trash bin.

Bob began to look restless. "I think I'll take Sundae to the park for a long walk," he told Bonnie. "That'll be his Christmas present." The dog, a big smelly sweet old mongrel, perked up as if he had understood. They went out together, the dog's shoulder bumping companionably into Bob's calf.

Bob parked his car near the drop site called "Bob," opened the trunk of the Volvo, took out the package, wrapped in plastic, put it under the footbridge in the agreed-upon corner, and dropped some pepper over it. He and the dog then walked back to his car. Both were sneezing. In the package that the KGB had left for him was $38,000. There was no getting around it. Despite the remains of the pepper, he could hardly wait to get home to Bonnie. He had a hard-on worthy of a stallion.

"I'm glad you're back," said Bonnie. "It's been a wonderful Christmas."

"Hasn't it?" Bob said.

The drop, all the way from out the door and back again to the house, had taken only an hour—one more ingredient to his pleasure.

There were days when Bob hated going to Confession; he came out feeling sick at the thought of how few deeds he confessed. On other days, though, for no reason he could name, he felt as if he had aced the process so well that afterward he could pray right out of the passion of his heart.

"Oh, my God," Hanssen said, "I am heartily sorry for having offended Thee, and I detest all my sins because I dread the loss of Heaven and the pains of Hell, but most of all because they offend You, my God, who are all good and deserving of all my love. I firmly resolve with the help of Thy grace to confess my sins, to do penance, and to amend my life. Amen."

When Bob stood up, his face was shining. He went to Jane.

"Darling, I feel it every time," he said to her. "Confession is the key. Always go to Confession. It takes care of everything."

That same night, before the mirror, the draperies of the shawl up on the hooks above the sink, he spoke out of another presence in himself: *Is it possible that all my life, I, like Kim Philby, have been preparing to become*

201

*the perfect spy? Do I truly care about the Church? I
would swear that I do. But I have to wonder. Am I such
a dedicated actor that I immerse myself in the role?"*

Hanssen looked at the mouth speaking back to him
from the mirror. It was as if that mouth came from another person.

*"An interesting question. Can it be that there are
more things in heaven and earth than You, God, have
ever dreamed of?"* He paused. *"Bob, ask yourself. Why
do you not fall to the ground for such blasphemy?*

*"The answer is simple. It is not blasphemy. Life is
much too complicated for that.*

*"I want to keep doing all that I am doing—spying,
Bureau work, my family, my small secret with Jack—I
want to go in every direction at once. Despite the stress.
Let's face it—I am truly a man. I feel open to every kind
of action. Truly a man. I feel strongest when I can go in
two directions at once."*

16

1990

Six or seven top counterintelligence experts, Special Agents, and analysts were sitting around the conference table. Hanssen addressed them.

"It is," he said in answer to a question, "not impossible that there is a mole in the woodwork right here in the Bureau."

"Do you say that it is likely, Bob?" Mike Shepard asked.

"I don't think I would go that far. But lately there have been a few unexplained Soviet moves. Occasionally, they do seem to be holding an ace to our king."

The big blue-flamer who had once told Bob that he looked like Digger O'Dell now spoke up: "Yeah, on the evidence, I definitely have the impression that there is a mole, but I think he is in the CIA."

"That is the likelihood," said Bob. "Of course, we can't be certain."

"I am. No FBI man could ever be that kind of scumbag," said the blue-flamer.

Bob waited until evening to reply. Just before going into the bathroom, he had been rereading *The Man Who Was Thursday*, by G. K. Chesterton. It was his favorite novel, and it always left him feeling eloquent. To the mirror, he now said:

"I am amazed by myself. It is as if something in the scheme of things wants me to live in a land of ice and mirth and exquisite privacy, totally removed from other people's feelings."

A day after the meeting, Mike called Bob to his office and told him that he had good and exciting news. Bob had been one of the Special Agents selected for the inspection staff for the last six months of 1990 and most of 1991.

Bob, however, did not look happy. "Michael," he said, "I don't know that I want to move. Things are good at home, and I've never been that keen on travel."

"I guess I can understand your reluctance," Shepard told him, "but you have no choice. This is not a dance card. The FBI tells you where you are going."

"I know that, but is there no way to get out of it?"

"You could find a trapdoor somewhere, I suppose, but Bob, you don't want to, believe me." He went on as if this was not the place to stop. "Bob, I think I know you fairly well. For all your cool, it's obvious to me that your ambition is as sharp as a razor. So don't tell me that you have no desire to pull up from 14 to 15. But I guarantee you, there's no way to reach Grade 15 unless you've served on the inspection staff. It's essential to promotion."

"All right," Hanssen said. "I obviously have to come to terms with this."

"Do it quickly, Bob. Think hard! We'll talk more tomorrow."

In the kitchen, Bob and Bonnie were having it out. "All right," she said. "So you take it, and then maybe you will be a 15 next year. But what I want to know is why are you always thinking about money. Don't we have enough right now?"

"Bonnie, be fair. You are the one who's always fearful

204

that we are on the edge of bankruptcy. And yet you couldn't even keep the checkbook straight. I had to reduce your check writing. I had to put you on a budget and have you pay almost everything in cash. And we're still on the edge of bankruptcy year after year."

"I don't like that word, Bob."

"Do you think I like it? I hate it. That's why I'm always thinking about money."

"I'm sorry. You're right." She touched his cheek lightly with her fingertips. "But, Bob, I hate the thought that you'll be away for two or three weeks at a time. You'll always be out in some faraway field office. How many do you have to do?"

"There'll be a good many, Bonnie. Part of the month I'll work out of D.C., part of it I'll travel to the designated field office."

"And you'll be on this kind of work a whole *year*? A year of being away from home more than you are here?" She was looking very upset now. "Tell me, is it only because of the money? Why is it so important for you to get up to Grade 15?"

"Because that is equal in rank to being a colonel."

"Oh, now I get it. Colonel Hanssen will be higher in rank than Lieutenant Colonel Hoschouer. Well, Colonel, just the other day I was having tea down the street with Sally Taylor, who is getting a divorce from her husband. You know what? He was on the inspection staff and met some bimbo. Now her marriage is gone."

"Bonnie, that could never happen to us. How can you even conceive of that?"

It was the only matter he took up with Shepard the next day. Walking the hall with him, Bob asked Bonnie's question.

"Is the inspection tour really hell on marriage?"

"That's the negative. I won't b.s. you. Marriages are hurt. A lot of philandering goes on during that period.

One time on the inspection staff, there were twenty-five of us sitting in the field inspectors' lounge, all of us ready to leave in a day, a week, whatever. And of those twenty-five men, twenty-three of us had been divorced."

"I will never be a part of those statistics," Hanssen answered.

"I believe you. But watch out. Wives get mad because the washer breaks down and you're not there to fix it." Shepard actually let out a sigh. "Bob, let's talk about the positive. Out in the field, the inspection staff is looked upon with a lot of respect. With one report, you can affect careers in Albuquerque, Omaha—you name it. Give somebody a Schedule F and he's in trouble. Give a good rating and the guy loves you forever. But, man, you can certainly exercise your intelligence." When Hanssen didn't reply, Shepard continued, "Are you still hesitating? Let me give you the pep talk. The key thing from the positive point of view," he said, "is that you will finally have a real chance to make the Bureau a little better. Remember those guys you complained about back in New York who wouldn't work on Sunday. You were frothing at the mouth over how impotent you felt. But now you can be a force for *good*."

"All right. I'm perking up. It does sound effective."

"It is. It's our best management tool. But it's not easy," warned Shepard. "If you don't do it well, your career could be at a standstill. On the other hand, do it right, and your future will get a powerful shot in the arm."

With his next drop, Bob enclosed a message:

BECAUSE OF A PROMOTION, I WILL BE TRAVELING FOR ONE YEAR AND WE MUST DISCUSS COMMUNICATION PLANS FOR METHODS OF RENEWING CONTACT.

At the KGB offices in Washington, Fefelov decided that it was just as well that Ramon would be inoperative.

What, after all, could they do with his information now? The game was running down. The Soviet Union was falling apart. It was a total mess. There was dissension everywhere. Too much freedom.

"Yes," Fefelov sighed to himself, "let Ramon have his year off. Soon these Americans will be our best friends." Now, another message from Ramon:

MY SYMPATHY FOR THE DIFFICULTIES YOU ARE EXPE-RIENCING IN RUSSIA. CONSOLE YOURSELVES WITH THIS THOUGHT: NO SYSTEM IS PERFECT.

Fefelov replied:

DEAR FRIEND, WE APPRECIATE YOUR LETTER EX-PRESSING YOUR SYMPATHY FOR OUR DIFFICULTIES IN RUSSIA. CONGRATULATIONS ON YOUR PROMOTION. WE WISH YOU ALL THE VERY BEST IN YOUR LIFE AND CAREER. WE APPRECIATE YOUR SYMPATHY FOR SOME DIFFICULTIES OUR PEOPLE FACE. OF COURSE YOU ARE RIGHT: NO SYSTEM IS PERFECT AND WE UNDERSTAND THIS. THOUGH WE CAN'T BUT REGRET IT, OUR CON-TACTS MAY NOT BE SO REGULAR AS BEFORE.

WE CAN TELL YOU THAT SOME OF THE MATERIALS YOU PROVIDED ABOUT POLITICAL ISSUES OF INTER-EST WERE REPORTED TO THE VERY TOP. YOUR POLIT-ICAL INSTINCTS ARE ACUTE.

17

1990

The inspection tour proved demanding. Before going out to each field office in each big city assigned to him, Hanssen would be cooped up with about twenty guys like himself, all of them close to senior, trapped together in a big bullpen in the field inspectors' section at D.C. Headquarters. They would all be reviewing the cases that had taken place over the last year or two within the field office they would visit next. By the time Hanssen arrived at his designated inspection, whether in Kansas City, Seattle, Houston, or wherever, he would come in on his first day with a huge stack of files—there to look over the work of every agent in the place, there to determine who was efficient and/or effective and who was not. He would interview every one of them, including the supervisor. He was now the one to make the judgment whether each agent was on top of things or was coasting.

The senior agent of the local office was often a little in love with himself. He might not have gotten to the top of the Bureau, but he had certainly worked his way up a well-cushioned position in the area that he supervised. Arrogance grew on such guys like mold, and Bob loved scraping them down a layer or two. He would say, "Look, I've been reviewing the operations of the crime squad, and I have a few questions." The inquiries were often brutal. "Did you check the Intelligence Base when you were dealing with this

208

bunch? What did you find out three years ago on that potential defector described here? Where was the follow-up? I don't see any further detailing. Do you have any?"

In his hotel room, he would often be up late writing, working weekends to justify his findings in anticipation of counterattacks by the local Bureau people.

He enjoyed the work. Once, in August, he actually copied some files from Bureau Headquarters in D.C. and mailed a diskette to the KGB, but his attention in late 1990 was mostly focused on the work for the inspection staff. It was in no way a substitute for espionage, but he certainly didn't mind being able to look middle-aged macho fools and pumped-up management types right in the eye while he slowly made them sweat off their fat.

Now Hanssen was in San Francisco talking to two operatives.

"I'm having a little trouble believing what I just heard," he said to them. "Your superior wanted you to get a contact in the Soviet Consulate here . . . ?"

"Yes, sir," the first Special Agent answered. "The way he put it was, 'Lasso up a source or two.'"

"And so a year ago you obtained permission from D.C. to mail classified information to the Consulate?"

"Yes, sir," said the second Special Agent. "Just a couple of unimportant papers. But he liked his idea. It was to enclose no note. He figured it would travel faster that way. Get a lot of these local Sovs pretty nervous."

"What came back?" Hanssen asked.

"Well . . . nothing," the first operative said, "but Herb—"

"Herb is your superior?" Hanssen interrupted. He made a deal of this by looking up the name in the papers before him. It was all for show. He had known the name even before he came into the office.

"Yes. Herb told us to do it again. So we sent out some more information."

"Nothing came back? Correct? I see nothing here to indicate returns."

"Well, Herb was transferred and we weren't sure how to continue. Herb said, 'I'm leaving it with you fellows.'"

"So you still decided to send out pieces of information?"

The two agents spoke together: "Yes, sir."

"You mean this office has been sending classified material to the Soviet Consulate here for—how long is it now?"

"We tried about every three months."

"For the last nine months—and still nothing has come back. No potential sources?"

"Well, they seem to be very cautious over at the Soviet Consulate here."

"So you were doing no more than hoping one of the Soviets would pop a letter back to you one of these days."

Again, they spoke together: "Yes, sir."

"For nine months, then, you have been giving away material." He looked at a paper. "Permission, I see, was granted for three times, but I can count five times that you sent information to them over the course of a year."

"I guess it was five times." The second Special Agent managed to get the words out.

"If you don't close down this operation permanently," Hanssen said, "it will bring a Significant Deficiency down on this office. I'll check back with you on this in a couple of days."

"Yes, sir."

Hanssen was close to quivering with rage. He almost said aloud, *This has been sloppy! What kind of idiot will go ahead and churn the waters without knowing whether any fish are feeding!*

That night Hanssen enjoyed himself. He had a room high up in a hotel on Nob Hill, and it overlooked the bay on two sides. He was finishing his dessert, some kind of red-colored pudding, and all the while he was looking at erotica on the tube. When a knock came at the door, Hanssen calmly changed the channel, dropped his napkin over his lap, pulled the table a little closer, and called out, "Come in." The waiter entered, and Hanssen, without moving from his chair, said, "Could you bring me another cherry pudding?"

After the waiter left the room, Hanssen removed the napkin, touched himself, and went back to looking at the erotica. There was something so quietly powerful about living this way. After ejaculation, he called Bonnie. By the end of his call, the waiter was back with the pudding.

After each inspection tour, Bob would be back in Washington with little idea of what to do with himself next. The field inspectors, relieved of all other duties, did have to report to the office every day, but then it became a matter of walking the halls or sitting around in the lounge reserved for them, reading newspapers, talking to one another—which with few exceptions was not particularly enjoyable for Bob—and then he could take off early. After the inspectors had worked so hard out in an unfamiliar city for two or three weeks, nobody minded that their time in D.C. should be their own—some of the working day at any rate. They did spend time boning up for their next assignment, but that kind of research could hardly fill five working days once you got the hang of it. Finally, Bob became so bored in the dog days of August that on the twentieth, he put some stuff together, made a diskette, and mailed it to Malkow. Not two weeks later, on September 3, after seeing a tape signal on the post they had agreed to use while he was away, he went to the dead-drop site he had specified in the letter and picked up $40,000 in cash. He could never figure out how they decided how much to give him. Important, valuable information might bring him back $12,000 or $15,000, and then some casual collections, equal to no more than this last hurried one, brought him

$40,000. Could this be just an expression of their grati-
tude that he was staying in touch?

Sometimes when he was back in Washington, he would
drive to work with Walter. One October morning, Ballou was in a good mood and made the mistake of saying,
"You know, I went to a neat going-away party with
some Bureau people last night."

"Where?" Bob asked in passing.

"At the Good Guys bar on Wisconsin Avenue." By
the look on Bob's face, Ballou decided too late that he
shouldn't have gotten into this. "It's a strip club. We really did have a good time," Walter finished lamely. Bob
didn't even try to hide his disapproval.

"I wouldn't," he said, "call that a good time."

"Bob, it wasn't the way you think it was," Ballou said.
He was talking rapidly. He felt as if he was sitting next to
a grand inquisitor. "It wasn't about looking at the
women—it was just the guys being together. You know,
for the camaraderie. It's not a sex thing; it's a male thing.
The girls are like the wallpaper in the back of the room."

Bob was acting like a priest who had heard more than
everything for the last twenty years. "Walter, when you
go to a place like that," he said, "you are, in effect, paying the girl's salary. You are contributing to the money
she gets for taking her clothes off. That's a sin for her.
You are paying to induce her to continue to sin."

"I'm not sure I have an answer for that," said Walter.

"Well, don't try to avoid the thought. It's an occasion
of sin."

Actually, Bob knew the Good Guys strip club. Over
the years, he and Jack had gone there a few times. It occurred to him that now would be a good time to find another place. He had heard of one that was supposed to
be pretty neat. It was called 1819.

PART THREE

1819

1

1990

There were photos of Tracey Starr on the marquee outside. Hanssen stood, hands in pockets, and studied the pictures before he went in. It was the lunch hour and the house was half full with businessmen and government people. Bob was ready, supposing he ran into anyone he knew, to make a face and complain about the kind of joints he had to visit when meeting contacts who were on the sordid side.

As he entered, Tracey Starr had just come onstage to do her strip. Bob took a table and watched. At the end of her act, there was a fair amount of applause, much more than the dim pattering that is common in the lunch hour for the average stripper. There were even some whistles and cheers, and someone threw money on the floor. As Tracey exited, Hanssen called the waitress over and whispered to her.

In the dressing room, Tracey had changed to a silk slip with chiffon and a silk robe. The waitress who had been talking to Hanssen came in and handed her ten dollars.

"That tall, dark guy sitting on the right, said to me, 'Tell the young lady'—get this!—he said, 'I never thought I could see such grace and beauty in a strip club. She's fabulous!'"

"He said that?" Tracey said to the waitress.

"Absolutely!"

"Which man was that again?"

"The very tall one. Eighth table on the right."

"Is he there now?" she asked.

"Better hurry—he just paid his bill."

Tracey got up fast and caught him just as he was going through the door.

She still had the ten-dollar bill in her hand.

"I want to thank you for the compliment. That means much more to me than the money," she said.

"I'll be back," he said.

"Yes, please be back. Soon," she said.

Not too many days later, as she was dancing onstage, she saw Hanssen and gave him a subtle smile and made a point of flashing her eyes.

After her dance ended, she went back to change into her after-act outfit, a fancy club dress, and emerged to sit down in the chair beside him. She had to admit to herself that she was feeling pretty feminine.

"You came back," she said.

"I told you I would." He ordered a drink for her and coffee for himself. "What do you think I do for a living?" he asked her.

That was pretty abrupt, she thought, but then maybe he was a little shy. Guys like that were sometimes afraid of a lame conversation, so they zoomed. But she was used to handling a variety of types.

"Men always ask me to guess," she said, "and I'm pretty sharp. But with you"—she shook her head—"no clue. What *do* you do?"

"I work for the FBI."

"Come again?"

"You don't believe me?"

"Could be. You look very mysterious and important and . . . and deadly," she said.

"I don't want to scare you." He made a point of smiling.

"I won't stay scared for long. You do have a nice smile." There was a pause as they looked at each other. "I don't know if I believe you're really FBI. If you are, you must have a card." She looked him right in the eye. "Show me your ID."

He actually had it ready. She studied it, then looked up. All right—he wanted to zoom. She could do that, too.

"I've got a job for you," she said. "Can you help me find my father?"

He smiled. "Well, I could use a few details."

They drew closer to talk this over.

"All right. First let me tell you. My name is not Tracey Starr, but Galey, Priscilla Galey."

"Where were you born, Priscilla?" he asked. It was the first time he had spoken to her by name.

"In Indiana, in a very small little town. Boonton, Indiana."

"What does your dad do?" Hanssen asked.

"I only met him once. He left when I was a baby, and my mom got another husband, a truck driver. Then after him, another boyfriend. You don't want to know all this, do you?"

"I have to."

"One of her boyfriends ran me off. He hit on me. I told my mother I was pregnant—I hadn't even had sex! It was run away or get raped."

"Your mother couldn't protect you, Priscilla?" He obviously liked calling her by her real name.

"She would never have believed me. She couldn't afford to."

"So did you run away all by yourself?" he asked.

"No. I had been thinking of getting married to the fellow I was going with, so, we eloped. I was sixteen. I certainly didn't plan on sex that early. At that age virginity was very sacred to me."

He believed her. He was intrigued. She had this easy way of talking about herself, as if she had no reason to hide anything. He couldn't believe how much at ease he was with her. She was tall, with an exceptional figure, good features, and open blue eyes—she should have been alarmingly beautiful, yet he was as comfortable as if he was with Jack.

"It is very interesting," he said, "that virginity was so sacred to you then."

"Why do you say interesting?"

"I think it means you were thinking of your soul."

"Come again?" Priscilla Galey said.

"I am certain," he said, "that it would have made a huge difference if your real father had stayed."

"The only memory I have of him is the one time he came to visit. We went out to the garage, where we had this beat-up old piano, and my dad said to my mother, 'Can she play by ear?' Mom said, 'Yep, she can do it. She's your daughter.' I guess he didn't believe I was his daughter. So he marches me over to the piano, and hums a song. 'Stardust.'" She hummed a little phrase or two for Hanssen. "I played it. For a few minutes we were playing together. It was wonderful. He could really work an old piano. Then he turns to my mother and says, 'She's mine!'" Priscilla laughed. "That was it. That's all I ever saw of him. A tall, good-looking man." She looked at Hanssen. "You have tears in your eyes. Oh, that's beautiful."

"I guess your story got to me," he said.

"Well, is it possible to use the FBI to find him? You do these sort of things, right?"

"I would need much more information."

"My mother doesn't even know where he is."

Hanssen shook his head sadly. "In that case, you might never find your birth father, but you *do* have another. A true father who loves you very much."

She was puzzled. "Who are you talking about?"

"Jesus Christ."

She drew away, obviously disappointed. "Oh, that's so far away from me." Now she took a careful look at him. "Are you a Catholic?"

"The only true religion."

"Well, okay, that's your opinion. You're entitled. I'm a Catholic, too, I guess. At least I used to be. I used to go to church with a girlfriend when I was a kid. It never meant much."

"Did you like it?"

"Not much," she said. "You go in and it's, you know, a drill."

"There's a lot there. You learn as you go." When she didn't respond, he said, "Well, let's not decide too quickly." He nodded as if the subject would still be there for them, and then asked, "How long did this early marriage last?"

"Nine months. To the day. I left him out on the West Coast."

"When did you start stripping?"

"Oh, not for a long time. I was too shy. The first time I went onstage in a topless bar, I let down all my hair in front of my face. I couldn't see anything. But when I got to know what I was doing, it was exciting. I work for the applause."

"Not for money?"

"Money is always there," she said.

He cleared his throat. She could tell that the sixty-four-million-dollar question was coming.

"If I may ask, did you have a lot of relationships over the years?"

"I only have one boyfriend at a time," she said. She looked him full in the face, then continued. "I want to give it time, see if it will work. If it doesn't happen within five years, then, honey, see you around."

"Do you have a type?"

"Tall, dark, and handsome—like you."

Hanssen gave a big happy laugh. He seemed surprised at how much he was enjoying himself.

Priscilla continued: "But I guess there was a variety. Let's see—an Irish drummer, an Italian, a Samoan. I tried one Hispanic. . . ."

Hanssen sat and listened but didn't say anything. This was not exactly what he wanted to hear. Yet it wasn't really unpleasant. She had liked all those men, but she also seemed to like him.

After Hanssen left, Priscilla went back to the dressing room she shared with two other strippers. Since they went on before her, they were already putting on makeup for the next show.

"He works for the FBI, but he's not just an FBI man," she said. "We had an in-depth conversation."

"Would it bother you if he asks one of us to sit with him?" one of the girls asked. "He's not exactly cute, but I guess there is something there."

"I would be highly jealous," Priscilla said. "I'm putting you on notice, Cherise—I saw him first. He saw me."

"Okay. Don't get your panties in a wad. Did he say he would call you?"

"He gave me his office number, but I think I won't call. He knows where I am."

It was morning and Hanssen was standing on the street outside the club as Priscilla came in to work.

"I thought you were going to get in touch with me," he said.

"I don't phone men I don't know well."

"Then will you give me your number?" he asked.

"I can, but won't you come in to see the show?"

He shook his head. "I really don't have the time today."

"Well, come in for a minute. I'll give you the number."

"Let me tell the truth," he said. "I do have your phone number. I even know where you live."

"My God," she said. "Of course. You're FBI!"

Hanssen smiled. "Don't worry. It was just to check you out. You're very straight for a stripper."

"No trouble with the law. I don't even breathe wrong."

"That's the way to go."

"You have me curious," she said. "Why were you waiting here?"

"I want to invite you to lunch on your next day off."

The private club didn't have a sign outside, just a polished brass plaque that said MEMBERS ONLY. Hanssen inserted a key in a locked door and ushered Priscilla into the hallway. They climbed some stairs. On the second floor was a shabby, tired-looking lounge, bar, and restaurant. As he passed the hatcheck girl, he reached under his jacket and took out his Walther PPK and laid it on the counter for the hatcheck girl.

Priscilla had to admit that it stirred her up a little.

A waitress showed them to a table in the corner and handed them menus. Not much was said until they had ordered and the waitress walked away.

"Wow," she said. "I'm not all that used to men carrying guns."

"Are you scared?"

"Am I scared?" Priscilla looked at him and smiled radiantly. "I don't think so."

"Were you aware of me in the audience the other day?"

"I knew that someone out there was staring real hard at me. I could feel it."

"But you're used to that," he said.

"Yes. I like that. It's a personal love letter." She was surprised by the next thing he said. It was almost businesslike.

221

"How much do you make as a dancer?"

"Do you share your information with the IRS?" she replied. He had sort of hurt her feelings.

He seemed unaware of that, for he pursued the subject.

"I'd say it comes to fifteen hundred a week with tips," he stated.

"You can make that much. They throw tips on the stage, but, you know, I don't see that as part of my act. The girl who comes on after me picks up the tips. Tracey Starr doesn't."

"Tracey Starr! But your real name is Priscilla Galey. Which do you like most?"

"I like to switch back and forth. After all, who would want to see Miss Prissy take off her top?"

"All right. How did you choose Tracey Starr?"

"I had an old teacher who dated back to the burlesque days. He was the one who gave me the name. Oh, he used to work me like a drill sergeant, and it *worked*. And then I cured him of being an alcoholic. That is, I talked him into going to AA. We kind of helped each other out." She laughed happily at the memory.

"You have a good heart," he said.

"Oh, I hope so."

"Did you ever think of becoming a movie star?"

Her hand went over her mouth. "Never! I have bad teeth." She tried to laugh behind her hand. "I guess the best I ever did was win a prize. Stripper of the Year: Tracy Starr. Right here in D.C. They even gave me a medallion and some prize money."

"What did you buy with it?"

"A painting I had my eye on for a year. Unknown artist, but beautiful," she said.

"You're interested in art?"

"I don't know much about it, but I would love to study art. Because that's where my true interests are. May I ask—what are yours?"

"I'm mainly a family man."

"I guess you know religious art," she said.

"I do." He looked at his watch. "You know, there's time this afternoon. Want to go to a museum?"

"Nothing I would like more."

"Which one?" he asked.

"Surprise me."

"The National Gallery?"

"That's the one!"

2

1990

Priscilla's interest was in beautiful nude women. Hanssen stood before those paintings with his eyes downcast. All the same, she could see: he was stealing looks.

"You're shy about this, aren't you?" she asked.

"Let's say I feel more comfortable with religious art."

He stopped, however, at a work by Hieronymus Bosch. He seemed frozen by it. The villagers, the lechers, and the demons were all swilling at the same feast. When Priscilla approached, he said, "What do you think of these pictures?"

"They scare me."

"These are the nightmares that bring people to Confession," he told her.

"Why—do you have dreams like that?"

"I have all sorts of dreams."

"I hate to admit it, but so do I." She could hardly believe what he said next.

"Maybe your dreams are telling you not to keep tempting men. Not with the gift of your beauty."

What a statement! It had to give her a lot to think about.

In the café of the National Gallery, they had coffee. She didn't usually like to hear men talking about their families, but in his case, she was curious. And he was ready enough to talk about this part of his life.

"I've always been completely faithful to my wife," he told her. "And we have six splendid children."

"I guess it's wonderful to have the kind of life you have," she said. She felt a little out of her element, as if she was trying to please some guy who was a big authority. "In fact," she decided to add, "at this moment, I'm alone. I've just broken up a seven-year relationship."

"Really living alone?" he asked.

How much had he found out about her? She didn't dare to be too evasive. "Well," she said, "my ex is around. He hangs on like a bad cold. I tell him, 'Don't push it. We can have dinner and try to be civil, but don't tell me what to do anymore.'"

"He's always there?" Hanssen asked.

She took a chance and lied. Actually, he was a live-in ex. "Just once in a while I let him stay over. On the couch. I feel sorry for him. In fact, I haven't even seen him for a couple of months."

Back in her dressing room with Cherise and Edie Marie, she decided they must be a little psychic, because they started to ask her exactly about that.

"Does your FBI guy know about Reggie?"

"Cherise, do you think I'm going to tell him I've dated a black man for seven years? And that he still lives in my apartment?"

"You're amazing to still hang with him. It's over, isn't it? So watch out," Edie Marie said. "I knew a girl once who got messed up bad by a black guy who she let stay around too long."

"No, Reggie's gentle. Really gentle. He's opened my eyes to a lot. Back in Indiana, I thought the Ku Klux Klan ran the nation," Priscilla said.

* * *

225

In fact, that night she told Reggie about Robert Hanssen.

"This FBI man is out-of-sight," she said. "He is proud that he won't allow his kids to watch TV."

"That's hard to believe," Reggie said. He was tall and lank and kind of easygoing, all things considered.

"He and his wife read books to their children every night. I said, 'Not to let your children watch TV? I'm sorry, what kind of man are you?' Oh, Reggie, this was the strictness I ran away from, and I remember even we were allowed to watch TV."

"What's the wife like?" Reggie asked.

"He says he's never cheated on her. Says she's beautiful. Next to God, she is *it* for him."

The next day, as Priscilla walked by the sound booth at the club, the DJ stopped her.

"Priscilla, your FBI friend left this envelope. Asked me to be sure nobody gets it but you."

"If it's money, I'll give you a tip," she said. It was just that—a lot of cash, enough for her to give thirty dollars to the DJ. She couldn't wait to tell Cherise and Edie Marie. They were almost as excited as if it had happened to them.

"I can't believe it," she said. "He asked me—so casually—what did I want for Christmas. I told him about my teeth."

"Your teeth aren't that bad, honey," Edie Marie said.

"Well, I'm tired of covering my mouth when I talk. Read this note. Look what he says." She was so eager for them to know what it said that she read it out loud. "'So you can smile the way you should.' I think he is my guardian angel." She meant it. When she thought of him, she felt beautiful.

"And he's never made a pass?" asked Cherise.

"Not one," she said. She didn't know if she was proud or a little ashamed of that.

"He's got his head in a sling," said Edie Marie.

226

3

1991

Priscilla didn't see Bob for a few weeks, and he didn't call or tell her that he'd been off on an inspection tour. He just popped up on a cold January morning and asked her to have lunch with him at that private club. Once they were there, he couldn't have been more genial.

"By the way," he said, "I got you something for your birthday. I hope you like it."

He passed over a thin wrapped box. When she opened it, a pearl necklace on a black velvet cushion looked back at her.

"It isn't real, is it? If you want me to take it, tell me it isn't real." She looked at it. "No, I can't accept this."

"I insist. Take it."

"You make me feel like I've been crowned. Will you hook it?" She turned in her seat, lifted her hair off her neck, and succeeded, she knew, in stirring him up. His fingers were clumsy as he fastened the clasp.

"On second thought, you have six kids," she said. "You can't afford it."

"It's all taken care of. Don't worry. I received a large inheritance from my grandmother."

"So, I guess I accept it?"

"Of course you can," he said. Now she felt greedy. She wanted to know what it was worth.

"In that case," she asked, "what would be the least amount I could pawn this for?"

"At least a hundred and fifty dollars," he said.

"So it's worth fifteen hundred?"

"Do you really want me to tell?" He looked annoyed.

"No, I don't want to know," she told him quickly. "There's something magic about not asking what a present costs. Anyway, I was just kidding. I would never hock this. Even if I was starving." She looked to reach across the table and kiss him.

"No, no, no. That's not necessary," he said.

Back at her apartment, Reggie had the answer. "He's afraid of you. Some guys get all their kicks from hand jobs."

"Oh shut up, Reggie."

She really disliked Reggie at this moment. No wonder they hardly ever made out anymore.

About nine months after Bob had been assigned to the inspection staff, Mike Shepard called him into his office to present the good news: Hanssen had done so well that his last assignment would be a plum. He was going to be sent for a couple of weeks to the legal attaché's office in Hong Kong. It was a small installation and kind of collegial. He would be spending time with British Counterintelligence officials as well.

"You can almost look upon it as a vacation," Mike said.

"Well, I am pleased," Bob said.

"If you have the moolah, think of taking Bonnie along. That's considered okay."

He invited her that night. She had all sorts of practical reservations.

"Honey, it means weeks away from the children. We can't do that."

He could tell that she wasn't all that disappointed.

"Well," he said, "meet me in Hawaii at least. After Hong Kong."

"Let me think about that. It all sounds so expensive."

He had lunch again with Priscilla and told her that he was going out to Asia. Hong Kong, no less.

She was excited. That sounded magical. Hong Kong!

"Those Oriental people are so intricate," she said, "and so artistic. Their houses, their art, their gowns, their netsukes . . ." She actually pulled a netsuke about the size of her thumb out of her bag. "Isn't that fabulous?"

He looked at an ivory carving of a fat little old man hunched in a squatting position. It looked to be fine work. You could even see the wrinkles on the soles of his feet.

"You collect these things?" he asked her.

"Absolutely. I love Japanese art. Chinese, too, for that matter."

Hanssen absorbed all this. "You know, I have to pick up my travel tickets," he told her. "Why don't you come with me?"

"Sure," she said without taking a breath.

After he was done talking to the travel agent, he walked over to Priscilla, who was studying a poster of a Hong Kong cityscape, and handed her an envelope.

"You can use this," he said, "to go to Hong Kong. Or you can cash it in. But this is your round-trip ticket, business class."

She moved instinctively to hug him. He held her off with a smile.

"No, no, that's not necessary," he said. Same words as last time.

"I don't even have a passport," she said

"We'll take care of that."

"But I don't have a birth certificate. It's lost."

"You forget who I work for. We'll get you a passport and you'll be off to Hong Kong."

* * *

They traveled over on separate planes. It was one big un-believable dream for Priscilla. She spent a lot of the trip gazing out the porthole by her seat. Then she found her-self drawn to the windows in her hotel room on the eigh-teenth floor of her beautiful room that looked out on Hong Kong. She couldn't stop studying the city below, and the harbor.

The phone rang.

"You're here, right on time." Hanssen's voice came through strongly. "Terrific. Can we go to dinner tonight?"

"I'd love to. I brought a lot of gowns. But I thought you'd have to work a lot while you're here."

"I'll be free for breakfast most mornings, and cer-tainly free for dinner."

Priscilla came down the mezzanine stairs to the lobby wearing a sapphire dress with blue accessories, all to match her eyes. Hanssen met her at the foot of the steps.

"Fabulous," he said. They were both aware of the im-pression she had made on the people in the lobby.

"I came with two humongous suitcases," she told him, "plus my carry-on. Wait. You'll see. I plan my outfits."

At dinner, she thought he might get a little sexy at last.

"What," he asked her, "do you think about when you're on a stage dancing?"

She smiled. It was nice for once to feel like an author-ity. "I want to make all these men begin to listen to what I have to tell them. Without my saying a word."

He nodded as if she had delivered something pro-found. "That's the other face of religion," he told her.

"What do you mean?"

"Faith is exactly like that. You could say it's a thrill. A challenge. I feel as if it is my creative outlet."

"Is that why you never stray?" Priscilla asked.

Hanssen looked at her intently. "I repeat," he said solemnly. "My wife is the only woman I've known."

"Oh come on! You must have done *something* wrong. What about when you were a teenager? You never did anything?"

"I changed some test scores in college once."

With that, he gave his crazy horsey laugh. Priscilla could see that this night was leading nowhere.

On another evening, after she had made another dazzling entrance, during which every man in the dining room who looked at her had to be instantly jealous of Bob—which Bob loved, she could tell—he actually said to her, "I'm fascinated by the way you talk."

"Are you saying that you like my brain?"

"Yes. I do like it."

She laughed in delight. "That's a huge compliment to a woman. Especially in my business."

He gave the big smile she liked so much.

"Do you know," he said, "if people asked me, 'Where does she come from?' I would say, 'Well, I think she's from a well-educated family.'"

Priscilla glowed. "I have always had to convince myself that I could be as good as the person I see myself to be. So, I do try to be graceful."

"You are a lady."

She made certain that no tears came to her eyes—they would ruin her mascara—but she felt close to bursting with emotion.

Still, nothing happened after dinner. He shook her hand and went to his room.

Hanssen was talking to himself in the mirror over his hotel room dresser.

"*I am certain she is not involved with anyone else during this period, and that is good. My involvement is protecting her. My only question: Do I want to make love to her as badly as I wish to save her?*" The face in the mirror spoke: "*Real question: Are you totally scared*

231

of her? You have always been scared of the sexiest girl in class." He replied to the face in the mirror: *"Bonnie is the sexiest girl I ever met."* The mirror face responded: *"The exception that proves the rule."*

Shepard had been right—the work was easy. The British were indeed collegial, and the only friction, if you could call it that, came from Bob's reluctance to go out and get drunk with them at night. They kept saying after Bob showed them a photo of Bonnie: "Bless you for that wife you have. It gives hope to us old sticks."

He couldn't keep from smarting a little. He did have Priscilla back at the hotel and did feel pretty romantic. She was in a lovely red glittering dress, and after dinner they sipped tropical drinks while listening to "As Time Goes By": "A kiss is just a kiss / a sigh is just a sigh. . ."

"I love *Casablanca*," she said.

"That's the only movie for me," he replied. It was certainly one of the two or three he had always lived by. But the film he really loved was *Investigation of a Citizen Above Suspicion*. What a fabulous film! That Italian police commissioner who was seen as the epitome of integrity but who nonetheless gets away with murdering his girlfriend was really something. No point in telling Priscilla about that one, though.

Later, after they said good-night, Priscilla went out to see the town by herself and ended up in a bar. Yes, there she was, talking to Bob on the bar phone, having awakened him at one A.M.

"Bob, you have to come down and get me," she said. "I'm lost."

"You went out after dinner?" he asked.

"I'm blue that this wonderful vacation is over. So, yes, I went out. All by myself. And now I don't know how to get back."

232

"Well, where are you calling from?"

She looked through the window and called out the name of the street. The signs, happily enough, were in both Chinese and English.

"Priscilla! That's the red-light district!" he said.

She almost laughed. She was certainly drunk, because she wanted to laugh at him. She had heard the hint of a pipsqueak in his voice.

"I'm really in a very nice club," she said. "There are American servicemen here, and the bar even has my brand of liquor. Plus American music. Come on down."

"Are you drunk?" he asked.

"I don't dare get drunk in front of you, honey."

"I don't know if you should drink at all."

"I know, I can't," she said like a little girl. "Please come and get me." How nice! Her head was revolving oh so slowly. She had a truly rosy buzz. Buzz and glow. "Darling," she said, "don't be mad. I don't want to ruin your beautiful attitude toward me."

Hanssen got dressed to go out and meet her.

Half an hour later, she insisted they get out on the dance floor for a number or two.

He had rarely felt more miserable. "I have to confess, I can't dance," he said.

"Just this one," she said.

"Don't make me repeat myself. I don't know how to dance."

"I can teach you. It's easy. You listen to the music and you move! Simple as that"

"You can't teach me," he said.

"I can. All you have to do is loosen up."

Out on the dance floor, he tried. But he was not about to loosen up. He was studying the faces around them. A lot of them were bad faces. It kept him on guard. So tight! Finally, they had to walk off the dance floor.

* * *

Not too much later, alone in her room on the eighteenth floor, Priscilla was taking a nip from the in-room bar. Two small empties were already finished. She knew she was drunk. She kept talking to the wall in an I-am-good-and-sick-of-you voice.

"You want me to convert to the Church? I would like to convert you to a human being." She set down a third empty. She kept thinking of Bob all by himself in his room. "It's awful—I've never been turned down by any man before," she said to the wall.

He was alone, lying on his bed in a bathrobe. He felt as if he wouldn't get to sleep for hours.

There was a knock on the door.

"Oh no!" he whispered.

The knock came again. He heard Priscilla's voice.

"Let me in. I know you're in there, Bob. Let me in."

"Priscilla, go away," he called out. "You're drunk."

"Let me in or I'll make a fuss. I'm going to scream."

She let out a brief but powerful shriek.

"No need to scream."

"There's a lot more to come," she told him.

"All right, all right," he said. "I'll open the door."

Priscilla was ready for a long night and a great one. "I just dig you, Bob. I dig you . . . I can loosen you up," she said, putting her arms around him as he opened the door. The thought of turning the key in this sweet, generous, poor locked-up man had her turned on. It was always the way she had felt on those oh-so-rare occasions when the curtain was going up on a big, new romance.

"Priscilla," he said. "Don't do something you'll regret. Please don't." The weakness in his voice was turning her on even more. There was so much she could do for him. She'd nurture him all the way to strength.

"Please don't," he repeated as she put her hand on his crotch.

234

She couldn't believe it. He pushed her away. That did it. She turned off the light switch by the bed table and gave him a shove onto the bed.

Hanssen's voice came out of the dark. "For God's sake, Priscilla, stop that. Stop this instant! Good Lord, what the devil are you doing down there?" Then after a moment: "Where did you learn to do that? Oh, no, no."

In the darkness he pushed her away, but just a little late. He was surprised at how much came out of him. And the worst of it was that it was all awful. It had not only been against his will, but there hadn't been any surprise at the end to turn him inside out—just a painful ejaculation, dragged out of him, spewed all over her face in the dark. And now he was no longer totally—technically— faithful to Bonnie.

Priscilla left his room, closed the door behind her, and walked down the hallway to the elevator. It was a long walk, and her mascara was running.

There, from her hotel room, at two in the morning, Priscilla called Edie Marie, at the dressing room in the club. Considering how drunk she was, it was amazing that she could get the words out.

"I never wanted to stain this wonderful image that he thought he had of me. I didn't want to disappoint him."

She could hear the late-lunch-hour crowd in the background.

"Now, don't get into tears," said Edie Marie. "You're getting a deep, sad tone in your voice."

"I can't help it. I'm in a ton of tears," Priscilla said.

"You did the right thing. How could you know it would bomb?"

"This is killing me. Oh, Edie Marie!"

"Just think of him as a skull case," Edie Marie said.

"No, he's like a father. No, I don't mean that. I just thought I could be like a woman for him."

"Prissy!" The stripper paused. "Prissy, I don't want to

hurt your feelings, but there's something weird about the guy. . . . He's a dork. I mean, I think, deep down, he's a dork."

"Do you realize he's the second-highest man in Washington?"

"Who the hell told you that?"

"He did. He said that in terms of what he really gets done, he's next to the president. Over at the FBI, he's untouchable. That's how high up he is."

"Then why did he never try to find your father?"

"Oh shut up!" Priscilla burst into tears again and hung up. She looked around the room. "Good-bye, Hong Kong. Good-bye, beautiful Hong Kong."

In his room, Hanssen was speaking to the mirror.

"*Beware. She has to be embarrassed and she can make terrible trouble for you—but she won't.*"

The mirror replied, "*You hope she won't. . . .*"

"*At least it came to a head,*" he said to the mirror.

The other face replied, "*Cut off your relationship with Priscilla. Tomorrow, act as if it never happened.*"

At the checkout desk, the next morning, the clerk said, "Miss Galey, your bill is all taken care of," and handed her a note. She read:

> *Priscilla, I didn't know if you had enough saved to cover it all. Use the $150 for the gift shop in case you've forgotten anything. There's a limousine waiting to take you to the airport. Have a wonderful trip home.*

4

1991

In their Hawaii hotel room, with a view of the ocean and the sand, Bob and Bonnie embraced on the balcony.

"This is the best vacation we've ever had," Bonnie said, "and the best part is that you're the man I used to know."

"It's wonderful. So wonderful. Better than ever," Bob said. He meant it.

Holding Bonnie, he saw a flash of Priscilla's mascara-stained face as she closed the door to his room in the Hong Kong hotel.

He told Jack about it.

"Priscilla's idea was to look better each time as she came down the stairs into the lobby, and I've got to say she was absolutely successful."

"I can picture the look on your face."

Hanssen laughed. "Jack, when I would walk into the hotel's number one deluxe restaurant with that gal on my arm, every man in the room had to gape. Open jaws wall-to-wall." He heard himself laughing over that one.

The first time he allowed himself to walk up to 1819 and look again at the nude photos of Priscilla, he knew it wasn't over.

What can I do? he asked himself. *I've got to see her again.*

* * *

They were in this seedy little club, his gun left with the hatcheck girl, and neither of them felt any need to speak of their last night in Hong Kong. Instead, they got to talking about automobiles.

"If you had the money, what kind of car would you buy?"

"That's easy," she said. " A Lamborghini. Or a Pentara. Maybe a Lotus."

"Come on—realistically, what would you get?"

"My favorite," said Priscilla, "would be a long-front-bodied Jaguar with spoke rims. The old-fashioned kind of convertible. But practically? I guess I would look for a Mercedes."

"Why?"

"Mr. Hanssen, everyone's always ready to buy a used Mercedes."

"You do know what you're talking about," he said.

"I put a lot of thought into this. I love cars."

"Do you have a driver's license?" he asked.

"I used to. I had one for five years, but my brothers wrecked my old Javelin. I haven't had a driver's license since. I just let it expire. I was too depressed about what happened to the Javelin."

"Maybe someday you'll have a good car," he said.

"I don't even dare to daydream about things like that."

"Do you know, the next time we have lunch, I am going to have three surprises for you. That's a promise."

They were back in their old routine again.

A day later, he was having lunch with Jane and Sue in the FBI cafeteria. School was out for the girls, and they were working as summer temps at the Bureau. In the middle of the meal, there was a beep from his pager.

"That's my notice," he said. "The daily prayer."

"What is it today, Dad?" Jane asked.

238

He spoke it back to them as it appeared in the stamp-size window:

"'Direct, we beseech Thee, O Lord, our actions by Thy holy inspirations, and carry them by Thy gracious assistance, so that every word may be brought to its fruition through Christ Our Lord. Amen.'

"Every word in the prayer is as real as a living creature if you are really willing to listen," he said. The girls agreed.

That same night, Bonnie was talking to Jane and Sue.

"Isn't it a wonderful opportunity?" she asked them.

"Mother," Jane said. "I wouldn't call it wonderful. It's just a summer employment program for children of FBI agents."

"Don't be a spoilsport. I'm sure it's extraordinary," Bonnie assured her.

"Well," said Sue, "what Jane and I like best about it is that we can meet Dad for lunch. That's a lot more interesting than the typing."

Bonnie paused. When she spoke, she was sure to make her voice sound casual, as though what she said didn't count for much. "By the way, girls, what does Dad's secretary look like?"

Both girls at once: "Mom!"

"No, tell me. Is she at all good-looking?"

"Mom, please . . ." said Sue. "She's a nice, efficient middle-aged woman. How can you think that about Dad?"

Bonnie became angry. "I wasn't thinking anything about Dad for one moment. I'm just curious what his secretary looks like."

Priscilla and Bob were again at lunch, again at his favorite place. It wasn't even an FBI club, she had decided, more like a Mafia-type joint, where they didn't get excited if you checked a piece. It was interesting, because he was obviously kind of known there, but he never talked to anyone except the hat-check girl or the waitress, and none of the customers talked to him. It was as if everything was understood. You went there for privacy.

"We've been sitting here ten minutes," she said to him, "and I can't wait any longer. It's killing me! You said you were going to have three surprises for me."

Hanssen put an envelope on the table. He laughed at the subtle look of disappointment on her face.

"All right—that's just money," he said. "But now open the letter."

She pulled out an American Express card with her name on it.

"Well, I have to thank you for this." There was silence. She still felt vaguely disappointed. A credit card was wonderful, of course, but kind of anticlimactic. "I don't mean to sound ungrateful, but I thought you said *three* surprises."

Hanssen smiled and pulled out a car key attached to a small, elegant leather pad. Now she could squeal with pleasure.

"I tried to find a used Jaguar," he said, "but they are rare and hard to maintain."

Priscilla took a few bites of her food. Silently, she kept looking at the metal emblem on the leather pad. "A Mercedes. I'm too excited to eat. Is there really a Mercedes waiting for me?"

"You don't have to eat," he said. "Would you like to take a look at it?"

"Oh yes! I don't think I can wait."

"Well, let's stop off first and get you a temporary license. Then you go in for the driving test as soon as you get the car."

"Oh my God!" Priscilla said when she saw it on the lot. "It's a 190E."

It was champagne silver, with a red leather interior and a sunroof.

She couldn't help herself. She *oohed* and *ahhed* as if she were looking at an infant, and he seemed to understand her joy completely.

"When you drive up in a Mercedes to any place at all," he said, "they're not going to ask you if you went to college—they're going to treat you right."

Backing up for the officer who was testing her, Priscilla shifted into reverse and whipped the 190E into a reasonably small space. Did it with real skill.

"Very good, very good," Hanssen said. "Bravo! Terrific!" She beamed like a child at the praise.

That night, though, the other strippers were on her case. She made the mistake of saying exactly what she thought.

"I didn't buy this car," she told them. "*He* gave it to me."

"He!" said Edie Marie. "You make him sound like God."

"He is."

"Are you on loco-weed?" Cherise asked her. They howled with laughter.

"God, oh, give me a little kiss, God," said Edie Marie. She could have poked them, they got her so mad.

The car was doing it to everybody.

"Why are you always looking out the window?" Reggie asked her. "Is it really your car? Or is it hot?"

"It's really my car!"

"Well, let's get some cool about it," said Reggie. "You're just afraid his wife'll find out."

"I feel as if something's going to happen to my car," she said.

"Live in fear, that's the music," he told her.

"I'm ecstatic," she said. "And when you're ecstatic, you're always apprehensive as well."

5

1991

Igor Vladimirovich from the Politburo was meeting with Vladimir Kryuchkov from the KGB. Igor Vladimirovich was now six years older than he was when he had spoken to Shebarshin, and looked more certain of himself than ever. Kryuchkov, in turn, looked to be his equal.

"Four years ago," Igor Vladimirovich began, "I said to Gorbachev, 'You may be number one in the Soviet Union, but Kryuchkov has his KGB with him. And the army. Respect Kryuchkov as number two.'"

"You magnify my importance," Kryuchkov said.

"Chairman Kryuchkov," Igor Vladimirovich went on, "I will speak frankly. If something is not done soon, Gorbachev will oversee our ruin. Soviet society will cease to exist."

Kryuchkov lifted his hands slightly. "What do you propose?"

"We must show that Gorbachev works for the United States, not for Russia. That he has become our enemy."

"Objectively speaking, this may be true."

"Let me tell you," Igor Vladimirovich said. "Gorbachev's situation in our Politburo hangs by a thread."

"No!" said Kryuchkov. "Last year, we were certain he would fall. He remains. Why? Because if he topples, chaos follows. Our situation is complex. Too much so for direct exercises of strength."

"What if you were to find that Gorbachev's closest people are working for United States Intelligence? Even Gorbachev's best friend . . ."

"Yakovlev?" Kryuchkov mulled it over.

"Possibly."

"You have evidence on Yakovlev?"

"Not direct, not yet," said Igor Vladimirovich.

Kryuchkov paused. "Yet, you suggest that there may be a highly restricted file put together by the Americans on Gorbachev's best friend?"

"Yes. Something to show how much Yakovlev is involved."

Kryuchkov did a little imitation of Igor. Did it right to his face. "'Comrades, I am sorry, but now we know. We have seen the documents on these men. Gorbachev and Yakovlev are working for the United States.'"

"Yes. Exactly," said Igor Vladimirovich.

"No," said Kryuchkov. "I can promise you. If Gorbachev is working for America, there will be no file. No document will exist. Some things are not put on paper."

"Allow me to cross one very big bridge: When such paper does not exist, why can it still not be found?" Igor Vladimirovich paused. "I will say it: Who among your trusted sources is ready to provide us with such a paper?"

"It is possible," Kryuchkov nodded. "There may be one man we can call upon."

"If he comes back with what I want, we will buy him Hawaii!"

"Hawaii?"

"That is what all Americans dream about? A tropical island all their own."

"Igor Vladimirovich, let us speak frankly. One piece of paper, no matter how well it is presented, cannot produce the effect you envision."

"May I say: You understand your KGB. But our Polit-

243

buro is mine. Half of it, mine. Our Politburo is now in such extremity of confusion that one piece of paper *can* start a big fire."

Kryuchkov smiled. "This much I can promise: You and I are not wholly separated in our understanding."

In a stall in the men's room on the fourth floor, Hanssen was talking to his reflection in the polished steel.

"'Give us advice,' they ask. 'Help us to stop the mess. Can you find agents at the summit of Soviet government who work for U.S. Intelligence?' What do they want me to do? Make it up? I am in intelligence, not forgery." He could feel himself hyperventilating. *"They can go screw themselves."*

Later that day, he prepared a letter to send to them.

I WOULD SUGGEST THAT THE SOVIET UNION COULD BENEFIT FROM A THOROUGH STUDY OF THE SUMMER OF 1968 IN CHICAGO WHEN THE CITY WAS GOVERNED BY MAYOR RICHARD J. DALEY.

"What kind of answer has he given us?" Igor Vladimirovich complained.

"He says, 'Learn from Mayor Richard J. Daley'?" Kryuchkov said. "He suffers from American arrogance at its highest point. Ramon has gone crazy."

"Yes," said Igor. "Our Soviet is collapsing. Baltic republics, gone. Ukraine maybe, and he says, 'Learn from Mayor Daley'? He does not understand our civil war, our collectivization of agriculture, our Great Patriotic War."

"But Mayor Daley he understands," Kryuchkov said.

At home, Hanssen was working at his computer. He put a KGB diskette into the floppy drive. The legend "EN-CRYPTED. ENTER PASSWORD" appeared on his monitor. He quickly entered the keystrokes and a flash of English text appeared on the screen:

WE ALSO ACKNOWLEDGE AGAIN YOUR SUPERB SENSE
OF HUMOR AND YOUR SHARP-AS-A-RAZOR MIND. WE
HIGHLY APPRECIATE BOTH.

On August 19, the family was watching TV news clips of
Soviet military tanks in Moscow. A coup d'état was in
the making. Bob got up and went into the bathroom. He
locked the door and looked into the mirror. His reflection looked back at him and began to speak:

"If the KGB doesn't panic, maybe I won't either."

He put his finger on the lips of the man in the mirror.

"Are you crazy?" The mouth moved around his finger on the mirror. *"Of course the KGB is in panic. But
that has nothing to do with you. You will not panic."*

After a short time in the living room, Bob got up and
headed for the door.

"Where are you going?" Bonnie asked.

"Just restless. I'm going to take a spin," he said. He
had scheduled a drop for this night.

In the paved lane outside the park, he stopped his car, got
out, opened the trunk, removed a plastic bag, walked to a
nearby footbridge, looked around, placed the bag in the
arranged corner, stepped back, sneezed a few times, then
returned to his car. It had been a routine drop. A package
and a diskette on some new FBI surveillance methods and
some miscellaneous information on operations and technical matters. Sometimes when a death occurred in a family,
you carried on just as if nothing had happened. Indeed, in
the middle of July, he had grabbed the first thing he could
get his hands on and even told the KGB that he had been in
a hurry and did not want them to worry about his silence
after missing a scheduled meeting in June.

When he got home, Jane wanted to talk about Opus Dei.
Bonnie had suggested that she bring it up.

"Dad, sometimes I wonder about giving my whole commitment to it. But I don't know. Really, I think I shy away from thinking too deeply about it. Because it is a very big commitment."

"It is," he said. "Opus Dei is the real Church. But, Jane, you can talk to me about your reservations." He was so proud of her. She was nineteen now, and slim and blond and blue-eyed and quite attractive. At times like this, when she was a little troubled, maybe even a bit more attractive.

"Well . . ." She paused. "I heard whispering about . . . oh . . . some of the numeraries wearing, you know, like thigh bands with . . . some kind of teeth on them. Something of that sort."

"You're speaking of mortification."

"I guess I am. You see, that's what I've heard," she said. "Isn't that, um, maybe a little radical?"

"Jane, right from the early Christians on, mortification has been preached by the Church."

"But, Dad, you don't secretly wear belts or bands with spikes on them, personally on you, do you?"

He smiled. "The most intense mortification I go through is to pray with all my heart on these knees. They're getting a little old for that."

They smiled and looked at each other with tenderness.

The clarity and gentleness of this feeling encouraged Bob to bring her in on a serious talk about Opus Dei. He began by mentioning an article he had just read. It was called "Spirituality in the Professions and Workplace," by the Reverend C. John McCloskey III, who was with Opus Dei in Washington. It had been a wonderful essay, he told her—first appeared in *Faith and Reason,* a fine magazine, the 1990 issue.

"Here!" He even took it down from the bookshelf as they spoke.

"Right in the beginning of Father McCloskey's essay," he said, "is an excerpt from a book by Monsignor

246

Robert Hugh Benson. Wonderful stuff. It's really incredible. Monsignor Benson describes Christian life before the emergence of the monasteries, back in the second century. And it gives you a real picture. Benson is saying that those early Christians lived in the flesh yet they were never governed by the desires of the flesh. Why? Because they were citizens of heaven. Isn't that quite a choice of words? 'Citizens of heaven.' Splendid! They might have to dwell on earth, they might have to be obedient to the laws of the society they live in, but, Jane, they exist on a level that completely transcends the law. That's how pure they were."

"Is this the idea behind mortification?" Jane asked. "To make you more pure?"

"Some people need mortification of the flesh to get there," Bob said. "Some don't. But one way or another, if you belong to Opus Dei, the idea is to be able to work in the world in so fine and detailed and pure and considerate a way, and even at so quietly heroic a level, that a flow of spiritual energy can be felt all over." He paused to emphasize this. "Think of it as an overflow of holiness capable of permeating all Christian life."

"It sounds kind of huge," said Jane.

"It is. But it is necessary if we want to get there. It's the only engine of change for the better. It happened once; it can happen again. Look at the Roman Empire. A totally corrupt place, a degraded society, yet those early Christians understood what was possible. The world didn't have to stand in the way of holiness. It wasn't an impregnable obstruction. If there was enough faith, you could reorder any world, no matter how hideous; you could reach the essential goodness that God gave to all of us. Those early Christians were even powerful enough to convert that wholly pagan, evil-driven Roman Empire."

"I don't know if I ever realized before how incredible a change that was. They did, didn't they?" said Jane.

"They certainly did. Holiness can change the world. That's the real secret. Everyone goes around looking for the dirty little secret that will give them power and never realize that the answer lies in the other direction. Where? Why, it lies in the clean little secret that holiness can change the world. To be a real Christian is to be able to change the world."

"But I've heard you say there are so few real Christians."

"So few. That is why Opus Dei is tremendously important. Jane, it is the belief that you will commit your life in every way, large and small, to working in the Lord's vineyard. We were called by Christ to sanctify the world and transform it, even if we only do it quietly and in little ways. But we are committed in that quiet way to being an apostle for Christ."

Jane nodded. She did not know if she could speak. Her father's sentiments were so intense. One could simply burst listening to him. It made her love him even more. Because, at the end of all this, he did not ask her if she felt closer to Opus Dei. It was awful, but, secretly, she still didn't know if she would ever be ready. And he was so sensitive to her. He didn't push her. She knew how much he wanted to, but he didn't. That was kind of noble of him.

Priscilla was driving with Bob in her Mercedes, but he was choosing the route. He kept talking about religion and the miraculous effect it could have on one's personality.

"It would take a miracle to change my life," she said to him at last.

"God makes miracles," he told her. "He does it to show us that nothing is impossible."

She said to him: "I think miracles happen on a small scale. A life is saved, a baby is born."

"Yes, and there are also major miracles," he told her.

"But the first step is to go to church. Will you promise me that you'll come to Saint Catherine's here"—he pointed to it as they passed—"this Sunday?"

"Here is where you and your family go?"

"Every Sunday."

On Saturday night some men were in the 1819 club with their wives. The emcee spoke through his microphone:

"And in another hour, it'll be midnight—Sunday for all us good churchgoers."

A ripple of laughter passed through the room. Priscilla winced.

It was 4:00 A.M. when she got home from work and 8:00 A.M. when her alarm went off. She sat up in bed to put Visine in her eyes.

She came out of her house wearing a nice suit, got into her Mercedes, and drove out to the church.

Priscilla was first in the parking lot. She sat back and fell asleep.

She woke up to car doors being opened and shut all around her. She saw the Hanssen family van arrive and park at the other end of the lot. She could barely see Bonnie.

"She's pretty," Priscilla murmured to herself.

In the distance, she saw all six kids walk by. The oldest, she knew, was almost twenty; the youngest was six, a pretty little girl.

Reggie heard all about it that night.

"It was just the way I imagined it," Priscilla said. "A perfect Sunday, with the perfect all-American family going to church."

"Did you walk in?" Reggie asked.

"No. I sat in that car thinking of all that could go wrong. Like, what if there was a forced introduction?

She would know that I know him. She would feel the gravitational pull."

"Hey, lady, he was taking a very big risk by inviting you. Did he know you were coming today?"

"Well, I could see him looking around for me."

On Monday, Priscilla was having coffee with Hanssen before the lunch hour.

"Why didn't you come in? Why?" he asked. He had a huge smile. He was radiant.

"Oh, I tried to the best of my ability. I couldn't get out of the car," she said.

"I'm exhilarated that you showed up. Next time, you'll pass through the door."

"You know, I have to walk right by a church every single day on the way to work."

"Ever tempted to go inside?"

"No. How can I? Think about it," she said. "I would feel like I was polluting the place. I go to take my clothes off just a block away."

"Maybe that's the right way to feel."

"I don't agree. It's an awful feeling," she said.

"Priscilla, you have a beautiful soul. Give three promises to God. Promise three things. That's all you need—three promises that you mean to keep."

"What three?"

"Go to church. Don't live with a man if you are not married. And you have to stop performing in public."

"You said that what I do is beautiful."

"Not everything beautiful is blessed. Promise these three things to God."

She could not trust herself to reply.

In the dressing room, getting ready for the noontime show, Priscilla was talking to Cherise.

"He doesn't love me. He loves boredom. No TV, no clubs, no music. Nothing but work, family, and church."

"Deadly dull," Cherise said.

"No. No. I guess his life is very interesting to him."
Priscilla started to cry. "Today, he just broke something
in me."

The tears brought a stream of mascara down her
cheeks. It took right up to the last minute, but she pulled
herself together, repaired the damage to her makeup,
and went out to dance.

6

1991

Fefelov was writing:

> PLEASE OFFER UP YOUR THOUGHTS ON LEADS TO
> POSSIBLE RECRUITMENTS OF INTERESTING PEOPLE IN
> THE RIGHT PLACES.

Hanssen wrote back.

> THE RECRUITMENT YOU MAY BE LOOKING FOR IS AN
> ARMY OFFICER IN MILITARY INTELLIGENCE NOW
> STATIONED IN GERMANY WHO HAS FREQUENT CON-
> TACTS WITH RUSSIAN OFFICERS IN GRU WHO WORK
> AT HIS LEVEL. HE IS LIEUTENANT COLONEL JACK
> HOSCHOUER AND HAS BEEN DISAFFECTED SINCE HE
> HAS RECENTLY BEEN TOLD HE WOULD NOT BE PRO-
> MOTED TO FULL COLONEL.

The red shawl was on the hooks, and Hanssen was talking to his reflection. He did all the talking. The mirror
did not reply.

"*What if they recruit Jack? It's not impossible that he
could become a real confidant.*

"*I need a confidant for little things—the persistent
worries that eat into the lining of your stomach.*

252

"Except! Except that I can live without confiding in anyone. It is the secret of my strength.

"Why did I give Jack's name to the KGB? Why? If they hook up with him, they will learn my name. Who am I playing these games with? Them? Or myself? Or do I just want to get nearer to Jack?"

In a beer garden in Bonn, Hoschouer, in uniform, and a Soviet officer in uniform, entered to have lunch together. After they had finished their coffee, the Russian said, "Jack, have you ever wondered why I don't ask you something that has relevance to Intelligence?"

"I would say," Hoschouer replied, "that it's because we're friends. That, Yuri, is why I've never asked you anything that is relevant to Intelligence."

Yuri looked at him, smiled, stood up, shook hands, and walked away.

Christmas Day, 1991: The family was at home watching television. There were news shots on the screen of the Soviet flag coming down in Red Square. Bob and Bonnie and the children were all clapping and cheering.

"What a wonderful Christmas present this is!" Bonnie said.

Bob smiled to show how much he was in agreement with her. As he smiled, he could hear his own voice, full and clear, without the presence of the mirror: *What the hell does this mean? I just gave them a dead drop nine days ago and now their flag is coming down. What kind of trouble am I in?*

Opposite Directions

Part Four

Opposite Directions

1

1992

Priscilla's birthday was just two days away from Christmas, and she liked to celebrate the two events together. To be a Christmas baby was a really special feeling. So, despite everything, she had looked forward to this one. It could never be as good as last year, because around December 1990, a little more than a year ago, Bob had been so wonderful about giving her money to fix her teeth—and did it when he hardly knew her.

Now she felt as if all the gifts he had given her were wiped out by one remark: "Not everything beautiful is blessed." It was as if somebody had given her a mean jab in the stomach, and then, instead of getting better, it got worse. She would never forget those words. She had always felt that she could exhibit her body in public and not have to feel the least bit of shame. Now she did. Oh, he had ruined so much. She really didn't want to see him anymore. In her memory, she kept going back to that awful night in his hotel room in Hong Kong.

So, now, this Christmas, trying to get out of her bad mood, she agreed to go out for the evening with Reggie. That could be what she needed—a night on the town.

But it didn't turn out to be a big evening. Reggie's loyalty was no longer to her; it had gone back to his mother and father. He took her to their house for Christmas dinner, and it turned into one very long family occasion.

Out came a home-cooked meal and a bottle of wine. On top of everything, they were very religious in the special way black people often are. So intense in their praying. Very vocal. Yet every time a prayer ended, they all had to work to make conversation. She was a stranger in their house.

Reggie didn't take her out afterward, either. Instead, he brought her home and then took off to see some friends.

When your luck is running that bad, get out of your box! On impulse, she packed some things, got into her car, and drove all the way out to Columbus, Ohio, where her mother was living. No call in advance, no warning— just like that. Drove through the night. Arrived around ten in the morning. She was going to stay a couple of days and show off her Mercedes. When she thought about it later, she realized that she didn't know she was actually saying, "Good-bye, Bob, good-bye for keeps."

It turned out to be the most absolute change she could make in her life. Her mother lived up on the third floor of a run-down building in a rank neighborhood. Priscilla kept the Mercedes in a garage. But she wasn't there long enough to turn around when, much to her surprise, she met the man of her life. At a party on New Year's Eve! She couldn't believe it. He was so handsome and also brilliant! They spent the whole night talking about deep subjects like philosophy and science. It was only a ratty party that the girlfriend of an old friend of her brother's invited her to, but this tall, beautiful guy was there, and they just fixed on each other. He dressed in a cool style, very much his own, and mentioned books she had never heard of. He knew a lot about art. They got together big on Hieronymus Bosch. Before the evening was over, she also guessed that he was into drug dealing, but she had never met a man who turned her on so quickly. So intelligent—he was unbelievable. Like a criminal played by a movie star.

258

She was introduced to his father the next day, an old charmer, and told him ten minutes into the conversation that she was going to marry his son.

Her mother started in on her about that. "Is this guy the reason you're staying on in Columbus?" she asked.

"He's the only reason," said Priscilla.

"How will you earn any money?" her mother asked.

"I'm not thinking about a job."

"Isn't that just like you!"

"What if it is?"

"I want to know—what happened to your FBI man?"

"Forget him. It's about the new man now. Love has bitten me. Never this bad before."

"I thought the FBI man was treating you so good."

"He didn't really love me"

"Did you, at least, say good-bye?"

"No. I didn't leave any word for him when I left."

"Nothing?"

"According to Reggie, he has made no move to reach me, either."

"He will," said her mother. "Cops hate questions they can't answer."

After a while, Priscilla began to freak out a little. She understood that the new guy didn't love her in the way her feelings had moved over to him. She had to wonder if he just saw her as a useful asset, loved her Mercedes, all that. Yet once in a while, every two or three days or so, she had a night with him that was a record-breaker.

She finally decided to stay in Columbus. Yes, she would give up her job at 1819 and her apartment in D.C.—she would float on love. All the while, she felt weird. It was true. The new lover was a drug dealer. She was now on a lot of stuff in a way she'd never taken it up before. And she knew Hanssen was going to show. Sooner or later. What the hell, she was using his American Express card. In fact, by the time she went back overnight to D.C. for the big move to Columbus, she had to rent two U-Hauls and hire three people. There was certainly enough furniture in the apartment—a big L-shaped combination living room and dining room with a bar in the middle and a great big bedroom with walk-in closets. Ten years of gowns, along with everything else. She must have put a couple of thousand on the credit card just to make the move. Mr. H. would soon be on her tail for that. She knew that much.

He was. It took two months, but one day he pulled up in his Volvo to her apartment back in D.C., got out, checked the directory in the foyer, and rang. When the buzzer sounded, he entered, climbed a flight of stairs, and knocked. The door opened. On the other side was a black man, almost as tall as himself. That was a shock.

"I am looking for Priscilla Galey," Hanssen said.

"Oh, Priscilla's moved back to Columbus," said the black man. "Says it's permanent." Behind him, Bob could see an empty apartment with no more than a folding cot and a cigarette-scarred end table with a small alarm clock on it.

"And who are you?"

"I'm Reggie. An old friend. I'm cleaning the place out." He smiled. It was obvious. He knew who Bob was. "She owes rent," he said, "that they ain't gonna get."

Without one more word, Hanssen turned and walked away.

A taxi approached her mother's house on that rank street in Columbus. As Bob exited, he told the driver to wait. When Priscilla opened the door, he was formal.

"I've come to get the credit card I gave you," he said.

That was a chill! "Sure," she said. "Okay." She paused. "Well, hello! Won't you come in?"

"I'd rather not. I'm in a big hurry." He just stood in

the doorway and said, "Priscilla, you did not follow the rules, so I have to have the card back."

She knew that he could have just canceled her card. Why had he come all this way? But she knew. He had to tell her face-to-face. Had to have the satisfaction. Had to know whether she could be future trouble for him.

She opened her purse and handed him the card.

"Priscilla, it was our understanding you would use this only for car expenses."

"Yes. Car-related expenses," she said.

"But when the statement came to my office, there were other charges."

"Bob, I wanted to buy clothes for my two nieces. You know, Easter is coming. I want them to look nice for church. Couldn't you say that is religious-related?" She paused. "I'm telling you the truth."

The truth was that she would have no source of funds now. It was like the end of a show.

All he said was, "It had to be car-related."

"Thank you. I am sorry," she said. She needed to finish as a lady. "I didn't mean to make you mad."

"I'm not mad," Hanssen said. "But I do have to go now."

"Mr. Hanssen," she said, "I will never interrupt your personal life—you know that. I give you my word."

"I know, Priscilla. I trust you."

He got into the cab without a backward look.

Two days later, Priscilla and her sister were driving in her Mercedes on a two-lane street. Once this tank of gas was gone, she would have to buy her fuel with cash. Worse, they were arguing as they drove. It was a rotten fight.

"Stop lying to me," her sister said. "I know you slept with that FBI man."

"Is this what I get," Priscilla asked, "for spending six hundred dollars on my credit card for your lousy birth-

261

day last month?" Her sister was wearing the necklace Priscilla had bought and now, with a jerk, Priscilla yanked it off.

"Get out of my car!" she yelled. Her sister grabbed the necklace back and threw it out the window. Then they looked at each other in horror.

Priscilla stopped the car in the middle of the street, right after making a turn. She didn't care. Both of them ran back to where the necklace lay broken, cultured pearls scattered all over the asphalt. They bent over to pick them up, one by one.

"Listen," Priscilla said. "I've had men lay out hundred-dollar bills side by side and tell me every woman has her price. And I told them, 'Sorry, sir, I don't.' I'm telling you the truth. I did not sleep with Bob Hanssen."

At that moment, a truck came barreling around the turn and plowed into her car, whacking it right off the road and down into a gully. She could even see the last of it smash into a tree. The women were far enough away to escape bodily harm, but by the frightened look in her sister's eyes, Priscilla knew what her own face must look like. Everything was gone except for what the future would bring. A long, dark night, and Mr. Lightning, her boyfriend, in Columbus.

2

1992

For a time it looked like it might all turn out to be less disruptive than Bob had anticipated. Sizable changes were going on in the Bureau these days, but from his point of view, they were on the benign side. A new strategy was being designed for counterintelligence, and he had been in on the formation and design of it.

One night he even went so far as to explain the new approach to Bonnie. She was always eager to know what he was doing at the Bureau and his constant reminder to her that there were things he could not discuss proved acceptable to her—but barely. Her mood shifted; little household details already settled, like which of the boys should take the garbage out on a given night, came back to irk her.

So, he decided to tell her about his new position. He could probably do it without violating any truly confidential material.

"It's not common knowledge yet," he said, "but we are reassessing our point of view. It's no longer just Russia and the Warsaw Pact countries and China and Korea and Cuba—we're branching out. Bonnie, we're going to look everywhere in the world, not just at our enemies, but at our allies as well."

"Isn't that a little shocking, Bob?"

"No, Bonnie, it's just another face of the real world. Friendly nations also spy."

"I think it's despicable that they claim to be our friends but are not to be trusted. We do so much more for them than they do for us."

"Who can argue that point? The crux of the matter, now that Russia is making its transition to capitalism—"

"Do you trust the Russians now?"

"Of course not."

"Bob, I tell you—under everything, they are still Communists."

"You're right, but that's another question. What we're talking about now is that we have a brand-new strategy. It's called the National Security Threat list, and the bottom line is that we are going to focus on economic espionage and fix our sights on the French, the Israelis, on India and Pakistan—name any country in the world. Mike Shepard was talking to me about it and said, 'Bob, we need a very, very bright guy to take over the new unit. It's not so much a question of deciding who to target, but how much.'"

"Who did they choose, Bob?"

"Well, it so happens, Mike Shepard chose your husband."

"Oh, Bob, you are incredible. How long have you been keeping this from me?"

"Not long. I only found out a couple of weeks ago. It's a good deal. I'm now Unit Chief."

"What does that mean?"

"It's a real Grade 15, Bonnie. The next job up the line is to become an ASAC—that's Assistant Special Agent in Charge."

"And the next?"

"Hold your horses. It's SAC, and that is quite a post. Then you're speaking to the media and to Congress."

"I can see you on the tube. There'll be all sorts of assistants handing you papers while you testify."

"Something like that." He grinned his big smile. "Bonnie, this means I'm definitely going to get my

GS-15. Ninety thousand bucks a year and in addition a bonus of twenty-five percent."

"I can hardly wait to tell Liz and Jean and Mother and Daddy," said Bonnie. "You're such a big man, Bob, and you are just going to get bigger and bigger."

A Russian official wearing an oversized suit was walking down the hall on the fourth floor with two senior FBI officials together with none other than General Oleg Kalugin, formerly of the KGB.

They were being given a tour of the Bureau. One of the FBI officials stopped Hanssen as he walked by.

"Bob, congratulations on getting your GS-15."

Hanssen said his thank-you and gave another big smile.

"I'd like you to meet Mr. Bakatin," the official said. "He's now the head of the new KGB."

Bakatin smiled. It took just one glance for Bob to figure out the man was a politician. "Yes, we have a new name," Bakatin said. "No longer KGB. In English, we can now all say SVR. Democratic Intelligence Service, SVR."

"And this is General Oleg Kalugin," said the FBI official, "retired from the old KGB. He is advising Mr. Bakatin on how to reorganize and democratize the old KGB."

"Crazy times, are they not?" Kalugin said to Hanssen.

"We can agree on that."

The moment they moved on, Hanssen headed into the men's room, closed himself in a stall, and looked into the door's surface.

"I'm having trouble getting any words out. . . ."

He heard someone come in and stopped speaking. A moment later, he walked out of the stall and started down the hall to his office. Four doors away, Bakatin and Kalugin were visiting another office. They waved to Hanssen with the quick, easy warmth of new acquaintances.

In his office, he was able to stand in front of the window, which then reflected his face.

"You are a great spy at a time when spying has just become no more and no less than one more instrument of international business," he said softly.

He looked off into space and heard the voice in his head: *"But you still have to worry that the past does not catch up to you."*

For lunch that day, Hanssen and Walter Ballou were in a hash house eating hamburgers.

"Get this!" Walter said. "The Brits have hit a gold mine. One of the major archivists in the KGB, a fellow named Mitrokhin, just walked into one of their embassies and asked for asylum. From what I hear, the guy took a lot of prime stuff with him."

"The Russians must be having a fit," said Bob.

"I don't know about that," said Walter. "Given the atmosphere of today's visit, I don't sense any great allegiance to their past in these KGB guys."

In their bedroom, Bob was lying in the dark, his eyes open. His lips did not move.

If Mitrokhin knows about the existence of Ramon, the British could pass it on to the Bureau.

Hanssen touched Bonnie, who stirred and made a soft sound.

He turned back to his original position and said to himself, *From now on, I will devote myself to being more holy.*

As an inner remark, it felt genuine to him. It was as if he had gone through the test of seeking a real conversion and had found it, as if he was now what he had always presented himself as being—a true man of faith.

3

1993

The voice on the phone in Bob's office said: "This is Priscilla's mother."

"Good morning," he answered. "And why are you calling?" He was not going to spend time on this. No way.

"Mr. Hanssen, Priscilla really needs to have a little cash."

"What makes you come to me?"

"I'm going to tell you the truth, Mr. Hanssen. I'm worried. Priscilla has gotten hooked up with a bad fellow. I think he's a pimp. And I know he does drugs."

"I have nothing to do with your daughter's situation," he said, and hung up. The echoes of the conversation were about to rattle him when Elizabeth, his assistant, entered.

"Bob, I need your help," she said. "The new girl I have to work with is downright difficult."

"Who are we talking about, Elizabeth? Which girl?"

"The clerk that's just been assigned to us. She's very snippy."

"That is exactly what I need to deal with this morning."

"Bob, I'm sorry, but we've got to get her cooperation. Could you just take on a meeting with her and me?"

The young woman, Kimberly Lichtenberg, turned out to be an inexperienced blue-collar-family girl. With airs!

267

"I thought if we got together, it might be easier to find a modus operandi," Hanssen said. The three of them were gathered in a small conference room.

"I do not report directly to you, Mr. Hanssen," said Kimberly. "I'm just on loan."

"Well, we know that," Bob said. "But we are engaged, after all, in a project where we do have to cooperate."

"As I see it, cooperation is a two-way street," Kimberly said.

"Of course."

"I see no need to take orders if we're supposed to be cooperating."

"Now, Kimberly, you don't really want to come in here with that attitude, do you?" he said.

"Attitude? First Elizabeth and now you are trying to dominate my work. And you don't know anything about it."

With that, she left the room. Hanssen went after her. She was walking so quickly that he had to use his longest strides to overtake her, and when he did catch up, he had to grasp her arm in order to slow her down and protect his balance.

"Please come back!" he started to say, but she was so tense that at the moment he touched her, she tottered and fell. From the floor, she screamed.

"He was rude, and threw me down on the floor," she said to the two FBI inspectors who were questioning her.

"Threw you down?"

"He had his hand on me and next thing I knew, I was on the floor."

Hanssen was facing the same two agents.

"I put my hand on her elbow in a friendly fashion," he said. "In a quiet tone, I asked her to come back to the meeting. She wrenched her arm loose forcefully, when there was no need for force. In doing that, she stumbled and fell. I was only trying to restore a situation that had gotten out of hand. There was no physical assault. Just her insubordination."

"How would you characterize your judgment concerning this matter?" one agent asked him. "Considering, what is, after all, the end result."

"Perhaps it could have been less impulsive," Bob said.

Out in the hallway, a number of men passed him. Each one nodded gravely. One or two put a hand briefly on his shoulder in consolation.

In Shepard's office, Mike asked, "Why in hell did you grab her in the first place?"

Hanssen was miserable. "I didn't grab her, but I admit, I shouldn't have touched her. I used terrible judgment."

"That is why they suspended you for five days. For poor judgment."

"But I never threw her down," he insisted.

"Hey, they suspended her, too. Same five. For insubordination. You've got to get beyond this."

"I can't believe the Bureau couldn't recognize my side of it. After all these years."

"No way they could come back in your favor. They had to split the verdict."

"I can't accept that," Hanssen said.

"You have to. You are living in a politically correct world. You are not a woman, you are not an African-American. You are a regular white guy. No cards to play."

"Where's the fairness?"

"Get it straight: If it has to, the Bureau will chew you up and swallow you."

"I hate the way everybody knows about this episode," Hanssen said. He didn't know which was worse—the punishment or the pity.

"Of course everybody knows," Mike told him. "We're an organization of investigators. We ask and we talk."

"Bonnie can't forgive me. She pointed out that I'm going to lose a week of pay. Almost two thousand bucks. I didn't tell her that having this in my file also means I can probably give up the idea of any future promotion."

"That's right. No way you are going to get to the SAC or even ASAC. For that, you have to be one hundred percent sanitary. Why, the media would kill you if you were a spokesman for us and they found out about Kimberly Lichtenberg."

"Mike, you're there already. Can you realize how painful it is to give up the idea that in the future, up with the men who have some final say, I could have made a difference. But there it is. Now I can't. Why? Because one little hundred-pound girl—her mind polluted by all kinds of gender correctness—can lift more weight in the Bureau than I can."

"Ain't that the facts of life," said Mike Shepard.

Their conversation kept seething in Bob. It was still there when he half woke up in the middle of the night, yet remained in a dream where he was on television: *"I first met Bill Clinton,"* he said to Larry King, *"when he came to FBI Headquarters to speak. On that day, the Secret Service required all two hundred invited agents to give up their weapons. I can tell you, that was not a nice moment for us. When Ronald Reagan was our president, they never had to take FBI men's guns. They knew that we revered the man. But with Clinton, the Secret Service decided to take no chances."*

"What is your opinion of President Clinton?" Larry King asked.

"He is a sociopath. Everything he does is a lie," Hanssen said. It was such an agreeable moment that he hated to wake up entirely.

* * *

On Sunday afternoon, Bob and Bonnie were walking with the dog.

Sundae ran around, passed through a puddle, saw a man, walked up to him in a friendly way, and tried to leap up. In so doing, he smudged the man's safari jacket with his paw. The man marched toward them, his face contorted.

"Keep your damn animal on a leash!" he shouted. The man looked threatening.

Bob stepped back, opened his suit jacket, and pulled the PPK from his shoulder holster. "Don't approach closer or I'll shoot," he said. "I'm an FBI agent."

The man turned on his heel and walked away. When he had put some distance between himself and the Hanssens, he approached a policeman.

Now Bob and Bonnie were in the police station with the desk sergeant.

"All right," the cop began. "I know you've been here almost an hour, but it takes time to process this." He paused and then softened his tone. "Look, it's not a good idea to wave your gun in the park. You ought to know that, sir." He paused again. "And next time, please remember—we have that ordinance for a reason. We ask you to keep your dog on a leash."

Hanssen was cold. "Thank you, Officer."

Once outside, Bonnie was furious.

"That officer was absolutely right," she said. "You should not have waved your gun."

"Don't be absurd," Hanssen replied. "I know what I was doing."

"If you don't learn to control your temper, you will destroy everything we have worked for all these years."

4

1993

Bonnie, Bob, and Vivian stood near Howard Hanssen's hospital bed in Venice, Florida. Nothing had happened for a while and Howard was still asleep. Or so it seemed.

"Vivian and I are going to leave you alone, Bob, with your dad," Bonnie said.

In an old, rasping voice, Howard spoke up abruptly. "Thank you, girls."

Once the women were out of the room, the old man began to talk, but in such a phlegm-thickened voice that Bob had to bend over close to hear him.

"Look! Before I kick off . . ."

"You're not going anywhere yet."

"Don't try to bullshit a bullshitter." It took him a while to get that out, and then he laughed and nearly choked on his phlegm. "Look," he said. "I have to tell you something before I go. It bothers me."

Bob had been tense. Now it was worse.

"Okay, Dad. All right. What? What did I do wrong?"

Howard had to shake his head back and forth a few times. "Not you," the old man got out at last. "This time, me." He even made an attempt to sit up in bed. "Remember your driving tests?"

"Never forgotten them," Bob said. In fact, perspiration sprang up instantly all over his back, as if it had just happened all over again.

"Wasn't your fault. I bribed the inspector to flunk you."

"Each time?"

Howard held up three fingers. "Three shots. Ten bucks a pop."

"Why? Why, Dad?" He felt the pain again, the same pain he'd felt when his father would grab him by the ankles and whirl him around until he puked.

"You were getting too cocky."

"I thought you wanted me to act like a man."

Howard was able to take enough of a breath to say, "A man is no man until he knows he can fail and yet keeps going." He started to cough.

"You tell me now?" Bob forced himself to wipe his father's mouth. He would have preferred to throw the cloth in his face. "Why?"

"Got to get the record straight." It took him a while to say that much.

"Are you scared? Is that it?"

"Don't know." Howard tried to sit up in bed but Bob pressed him back. "Love you," said the old man. "I love you, Bob."

"Well, Dad, I love you, too." He had to say it, but he felt as if love and its absolute opposite were clawing away in him. All those years that he had awakened in a sweat because he'd flunked a car test three times running.

He was surprised to find tears in his eyes when he left the hospital room.

Bonnie and Vivian were at the other end of the hallway. As Bob approached, Vivian said: "Said your farewells?"

He nodded.

She looked back at him with her pretty old lady's face. Her eyes looked enormous behind her large eyeglasses. "I said mine a long time ago. A long time ago."

"Mother!"

In the mildest voice, Vivian said, "You and Bonnie

won't have to worry about your girls and boys getting a good college education. I'll be proud to help. I've saved for that."

Back in Washington, a huge crowd was on the Mall lawn. Posters were everywhere: THE FREEDOM TO CHOOSE IS DIVINE, GAY RIGHTS, RAINBOW COALITION. Off to the side of the Mall, Hanssen had decided to do a little observing of the activities during his lunch break. He could hardly believe what was going on. In a car parked nearby, a female FBI Supervisory Special Agent he knew by name was embracing another woman who happened to be a uniformed police officer.

He made a point of telling Walter Ballou about it as soon as he got back to the office.

"How do you rate this for news? I just saw our Supervisory Special Agent Tie Kingsford in a parked car near the Mall. She was with another female, a uniformed cop." Hanssen snorted so hard he had to use his handkerchief. "Walter, they were kissing each other. In full view. Take a look. It was disgusting. I tell you, the infection is everywhere. It's rampant."

"Bob, that must have been her sister. She's a park police officer."

Bob turned stone-cold.

"Frankly speaking, Bob, you haven't been the same since that . . . thing . . . happened with Kimberly Lichtenberg."

"No," Hanssen said. "I haven't."

"We should have a talk," Ballou said. "I have to wonder. Why are you still working here? You've been the first to say that that five-day suspension killed your future chances here. So why not resign? With your knowledge, you could make at least a hundred and fifty thousand working for some multinational firm."

"I can't resign. This place is in my blood."

274

5

1994

What a stir was created at the Bureau on the day in February when Aldrich Ames was arrested.

"Can you believe the guy?" Shepard said. "He's responsible for the deaths of at least ten Russians we had working for us."

"It could never happen here," Ballou said.

"I think you're right, Walter," Hanssen remarked. "It takes a career in the CIA to breed that kind of arrogant, self-centered, greedy bastard."

The tall, white-haired FBI man who had once mocked Hanssen now said: "You got to know it's serious when Digger O'Dell uses a swear word."

Bob was in bed, eyes wide open, while Bonnie slept. The voice started up inside his head. No need for a mirror tonight.

All right, now that Aldrich Ames has been caught, they're going to discover enough discrepancies between what he gave the KGB and what he didn't to realize that there's more than one of us in the woodwork. So I have to stick around. If I'm out of the Bureau, if and when the FBI decides to go on a mole hunt, I'll be a sitting duck. So I have to be there to guard the fort. I'm locked into the Bureau for the rest of my working days.

Bonnie rose out of bed while the voice was still in his

mind, and then she reached for the bottle of gel capsules on her side of the nightstand. When she came back from the bathroom, he asked:

"Did you take another NyQuil?"

"I need another one tonight. I have the collywobbles and nervous nellies all in one," she said.

"Darling, you have to stop thinking of all that's wrong in the world," he said. "You never get enough sleep."

"I can't help it. It's awful, Bob. I keep visualizing black helicopters descending on the houses of women everywhere around the country. Then these creatures come out and start removing the women's reproductive organs." She stopped. "All right, I know that's extreme. . . ."

"It is extreme, Bonnie, but it does have some basis. Things are getting extreme. There are an awful lot of U.N. birth-control initiatives being given a start-up right now."

"Do you still believe the Communists are infiltrating us?" she asked.

"Absolutely. Now that they've lost in Russia, they are proceeding to infiltrate every liberal movement in America."

"I wish you hadn't said that. The world is so totally exposed to godlessness by now. Everywhere you look—the newspapers, the television shows—it's full of pornography." She shuddered.

They would have conversations like this about once a week, usually in the middle of the night. That was the hour when it all felt so real you could touch it. How she needed the comfort of his arms. And he was happy to provide that. It was part of his own security, too. After 1979 and the GRU, he certainly didn't want Bonnie on a mole hunt in her own bed.

The next time Jack visited them, Bob showed him a piece of two-inch-by-two-inch cardboard that was about an eighth of an inch thick.

"You are telling me that this is a video camera?" Jack said. "I don't believe it."

"That is exactly what it is," Hanssen said. "A most advanced piece of technology."

"I don't even see a pinhole for the lens."

"It's there. This piece of cardboard is not only the camera, but it transmits images as well. I can set it up on a shelf in my bedroom at such an angle that the action will be entirely visible to you right here on the TV set in this room. We can try it out tonight after everybody goes to sleep. Just turn on your set. I've set the channel."

"Do I get to see what I expect to see?"

"Just about anything you'd like," Bob said. His eyes were bright.

"You're offering me the menu?" Jack asked.

"Tell me and you'll get it."

Jack spent an unbelievable half hour that night watching Bob strut his stuff on the closed-circuit TV. For a pasty, unathletic guy, Hanssen sure was a phenomenon. It made Jack wonder why he, a veteran army officer in good shape, was always working so hard to keep himself in splendid condition. It seems you didn't have to.

6

1994

In the morning, her face all flushed, Jane asked Bonnie whether she could invite a young man to dinner that night.

"This sounds special," said Bonnie.

That made Jane really blush. "It is. He is."

"Well, of course you can," said Bonnie. "And now you've got me awfully interested. But mightn't it be better to make it tomorrow night?"

"No, he has an evening seminar."

"All right, tonight, then. It's just that Jack Hoschouer will still be here."

"Mom, is there something about Jack that upsets you?" Jane asked.

Bonnie went still for a moment. "Yes," she said. "Jack does make me uncomfortable—I will say it. He always has. But, Jane, he is still your father's oldest and closest friend, and I don't want to take that away. As you know, it is not easy for your father to make friends."

"Is it all right to keep calling him Uncle Jack?"

"I guess you have to, yes," said Bonnie.

Around the family table at dinner that night sat Bob, Bonnie, Jack, Jane, Sue, Greg, Mark, Little Jack, and Lisa. Jane, the oldest, was twenty-one, and Lisa, the youngest, was now eight. Also present was a good-looking, well-built young man sitting next to Jane. His name was Richard Trimber, and right now his full attention was on Bonnie.

"Richard," Bonnie was saying. "Some people may call me old-fashioned, but I believe that AIDS is God's way of offering us a preview of the gate to hell."

Richard nodded. He had been having his difficulties trying to make acceptable conversation, and his next contribution went all wrong.

"You know," he said, looking neither to agree nor disagree with what Bonnie had just stated but rather to amplify it, "I read in the *Washington Post* yesterday that there's a network show where the actors auditioning were told they had to be filmed in full frontal nudity."

Full frontal nudity! That sure put a cloud over the conversation.

"Richard, we don't use terms like that while eating," Hanssen said. Bonnie shook her head. Jane looked down at the tablecloth.

After dinner, while the women did the dishes, Bob, Jack, and Richard were having a conversation in a corner of the living room.

"Jane tells me that you're going to apply to the FBI the moment you get out of law school," Bob said.

"I've been thinking about it," Richard said.

"I wouldn't recommend that," Bob replied.

"You wouldn't?" Richard was startled. He was not all that certain he would apply, but he had thought that mentioning the possibility might warm things up.

"The FBI is not what it used to be," said Bob. "Too many changes."

"What would some of them be, sir?"

"For one thing, the women that they now allow in are a joke." It was obviously no joke to Jane's father.

Richard kept listening.

"Most of the girls couldn't even make the percentages on the shooting range," Bob added. "The Bureau had to move the targets in closer. From twenty-five feet to seven feet. Seven feet," he repeated. "If I extend my arm, I'm halfway there." Given his height, he was hardly exaggerating.

"Bob," Jack said. "Tell him about the female agent who pulled her gun on a perpetrator and said, 'I'm an FBI agent.'"

Both men laughed. Bob obviously took some pleasure in telling and retelling this story.

"As it turned out, the perp was a real thug. So how does he respond? He grabs her gun and punches out her teeth. Then he takes her badge." That image had him laughing again. "'Maybe I can use this,' says the perp. In my opinion, all female law-enforcement agents ought to be at least six feet, two inches tall."

"What Bob is underlining is that once you get on an active criminal scene, it's crucial to maintain control," Jack said.

"Absolutely," said Bob. "You don't want a short, loud-talking woman whose sole aim in life is to chew up a man's ego. Once that type gets out there, it kicks up the level of crowd anxiety. That's guaranteed to increase the trouble."

Richard tried to shift the subject back to himself. He did want advice. "You know, I'm also considering the possibility of a career in the CIA," he offered.

"Worse," said Hanssen. "The CIA is a morally corrupt organization."

"Wow!" said Richard. "You don't mince words, do you, sir?"

"Take the Agency on its own terms. The CIA asks its agents to assume false identities. That is a license to manipulate other people."

"Wouldn't you say that only involves, at most, a small percentage of agents?" Richard asked.

"Those are the ones who poison the well."

What could he say next? It was important, Richard

felt, to encourage some kind of relatively relaxed back-and-forth conversation. After all, he was a law student—he could talk. He knew if they really got going, he would shine a little more. So he turned to Hoschouer. Jack seemed more open-minded. "Now that we're on it," Richard asked, "how do you in the army feel about the gays-in-the-military issue? You know, what the Clintons started."

At this, Hanssen shook his head. "In this house," he said, "we do not talk about homosexuals if we can help it. We feel that is about equal to bringing evil into the room."

Richard Trimber had a few conservative ideas of his own, but Bob and Bonnie seemed about as right-wing as anyone he had ever talked to.

Things got a lot better over the next couple of months. Jane explained to Richard that deep down her father was really very shy, so he sometimes seemed, well, maybe a little overassertive. You always had to listen to what he said, however. He knew how to get right to the root of a problem.

Richard worked at it. Bonnie, he soon discovered, ran the housekeeping side of things with an iron hand. He realized that was a cliché, but some clichés had real truth to them. Still, she was nice-looking, had kept her figure, dressed in a low-key way, maintained a neat home, cooked enjoyable meals, and spoke in a soft voice—almost always. If the kids didn't respond quickly enough to a request, though, or didn't set the table on time or wash the dishes or tidy up this or that—well, she could really yell in a voice that could hurt your ears. You really didn't want to get into a situation where you had to hear her yell. Even Bob, as Richard observed, was leery of crossing her. She certainly did run the house.

Bob loved his privacy. He liked to read, he spent hours surfing the Internet, and he was even something of a small-time computer guru, you might say. He definitely received lots of e-mail asking his advice on knotty cyber problems, and he usually had answers.

Richard managed to warm him up, though. Bob could tell hair-raising tales about a few of his exploits in the FBI. He told Richard a great story about how he had overseen a Sunday raid on a Soviet installation in New York, where he had stood in a doorway for hours, gun at the ready, so that he could cover all the people working for him if something went wrong. It was gratifying to see how this shy, reserved, highly opinionated man nonetheless began to warm up to him. It was clear that Bob now enjoyed his visits.

Actually, Richard had been practical about it. Whatever it took, he was going to make friends with him. He succeeded. Really, he had no choice but to develop a relationship. The alternative—to hang out in the kitchen with Bonnie and the girls—was not an option. There was only so much female conversation that Richard could take. So he approached it as a solvable problem and went out of his way to learn things that were of interest to Bob. They got to the point where Bob obviously enjoyed having conversations with him—stuff on guns, Bureau politics, G. K. Chesterton, foreign policy. Opus Dei was the only subject Richard skirted; he did not like Opus Dei.

On balance, Richard liked being with the family. There might be six kids in the house all at once on holidays, but there was harmony. They might squabble, but Richard never saw any flare-outs of hatred between brothers or sisters. They were truly a fine Catholic family. Richard came from a very different family situation—also Catholic, but with what you might call colder tendencies. So Richard loved being part of the Hanssens. It was not exactly as if he was marrying up, but he was marrying well, and he did adore Jane. In time, he came to respect Bob quite a bit—for his intellect, for his strong family feeling, and for his deep sense of privacy.

Bonnie was another matter. She was a little bossy. She could turn out to be a classic mother-in-law. He hoped not.

"Don't let Bonnie know how much I paid for the tires on Jane's car," Bob said to Richard in a whisper as Bonnie came down the stairs. She walked toward them with a look on her face that Richard recognized. You could call it "Battle Stations."

"Jane just told me," she said to Bob, "that you bought her four new Goodyear tires. She is ecstatic, and that is lovely. But, Bob, didn't you say that we have to tighten our belt these days, what with the wedding and all?"

"Bonnie, it was a fantastic sale."

Bonnie didn't have to watch television. The look she gave both of them was straight out of a sitcom.

"Richard, what did those tires cost?"

It was his turn in the barrel now. He was ready. "Bonnie, you won't believe it," he said to her, "but they were ten dollars apiece—forty dollars. This was a once-in-a-lifetime sale!"

Bonnie looked confused. "I hope I can believe that."

"Believe it," Bob said. "Richard doesn't lie."

The living room was jammed. Jane was in her wedding gown hiding upstairs, not wanting Richard to see her in it before the ceremony. Everyone else was all decked out in finery. Bonnie, dressed elegantly, was beautiful, and when Bob came walking down the stairs, he was dressed in a tuxedo. He did look awfully good—tall, and you could even say suave.

"Look, girls," Bonnie said. "There's my James Bond."

The family was toasting the newlyweds at the dinner table.

"God has never given me a cross larger than I can bear," Bonnie told Richard. She was slightly tipsy. "Sometimes I wish I had one, because it does make me nervous thinking about how perfect my life has been." She took his hand. "May your life with Jane be as perfect."

7

1995

Bonnie and Bob were in a marina and walking down to the middle of a wharf.

"Bob, why did you agree to go on this man's boat today? He's in television. He's a television man."

"Trust me, Bonnie. I have my reasons."

"How many times have you said, 'FBI men must stay away from all the media people. No exceptions.' You always say that."

Hanssen shrugged. He was about to let her remark pass in silence, but then he whispered as they started up a gangplank. "Over the last couple of years I've had lunch with this fellow several times. He's a respected writer, and he does consultation and investigative work for ABC. Bonnie, I'd like to get a few ideas across to this fellow. That could eventually find its way onto the air. Important ideas. It's sad but true. His people have the power to sway the American people's thinking."

It was a well-kept powerboat, about forty feet long. *Safehouse* was its name.

Hanssen, Bonnie, and the television man were sitting on the aft deck. The hired captain was up on the bridge. Food and soft drinks were spread out.

"I'm surprised you're so neutral," Bonnie was saying. "Planned Parenthood is a worldwide conspiracy." The TV man, James Bamford, had written a bestselling book, *Body of Secrets,* about the top-secret National Security Agency. His interest was not really in Planned Parenthood.

"I don't hear many people talking about it," he replied.

"The U.N. groups do all the time," Bonnie went on. "They could be behind that frightful Chinese policy of limiting births to one per family."

Bamford was accommodating. "Well, yes . . . but you know, some people do feel the Chinese have a population problem."

"I can't agree. Bob says there's enough room in Texas for everyone alive," she said. "I just don't see how Hillary Clinton dares to go over to Beijing and give the U.S. imprimatur to the U.N.'s conference on women."

"You can't trust either one of the Clintons," Bob offered. "They'd sell this country acre by acre to advance their own political agenda."

Bamford kept himself from giving any indication of what he was thinking, which was: *Whatever have I gotten into?*

The following week, the phone rang in Hanssen's office. He picked it up.

"Hello, is this Mr. Hanssen?"

"Speaking."

"This is Priscilla Galey's mother."

"It is? . . . Yes?"

"Mr. Hanssen—something awful has happened. Priscilla is in the lockup."

He took his time. "Well . . . what about?"

"They claim she was helping someone sell drugs. But, Mr. Hanssen, she didn't. Not a bit."

"How did she get into a situation like that?"

"She got involved with a man. The one selling drugs." She hesitated. "Can you . . . help her?"

Hanssen was silent for a while. Finally, he said, "She made her bed. I think she will have to lie in it."

He hung up the phone. Gently. But his stomach had turned sour on him.

Jack Hoschouer was now retired from the military and back in D.C. for a couple of weeks, working hard on his dissertation at the Library of Congress. As usual on these visits, he was staying at the Hanssens' house. One night when everyone else had gone to bed, he and Bob were sitting in their favorite corner.

"I'm ready to join Bonnie," Hanssen said at last.

"I'm ready to turn in, too," Jack said.

"Want to watch tonight?"

"Twist my wrist."

"What did you think of last night's show?"

"Exceptional," said Jack.

"Ever seen anything as gorgeous as my woman? Twenty-seven years of marriage and she still looks like a bathing beauty."

"She *is* beautiful."

"What did you like the most?"

"It was all interesting."

"No, what was most interesting?"

"You really like to pull it out of a guy, don't you?" He smiled. "I'd say it was when Bonnie got on top."

Bob whinnied. "I know exactly what you're saying. It's when she's facing the camera."

"Yes."

"Tonight I'll get around into the same position."

"I'll salute," said Jack.

The next day, before lunch, Hanssen was talking to Walter Ballou. "Clinton has a narcissistic personality disorder coupled with megalomania," he said.

"Watch out, Bob," said Walter. "A judge will never forgive you for a crime he's capable of committing himself."

"If you think I'm going to say 'Touché,' my friend,

287

you are way off base. A man with a narcissistic personality disorder can still be in love with a woman who has a paranoid personality disorder. Bill and Hillary."

That evening, as Bob drove out of the Bureau garage, he noticed that a good number of lights were on up at the seventh floor. He knew that three very high officials were consulting with one another that evening, and he had a pretty good idea of what they were talking about. In any case, he would be able to read the minutes of the meeting in the morning.

"Gentlemen," the first official said. "I've got to report to Mr. Freeh and he will be talking to the president. So, what are the probabilities now, post–Aldrich Ames. Are we rid of the moles?"

"I'd say there's got to be at least one more in the CIA," the second official said. "And I have to add, it's not impossible that we have one here. We had some odd losses a couple of years ago—every time we deployed a new collection device in the field, the Russian countermeasures team found it. And then a couple of our best moles were lost."

The three officials were silent, as if trying to catch the sound of a mole gnawing away, gnawing away. Hanssen could hear and feel that conference all the way home in his car.

In a modest restaurant, Hanssen and the television man, James Bamford, were having lunch. Bamford was eating a fancy salad. Hanssen had a hamburger. It was what he always ordered. Lunch was for hamburgers.

Hanssen enjoyed hearing Bamford talk about what he was doing. Also, he kind of liked being one of the journalist's sources. In the past, they'd talked about Felix Bloch, a State Department employee who had spied for and then defected to Russia. Hanssen had helped Bamford on that story.

Now Bob asked: "How did your trip to Moscow go?"

"On balance, it was successful. I was able to interview Viktor Cherkashin."

"Cherkashin? The famous KGB man? The one here in Washington who used to handle Aldrich Ames?"

"That's the guy," Bamford said.

"Tell you anything?"

"Not a word about Rick Ames. Which, I confess, was frustrating."

"You're saying Cherkashin did not make a single slip?"

"He's an old hand. 'I can't tell you whether we have spies,' Cherkashin would say to me. 'Obviously, we do our best to do a very good job.'"

"He didn't reminisce about moles he handled?" Hanssen asked.

"Just general stuff," Bamford replied.

"I'd love to see the transcript of his interview."

"Can't do that. Network rules. We don't show transcripts to non-employees, Bob. Anyway, there was nothing real dramatic in it."

Once in a while, the Hanssen children were allowed to watch an animated show or movie on video. The latest treat happened to be the Disney movie *The Fox and the Hound,* which Bonnie assumed would be innocent enough—it was Disney, after all. But it went wrong. Bob happened to come in while the two youngest, Greg and Lisa, were watching, and he only needed one look at the screen to turn it off.

"Why, Dad, why?" asked Greg. The boy looked about to become frustrated.

Bonnie was in the room before things got too heated, but Bob was ready to state his objections.

"Think about it. The male fox and the female fox are lying down side by side. Yet the kids know that they're not married."

"Well, Bob, after all . . ." Bonnie began.

Greg even got into it. "Dad," he said. "They're animals. They're not supposed to get married."

"That's not the point," said Bob. "You kids look at animals as if they are human. And these cartoons exaggerate that similarity. I don't want you looking at sewage like that."

No argument. Done.

Every time Hoschouer came to D.C. he stayed at Bob's. Their arrangement had gotten predictable. The others—the girls, the boys, and Bonnie—would go to bed; Jack and Bob would sit up and reminisce.

After a while, the mood would sometimes shift. Sometimes not. On many a visit nothing would happen. But every now and again, the silences would grow longer. Anticipation would stir. It was as if, each time, it had to happen out of a fresh understanding—as if Jack was being invited to look at the TV for the first time. And, in fact, even when they were ready, it didn't always happen. Sometimes Bonnie would not wake up in a reasonable mood—the sleeping capsules could prove more powerful than Bob's attentions. But usually it worked.

On this night, talk veered off in a new direction. Bob got personal in a different way.

"Jack," he asked, "if you were ever in bed with Bonnie, what would you be doing?"

Hoschouer said, "I'm not the man in the bed, Bob."

"No, but I know you well enough to be sure you've been having a few ideas."

"Do we have to talk about this?" asked Jack. It just wasn't the night for Bob to push the envelope.

"Yes, we can. It's arousing to talk. Jack, I am asking you flat out: What would you do with Bonnie?"

"I might not even touch her," Jack said. "It could put a bad dent in my friendship with you."

"No it wouldn't, Jack. Because I will tell you the

truth: I would like to see you making love to Bonnie."

That called for a special silence. They could hear each other breathing.

"You would?" Jack said at last.

Bob was not embarrassed. Not at all. "I'll tell you this," he said. "I wish Bonnie could have your baby. That is how close I feel to you."

"You're forgetting," said Jack quickly, "that this baby has to grow up."

"Jack, I would be a great father to that child. I've always felt for you because your marriage is childless. It'd be wonderful for you to have a son. In secret, of course."

Were they living on the craters of the moon? "This is ridiculous," Jack said. "Bonnie would never go to bed with me."

Hanssen was smiling. "Have you ever heard of Rohypnol?"

"No," said Jack.

"It's a new date-rape drug in Europe. From what I've heard, Rohypnol takes away all the internal inhibitions. It's supposed to be amazing. We could slip a small amount to Bonnie."

In these conversations, Jack always came to realize that his feelings, like it or not, were divided. No matter how much he thought that he didn't want to buy into any of Bob's schemes, there was always the other part of him that did say yes. And Bonnie, courtesy of Bob's closed-circuit TV, had gotten damn attractive.

"Where is this drug sold?" he asked at last.

"The Netherlands. Once you're back in Europe, why don't you try to pick it up?"

After Jack returned to his home in Germany, Bob sent him a copy of a story he had written and posted on the Internet. With no dead drop to distract him these days, he did that from time to time. He liked using the names Bob and Bonnie for his characters. If someone in the FBI ever picked it up on the Internet, he could claim that tricky, evil, unspeakable people were trying to destroy him. That would be a game to play!

Bonnie sat [Bob wrote] freshly showered and still naked, in the warm summer light which streamed through her apartment's large bedroom window . . . it was time for her to fix her hair. Her little ritual, a time to fix herself all pretty for Bob. Bonnie looked gorgeous, but she saw only the flaws. Bonnie wanted to be pencil-skinny like those models in the women's fashion magazines, but she looked more like those slutty buxom girls in Playboy *magazine.*

Still naked, Bonnie was trying her hair in different ways. When she looked out the window, there were five workers leaning on their shovels looking at her. In a panic, she tried to grab the shade and pull it down, but this move necessitated her standing stark naked on the bed to reach up for the shade-pull. There she was, in full view of her suddenly-bemused audience. Then the shade flapped up again. She sprung back, her cute little bush fully exposed, and again the shade flipped open.

The men were looking right at her and she was totally naked. It seemed like forever while Bonnie stood in that window, trying to unroll the shade, but she got it finally.

Bonnie felt galvanized from the experience. If only Bob were here, she thought. I'd show him even a better time than the workers on those tracks.

Jack sent an e-mail back, using their special encryption: *"You told me that story close to thirty years ago. You're unbelievable."*

Hanssen wrote back: *"Isn't it time for a visit?"*

* * *

A couple of months later, when Jack was in D.C. again, Bob asked him if he had gotten to the Netherlands.

"I did," said Jack.

"Pick up any Rohypnol?"

"I was near the Dutch border," said Jack, "so, yes, I did get on my bike and cross over to the nearest border town. Just a small town—nothing like Amsterdam. I didn't see any characters selling anything, and there was not much to do. So I rode back."

"That's it? All of it?" asked Bob.

"Let's drop the idea," Jack said.

Sometimes it got to Richard how much control and super-control you had to cope with in the Hanssen family. He would wonder how much it had to do with Opus Dei. Jane kept telling him that she'd had very pleasant experiences at Oakcrest, the Opus Dei high school she went to, and it helped to form her life, but Richard had had the exact opposite experience. His father was devout, and damn if he hadn't sent Richard one summer to an Opus Dei day camp, and that had been a misery. They could exercise you all morning under a hot sun and never allow you to take a drink. The counselors were numeraries, Opus Dei men who had taken a vow of celibacy, and they were gung ho on character formation. Richard had never met a bigger bunch of intense guys who needed to go on a date. Remarkable zealots, they really believed they were forming an army to fight a cultural war in America. In principle, it was difficult to argue with Opus Dei's idea that you should be a better person, a better Christian, but in practice, they attracted a compulsive type of personality who needed exactly that kind of heavy order in their day to help get through it.

If much of that spirit could often be found in Bonnie, there was even more of it in her mother, Frances Wauck, who was totally committed to Opus Dei. He happened to meet Frances in the kitchen of Bonnie's house, and there she was rearranging Bonnie's kitchen drawers. He couldn't believe it. Bonnie was a fifty-year-old woman, and her mother was explaining to her how she had not done it correctly.

Then Bonnie started in on Jane. Richard and Jane had just moved into their newlywed apartment when Bonnie came over to rearrange the furniture. They had it all wrong, she let them know. Control was such a big issue for Bonnie that Richard actually had to tell her, "You've got to stop commenting on how Jane's hair is cut. We're adults now. We're married."

This kind of micromanaging had its offshoots. The only time Jane could remember her father speaking to any of the children in a loud voice or spanking them was when they were rude to Bonnie. Her word was law.

That carried over to church in the weirdest way. The family always sat in the front row, but they certainly weren't making any show with money. The collection plate was still empty by the time it got to the second row. Richard couldn't decide if they were giving the money privately or if they were just above it all. For instance, they couldn't be bothered with making the sign of peace at Mass. No need to turn around and hug and kiss your neighbor. Bob disapproved of that. It disrupted the sanctity of prayer. And none of this neutralizing of gender, changing "Our Father in Heaven" to "Our God in Heaven." None of this face-to-face, person-to-person stuff that Vatican II had inaugurated.

8

1997

On the day Earl Pitts was arrested, the shock wave that rippled through the FBI was even larger than the one that took place when Aldrich Ames was caught. Ames was CIA—one could expect them to have such disasters. But Pitts was in Counterintelligence at the Bureau, and since 1991 had been responsible for supervising personal security investigations of FBI employees.

Hanssen and Pitts had first crossed paths in New York City, but never became friends. In D.C. both were Supervisory Special Agents, and when Bob returned from his duties on the inspection staff, his office was just five doors down the hall from Pitts's. They used the same elevator and men's room.

Bob, in the absence of a Soviet threat, had first been moved to Chief of the Economic Espionage Unit, known as the National Security Threat Office (before Kimberly Lichtenberg, that is), and by 1994, he was relegated to solving technical problems with teletype processing at the Washington Field Office while he retained his GS-15 ranking. In 1995 he was detailed to serve as the FBI's senior representative to the Office of Foreign Missions over at the State Department, where he even had an office these days, but he was still out of the action. But that morning he came over to the Bureau to talk to Shepard and Ballou about Earl Pitts.

295

"He worked right down the hall," one or another of them kept saying.

"Too creepy," said Ballou.

"I've heard he's a bit of a sexual kook," said Hanssen. "That could account for it."

It was good that Bob didn't hear the interrogation of Pitts or the reaction of two of the investigators.

"Pitts is going to give me a migraine," said the first.

"Doesn't he satisfy our mole problem?"

"I was hoping he would, but he keeps insisting there is another mole in the Bureau besides himself."

The second official said, "Are we supposed to take his word for it?"

"Of course not. But Pitts keeps complaining that the Russians treated him casually."

"They don't throw anyone away."

"It's possible the Russians were protecting a more important asset right in our midst."

In a closed room with no windows and a steel door, Pitts sat on one side of a desk. Two interrogators, sitting side by side, were facing him.

"Of course I'm a throwaway!" said Pitts.

"Have any idea who they might be protecting?" asked one of the interrogators.

Pitts took his time to answer. "I'd say Robert Hanssen."

"Hanssen?" said the other interrogator. "Why him?"

"Call it sheer animal instinct."

When the interview was finished, one of the interrogators said to the other, "I wouldn't trust Pitts as far as I could throw him."

The second man agreed. "I don't think we should even pass this on. It would tear the Bureau up if Bob is suspected. The very idea of Hanssen . . . that is real nonsense!"

"It's worse than nonsense. It's nauseating. If there is another mole, he's got to be in the CIA."

That Sunday, as always, the Hanssens were driving in their van along a small paved road toward Saint Catherine of Siena Church in Great Falls, Virginia.

All the children were with them, plus Richard, who had come along with Jane.

Bob had to drive very carefully on this road, because everywhere around him people were jogging, rollerblading, riding bikes. Bonnie, sitting next to him, was vociferous about it.

"What are all those people doing with themselves? They ought to be in church."

"I could run them over for you," said Bob.

"I know you think it's a joke," she said, "but that's not funny for the children."

I get up at five in the morning, he was saying to himself. Perhaps it was the reflection in the windshield, but he felt as if he were speaking silently to the mirror. *I shower, shave, dress, drive to church. I go to Mass, grab a quick breakfast, then go to work. I come home, eat dinner, go to bed at nine-thirty, make love or don't make love, sleep or don't sleep, and get up the next morning at five. I'm devoted to routine. This may not be enough. I think I would like to run those joggers down.*

That gave way to other thoughts. In his mind, he was speaking on television. In fact, he was holding the attention of a large audience. He decided he was about as good as any religious speaker he had ever heard.

I want to live my life, he said to that TV audience, *so that every single thing I do is for the greater glory of God. Do I wish to have a glass of water because I am thirsty? No! I will wait, and mortify myself. Thereby I will come closer to the great thirst of our Lord Jesus Christ when they put Him on the cross.*

He closed his eyes for a moment, then opened them before he almost sideswiped a passing car—just in time to keep Bonnie from crying. The incident was not about to put a dent in his reverie. *Folks,* he continued, *is it not possible that someone can continue to sin for many years, knowing all the while that he can make it right in the end?* He laughed aloud, startling all the others in the van, and went right back to the audience in his head. *Uh-oh, watch it, boys and girls. I feel drawn to spying again. It's been seven lean years, as the Bible says. Remind me of the prayer of Saint Augustine: "God, make me good—but not yet." Thank you, you stupid TV audience. You maggots. You larvae!*

He roared with laughter and continued to drive. Bonnie turned around and signaled to the children with her eyes: *Let's not make anything of this.*

Much later that day, long after church, and after Bonnie's Sunday dinner, he was still alone with himself in a far-off mood:

Deep down I've always seen myself as a warrior—yet here in this house, I serve as a nanny. Since Bonnie does most of the work, you could say I am a lazy nanny. The kids are terrific. She has done a marvelous job, and I have done a good one. In my fashion. All the same, life eats at me. I want to spy once more. I do. A brain surgeon continues to be a brain surgeon because very few people can do it. Where is the spy who could equal the job I used to do? Who else could equal me as a phenomenon?

He stayed up late thinking about a movie he'd just seen with Catherine Zeta-Jones. She had been wearing a skintight black outfit while Sean Connery taught her how to be a cat burglar. A little later into the early morning, while he was in the bathroom, he kept looking at a

298

photo of Catherine Zeta-Jones he held in his hand while gripping the Walther PPK in the other. To the face in the mirror, that perfect reverse of his own face, he said:

"If only I had had Catherine Zeta-Jones by my side. Brother to James Bond. Brothers forever." His mind wandered. He said: *"Evil has its own energies. It is not the absence of good. It is a lively presence. I know. Evil is exciting."*

When at last he went to bed, his sleep was a montage. Nothing but broken dreams. Jack was in bed with Bonnie, while Bob crouched in a corner beating his dummy. He watched and he watched. He whipped the dummy to lathers in his dream. Then Jane and Sue were in the back of the car and Bob had his arm in a cast. The girls were screaming, "I want a sports car, I want a sports car, I want, I want!" He saw FBI agents and Russian officers marching to Wagnerian music. On came "The Ride of the Valkyries," then "The Fest March" from *Tannhäuser*. He saw his father in peasant garb. Howard could have been at a feast arranged by Hieronymus Bosch. Howard was surrounded by demons. Then he rose up in the middle of them, his face distorted, and screamed: "I'm not as dead as you think! I love you!" Bob woke up. His throat was full of phlegm.

In the morning, at six A.M. mass, he was on his knees, praying powerfully. Indeed, no one could pray as powerfully as Bob Hanssen. At one point he began to sob. People turned their heads to look at him. He didn't care. He raised his head as if to defy them and saw his face reflected in the gold of a chalice. That was enough of a mirror for his mind to speak.

I am in a dark forest, and no longer do I know where danger is lurking. All I know is that I must go back to spying. That is the only reply to the oppression of my demons.

His thoughts stopped. His sobs began again. He had to control them before he could look again at his reflection in the chalice.

Will I pay a terrible price? Am I in danger of hating God? Why is He so unwilling to release me from my demons?

He continued to rock back and forth.

9

1998–1999

A few days later, he found himself writing pornographic accounts of sex with Bonnie. On June 5, he posted them in a newsgroup on the Internet.

His first piece was a rewrite, with embellishments and exaggerations, of the story he had sent months before to Jack Hoschouer. It was about the two hard hats who had seen Bonnie naked back in 1968, when her window shade flew up and she couldn't get it down and so, out of necessity, kept exposing herself. This time, for his story, Bonnie gave five workers a show, and he had her strutting around for them.

The second piece was a close description of Bonnie's body parts as Jack had seen them on the closed-circuit TV in their house. Hanssen used their real first names. It was all about Bonnie, Bob, and Jack.

If there was even one Special Agent in the FBI who happened to log on to that Internet newsgroup and knew Bob Hanssen, he would, given the investigative resources available, be able to trace the porn offering back to Bob's computer. Hanssen would not be able to make the claim that someone unknown to him was trying to sabotage his reputation in the Bureau.

Nonetheless, Bob went ahead. It was not unlike spying. The act gave him some measure of peace. The demons went to ground. He knew that if any of this was

301

discovered, it would enrage Bonnie, yet, somehow, that seemed beside the point. He loved her, but as he knew, he could betray her. So what? In his own way he did care for the FBI, yet he was ready to betray them, too. Sometimes, when alone in his car, he would hum "You always hurt / the one you love, / the one you should treat best of all." He had to laugh. The song was old and so corny, but he sang it, anyway. He was in a good mood. Nothing had ever come back to haunt him from those two postings on the Internet. And it helped to keep him from thinking that sooner or later he must go back to spying again. Coming up on the horizon soon would be the need for more money.

Once in a while, he would log on just to look at his contribution on Porn Star. He loved reading the hard sell at the end. It went:

> *If you liked this one, you're gonna LOVE "Exhibitionists' Haven" at http://www.netcom.com/ -ntrtainr/showoff4me.html. The site features TRUE, sent-in stories (and even some REAL wives' pictures) submitted by their husbands and boyfriends who LOVE to have their wives showoff for other people!*
>
> *Your Adult Check password will get you into this TOTALLY FREE and VERY popular site, now with over 190 stories.*

10

1999

He knew he could not trust his frame of mind, but he had kept on a reasonably even keel for months. Then he began to feel the gradual return of what he thought of as "the uncontrollables."

They took so many forms—not only the demons, but the migraines tortured him. Pornography or spying relieved him. And when he wished to avoid all of that, he came closer all the time to his last resort. Depression became his last resort.

He felt closer to that condition every day.

On impulse, he went to have a sandwich with Mike Shepard and was surprised by how glad he was to see him. Mike, by now, was retired. He had become the chief guru of a think tank he had started to which the FBI and the CIA now sent many of their people. The idea had really worked, Shepard explained. Counterintelligence, if you looked at it objectively, was often a sorry history of egregious mistakes made by its practitioners. So much was speculation. That was in the very nature of the business. It was too easy, then, to get lost in false premises. How, then, could you teach it in-house at the Agency or the Bureau? You would have to name names while pointing out the big and little boo-boos of people who were now running the works. So, as a safe play, both organizations sent their students to Shepard. He, being retired, could afford to name those names.

That proved to be a lively conversation for Bob and Mike, but by the second hour of their lunch, Hanssen could feel himself sagging again. "You look down in the mouth, Bob," Mike said.

What was the use of pretending? "I am a little depressed," he said. "I was feeling pretty good last year, but my assignment at the State Department is finally getting to me. I'm tired of checking out the petty shenanigans of foreign diplomats."

"Why don't you consider retirement?" Mike said with a full share of enthusiasm. "Bob, recognize your worth. You are losing money every day that you keep working for the FBI. You could make twice as much out here in the real world."

"I guess I could."

For a moment, Shepard considered offering a job to Hanssen, but he reined himself in. The opening salary would have to be large, and besides, Bob was too gloomy to be a good teacher. So Mike said nothing more about it.

Hanssen looked a little more depressed.

His mood picked up, however, that night. Jack was there, and after dinner they began to talk about politics. He seemed to enjoy this more and more. In the old days, the best part of Jack's visits with Bob, aside from the extracurricular events, often came down to the good but simple pleasure they took in each other's company. They were such old friends when all was said. They could sit in the living room for an hour or more at a time without a word. If the book either one happened to be reading proved particularly interesting, then he might read a passage aloud to the other. Time spent together was that easy, except, of course, for the extracurriculars, which were off the chart.

Yet now, over the last couple of years, a new element had entered their conversation. Bob had been getting more and more right-wing, and Jack, who saw himself as somewhere on the cusp between liberal and conservative, was beginning to look upon the more extreme of Bob's ideas as probably related to his increasing trouble with blood pressure. Whatever the cause, they were certainly beginning to have some pretty intense discussions.

Bob, for instance, was convinced that with the Cold War at an end, Soviet Communism was now being reconstituted in more palatable, and therefore more deadly, forms among American liberals, who were being motivated to drain the strength of American free enterprise. They were doing this by every means at their disposal. He often got pretty obsessive about Cuba and would even speak of Castro as a deadly threat, but as Jack saw it, you could still attempt to argue with him.

"Come on," Jack would say, "you don't really think we should invade Cuba again, do you?"

"What you don't see," Bob would reply, "is that their threat is real. There is a linkup between Fidel and American liberals. He imparts his virus to them."

"Give me a break," Jack would say. "Maybe Castro still believes in the final triumph of Communism, but he's no threat to the United States. Certainly not in any physical sense."

"The real threat," Bob said, "comes from the ideological rot Castro implants in us. The Clinton administration is the vehicle, and Castro has his hand on the wheel. He loves everything the liberals are doing. All that garbage about global warming, all those mushy international conferences and those insidious U.N. initiatives are designed to destroy big business and bring down the United States."

"Are you going to argue that big business is always on the good side of everything that happens here?"

Hanssen nodded. "Yes. Big business is a good thing."

"Unconditionally so?"

"Always."

"Like the tobacco companies, for instance?"

"Why not?"

"Come on, Bob. If the tobacco companies knew that their product was poisonous, then they are morally out of line to sell cigarettes without warning. And the internal documents the courts had to pry out of them show that they damn well knew."

"So what? If people choose to smoke, that's that. We have a right to poison ourselves. Under everything, this is a primitive conspiracy on the part of Socialists and people who think like Socialists, to screw big business."

All right, he had been talking that way for the last four or five years. But these days he was going further.

"When people do evil or bad things, or commit crimes," Bob said now, "the best treatment is to tromp on them with both feet."

"Without respect for the rules of evidence, I suppose?"

"Well, there you've got it," said Bob. "Basically, that is the fruit of the poison tree. The exclusionary principle."

"You're not serious?"

"Absolutely, I am. If, by chance, a cop asks a driver for his license, and happens to see drugs in the car, the cop can't arrest the driver. Why? Because he didn't have reason to suspect any drugs in the car."

"Cops violate that principle all the time."

"Maybe so, but in fact, the perp often gets away with it later in court. The exclusionary rule of evidence is nothing but a legalistic tool for liberals. It enables them to put handcuffs on the police. Why, the Bureau can't even use a wiretap unless we follow an unbelievable rigmarole. One restrictive rule after another. That can get to you. I tell you, it brings out the Stalinist in me."

"I agree with you. You sound like a Stalinist. What do you want—a society where the government is able to look into everything and know everything?"

"Perfect."

"What are you saying?"

"I want a society that's transparent. Completely transparent. So we can figure out in advance who is going to commit a crime and catch him before he does it."

"Bob, just about every cop thinks about it once in a while. But they give up on the thought. They're sensible enough to realize that it's too easy to misuse that kind of power. You're looking to bring down on us the worst excesses of banana republic dictatorships."

"No," said Bob. "We just need people who are properly and morally trained."

Jack began to feel as if there would soon be no point in talking to him at all.

Then the family went to Rome in 1999. He felt as if the trip had rescued him. For four years, the Wauck family had been planning it. Leroy Wauck's son John had entered his Opus Dei seminary in 1995 to study to be an Opus Dei priest. In 1999 he would graduate. Since Opus Dei was a special prelature under the guidance of Pope John Paul II, John Wauck would be ordained in Rome by the pope himself. For the Wauck family, it was as close as a Catholic could come to Nirvana. They would now have a commando in the special forces of God's most sacred army, endorsed and honored by the pope himself.

So, over they went to Rome that spring, the entire family—Frances and Leroy Wauck and all of Bonnie's brothers and sisters, with their wives and husbands and children. Bob took pains to put it up on his family website with photographs of all the Waucks and Hanssens and shots of the ordination, of Rome, shots of the Vatican, and passing shots of little events on the trip. It proved to be a pretty thorough assemblage, and it was available to everyone in the family, and to friends of the Waucks and the Hanssens, to look upon at their leisure.

Bob and Bonnie were the only ones to go over and return in first class. Leroy and Frances had come up with the airfare for all the other travelers, but something curious happened to the tickets for Robert and Bonnie Hanssen (who was traveling on this occasion as "Bernadette" Hanssen). It seems the travel agency had made a mistake. Somehow or other, the Hanssens had been given first class. None of the Waucks quite believed it, which is why they would always refer to it as "the mistake."

For Bob, it had been awfully important to travel in style. To Bonnie, Rome was Mecca. She regarded John Paul II as a saint. As Bob saw it, he could give a little nudge to heaven and earth, make all of it a special experience for Bonnie. He even chalked up his decision to spy again as a need for some more dollars. He did do the trip in style with her.

At the time, Leroy, Frances, and the rest of the Wauck family hardly knew what to make of it. Bob had always been grumbling about his situation, but now he was spending money. First class! Who ever heard of a travel agency making that kind of mistake? His in-laws found it hard to believe.

On balance, however, the trip was close to perfect for Bonnie. She felt that she could look upon her life as fulfilled. Nothing could compare to the occasion, with the exception, of course, of the birth of Jane—that miracle! The only flaw had been a small one. She did return with a few complaints about the moral decay of some of the Italian people she had met in Rome.

Bob had been living for years with one ongoing concern. Ever since Aldrich Ames's debriefing began in 1994, there was a danger that some little fact might lead the Bureau to his doorstep. Now that the FBI's Automatic Case Support (ACS) database system was up and running, it wasn't difficult for Bob to search its contents for words or terms that related to his activities with the Soviets. His use of the system was authorized. If his name or some name related to his operational locations came up, he would know whether he was in danger of being exposed.

Back in July of 1997, he ran the name "Hanssen" and "Robert P. Hanssen" for the first time. Nothing came up. Every so often he looked for words like "dead drop and KGB" or "dead drop and Russia," or he ran the name of the street he now lived on. Still, nothing came up.

Just before and right after he returned from Rome, he ran his list of names again. The search results showed nothing. He was clean.

One afternoon, Bob paid a visit back to the fourth floor and walked down the corridor, Coke in hand, shaking hands with some, smiling at others. All the while he could hear the voice in his head. Was that voice getting to the point where it could dispense with the mirror?

If I spy, escape would be easy. I've got my passport. Now that I've been to Rome, I see how easy it is. I could go to Vienna. From Vienna, Virginia, to Vienna, Austria.

He paused to enjoy the laughter within himself. But it did not come. It wouldn't work. He would have to leave the kids behind. *Only the demons will travel with me,* he told himself, and then declared, *What the hell. Come what may, I am resuming contact with the Russkies. I hope the new batch is as good as the old ones got to be. Once they learned how to deal with Mr. Garcia.*

He could see it all in advance. He could hear the Russian voice: *We express our sincere joy on the occasion of resumption of contact with you. More communication will follow.*

By October 1999, he was back in business. Two months before the millennium, he took up contact with the SVR in Washington. But now he was cautious about it and so were they. It was not at all like the old KGB days when he was making a drop every three or four weeks. Now he arranged for only one in 1999 and but a couple in the year 2000. Minor material if you got down to it—a few small-fry in the SVR who were working for the U.S. and a few confidential papers that came his way at the State Department. The old excitement was hardly there. He did like, however, walking in as the FBI's State Department liaison when there was an occasional conference at the Bureau on the possibility of a mole still lurking in the woodwork. One time, to his enjoyment, there was a mirror behind the other side of the table, and he couldn't take his eyes off himself. Sometimes his lips would quiver just a little. Once in a while one of the other officials might wonder: Is Hanssen developing a facial tic?

Here we are discussing how to catch our mole while all the while I am the one they really want. This is an intense stimulation for me. Sometimes it even feels like a captain's paradise. The demons do seem far away.

One Saturday, Bob told Bonnie that he was going to a gun show, but instead, on impulse, he drove all the way to a town with an airfield, in the western part of Virginia. Once there, he went up with a pilot in a two-seater plane and took a quick lesson, which even gave him a shot at the controls. All the way back in his car, he was exhilarated, and his mind began to play with the thought that if there was ever a crisis that called for a quick getaway, he might be able to steal a light plane and fly it all the way down across the border to Mexico. He'd have to make a couple of landings for gas, of course, but he could probably pull that off.

As a practical possibility, the idea got heavier and heavier the more he thought about it. By the time he was home, he had given up the notion.

11

2000

In Moscow, one-third of the distance around the world, Cherkashin and Shebarshin were in a bar commiserating over their vodka.

"You remember? Back in '91?" Cherkashin was saying. "Everyone here was saying, 'KGB is a barbarous organization.' It was not a pleasure to hear."

"It still angers me," Shebarshin replied.

"All right, let's admit it—Soviet gulags were not so good, but our KGB Intelligence was never close to gulags. In America, do they go up to CIA people and say, 'How about black people you torture in your prison system?' The CIA would look at you as if you were crazy."

"There used to be honor and order in our Intelligence. High standards," Shebarshin noted.

"Before perestroika."

"Yes. And after perestroika came that big pack of robbers with their fat tongue in Yeltsin's ear. Stole everything."

"Banks, industry, trust," Cherkashin said.

"A wolf pack," Shebarshin said. He put his hand over his mouth to muffle the next few words. "Even our KGB archive was rifled."

"Our archive! What was stolen?"

"No need to ask," Shebarshin said. "We know. It had to be valuable stuff. Somebody who said to himself,

'Whenever I am ready to make ten million dollars, this archive will be my passport to America.'"

"Is it possible that material on Ramon Garcia was stolen?"

"I would expect as much," Shebarshin said.

Walter Ballou, in a conference with a top FBI official, learned that during the Bureau's latest mole hunt, a CIA agent had purchased materials from a former high Soviet official.

"One of the items," said the FBI agent, "is a dark green plastic garbage bag that—hard to believe—was actually kept in the Moscow Center archive. It has a couple of latent fingerprints on it. The bag is in the lab right now. The other items are unique. We have a rarity—a complete dossier. Original documents, letters, locations of dead drops, computer disks, all the details of an ongoing espionage relationship that went on from 1985 to the fall of the Soviet in 1991. All done by a man who calls himself 'Ramon.' We even have the tape of a phone conversation that took place between Ramon and a KGB Intelligence officer who we've already determined is Aleksandr Fefelov, who, you may remember, worked in D.C. during that period."

"Is the tape clear enough to get a voice identification of this 'Ramon'?" Walter asked.

"Clear enough. Our lab people say they can remove most of the background noise. You're one of three men we're putting on this."

By the next day, Walter Ballou had learned a lot. He considered it a tribute to twenty years of professional work that he was not bouncing off the walls of a padded room. All the same, as he talked to the senior agent who had given him the assignment, he had to stay in control of his voice.

"The lab states," Walter said, "that there is a one

hundred percent certainty that the fingerprints on the dark green plastic bag belong to Bob Hanssen."

"No variables possible?"

"It is conceivable that the prints were lifted from a glass, let's say, that Hanssen was holding and then were transferred to the plastic bag."

"Do you consider this likely?"

"Technically speaking, it is difficult, but it can be done."

"You worked with Hanssen for years?"

"Yes."

"Is it fair to say that you don't want it to be Hanssen?"

"I can't begin to calculate the damage this will do to Bureau morale," said Walter. "If I were working for the Soviets and said to myself, 'Who is the best FBI man for us to discredit?' I would certainly choose Hanssen."

On the other hand, left to himself, Walter had a serious problem with one remark in the KGB's files. He felt a detectable drop in his stomach when he read it. Ramon had told the Soviets that he didn't like procedures because they caused rules. *"Rules,"* Ramon then said, *"create patterns and patterns, are detectable."* That sounded like Hanssen. It was the way he talked in conference to cut off opposition. Short, concise, power-packed.

Over the next couple of days, they went back and forth in conferences. At one point, the mole hunter from the seventh floor said, "See if you can find even one item that would prove that Bob Hanssen cannot be Ramon Garcia."

"What if I can't?" Walter asked.

"Then get together every bit of evidence we can find that pinpoints him. Be able to prove it beyond any doubt. Otherwise, we could end up with a Free Bob Hanssen committee demonstrating in the street."

Walter continued his probe. By the time of their final conference, he was certain. "Look," he told the man from the seventh floor. "I've got to unburden myself. We

313

cleaned up the tape that we have of Fefelov talking to Ramon Garcia. Ramon tried to muffle his voice, but there is no doubt: it is Bob. I know his voice better than my own."

A few decisions were made. The first was to bring Hanssen back from his State Department job to full-time Bureau status. They would give him a nice private corner office with two good windows.

A new title came with the office. He was now Special Assistant to the Assistant Director in Charge of Information Resources.

The moment Bob was alone in the office, he put his face in his hands, then stood up and looked out the window.

"It's over," he said to his reflection.

The face spoke back to him. It had a wild grin that reminded him of an expression he'd often seen on his father's face.

"Suck it up, boy," he said in a voice much like Howard's.

At the first opportunity, he wrote to his contact in the SVR:

SINCE COMMUNICATING LAST, I HAVE BEEN PROMOTED TO A HIGHER DO-NOTHING SENIOR EXECUTIVE JOB OUTSIDE OF REGULAR ACCESS TO INFORMATION WITHIN THE COUNTERINTELLIGENCE PROGRAM. IT IS AS IF I AM BEING ISOLATED.

After he sent that message, he did not hear from the SVR.

12

2000

In the dining room, only Bob and Bonnie sat at the table with Greg and Lisa, the two youngest children. Jane was married and the others were away at college. There was no conversation. Bob was staring into space.

"Is there something you want to tell us, Bob?" Bonnie asked. He looked at her but did not answer. "Is there something you want to tell us?" Bonnie repeated. Her voice was strikingly louder. He looked at her and very slowly shook his head.

At Oakcrest, where Bonnie taught an eighth-grade class in religion, she was giving a lecture on success in marriage.

"Communication, children," she said, "is the key to success in a marriage. Think about this word: *communication*. God intends us to share our thoughts and feelings with our mate." It was a lecture she gave every year and it had always worked well, but on this day she left the classroom as soon as she could and rushed to the ladies' room, where she began to redo her makeup. She had difficulty, however. She began to cry. Leaning over the sink, she found herself actually speaking to the water gurgling down the drain: "I do not have good communication with my husband," she said. "He doesn't tell me anything anymore."

As soon as she got home, she was on the phone with Jane.

"I want you and Richard to come over for dinner tonight," she said. "I don't know why, but Dad is awfully depressed. We have to cheer him up."

That night there were six of them at the table—Richard and Jane, Greg and Lisa, Bonnie and Bob. And Bob was no longer silent. He was talking with some urgency, although in a flat voice, as if half of him wanted to get his message across while the other half was somewhere else. He was restating the lines Walter Ballou had used: "Most Catholics are nothing but cafeteria Catholics," he said. "They choose what they think is palatable for them. But Opus Dei makes you recognize what your duties in life must be before you can serve God."

Richard groaned within. On nights like this, he could hardly talk to his father-in-law. Bob was like an ox. Heavy, mentally overfed, and dull.

"Yes, Bob," Richard said. "That is a strong and powerful point of view."

Here was one more thing not to talk about. Being around Bob when he was like this was just another form of mortification. For everybody in the room.

"Remember," Bob was saying, "Opus Dei holds the answers to everything."

Before they left, Bob went over to Jane and hugged her hard. He still looked morose, but he said, "Just remember, Jane, your father loves you."

Then he turned around and hugged Lisa. "Your father loves you, Lisa," he said. "Remember that."

He did the same thing with Greg. "Before I go to bed, son, I just want to tell you, your father loves you." He held the boy by the shoulders for emphasis.

* * *

The next time Jack came to visit, Bonnie made a point of taking him aside.

"Bob is more gloomy than I've ever seen him," she said. "The other night, we were coming back from visiting my sister and he drove right by our house. I had to scream at him, 'Bob, stop! You're passing our house!' See if you can find out what is wrong with him. I'm awfully worried. He could be keeping something from me about his health."

At the dinner table on this night, the conversation almost got away from all of them.

At one point, Bonnie said, "Last month I kept thinking about Florida and I couldn't sleep. I am so thankful that George W. Bush will be our next president."

"Yes," said Hanssen. "Anybody who voted for Gore ought to be executed."

"Come on, Bob," Jack said. "You can't mean that!"

"I can. The very thought of Albert Gore daring to be president after eight years of putting up with that sociopath Bill Clinton . . . my blood boils."

"Your blood pressure," Jack said, "is high enough as it is."

"Yes," Bonnie said. "He is absolutely right about Al Gore, but he does have to do something about his blood pressure. It worries me."

After she had gone to bed, Bob and Jack sat as usual in their corner of the living room. Hanssen told him solemnly, "Jack, I don't know whether anything will happen tonight. Bonnie has been out of it lately."

Hoschouer laughed. "Well, we're getting a little old for it, anyway."

Hanssen just looked gloomy.

Once they said good-night, Jack went as usual to Jane and Sue's room, which was available now that Sue was in graduate school and Jane was married and had children. Still, before he knew what he was doing and out of habit, he flipped on the television. He saw Bonnie sleeping. Bob lay beside her motionless, his open eyes gleaming in the light of the lamp.

On Christmas night, Bob and Bonnie went over with their family—just about grown up by now—to visit Richard and Jane, who had bought a DirecTV satellite dish. Looking at it, Bob was spellbound. "It has such power," he said aloud, and before long was totally engrossed in watching a classic *Twilight Zone* episode from the fifties, when TV was still in black and white.

Richard was struck by the fact that this was a family gathering, and yet Bob could not take his eyes off the screen. From what Richard could see in passing, this *Twilight Zone* episode was about a wealthy family who was obliged to put on masks that revealed their true and evil natures. By the end of the story, when they took the masks off, their real faces had become contorted into exact replicas of the ugly masks. Bob sat there for quite a while after the show before he roused himself long enough to turn off the set and join the others.

13

2000–2001

A car drove up to the house across the street from Bob's house, stopped, and parked. A real estate agent got out, followed by the buyers, a woman and a man. A For Sale sign was on the lawn. Not even an hour passed before the man and woman came out, shook hands, and the agent removed the sign.

A couple of days later, all the shades were drawn in the just-purchased house across the street. Inside, a big mattress was laid on its side against the picture window. A couple of men were installing telephones. Another mattress, covered with a blanket, was on the floor. A few folding chairs stood around the room. Two FBI agents, the man and woman who had pretended to be a married couple, were now joking.

"We ought to make it a little more convincing. Bring in a few kids," the woman said.

"Yeah," said the man. "Let's whip up a family. Get some rent-a-kids."

"He's got to know we're observing him."

"Not the worst way to increase the pressure."

In one of the empty second-floor bedrooms, another FBI man was sitting on a folding chair looking at a TV set. The set was connected by cable and jack to a camera sitting on a tripod. The camera was focused to look

319

through the slats of the venetian blinds in one window, and the TV screen showed a view of the exterior of the Hanssen house. The man in the chair would get up from time to time to pan the camera from window to window or zoom in on the big, beautiful door Bob had bought for the house years ago.

In turn, Bob would peer through a window of his own home and study the house across the street. All the while, the mattress blocked the ground-floor picture window.

On another night, Bob was at his computer encrypting a message for a diskette that he would leave on his next dead drop. If there ever was another dead drop—why didn't he hear from them?

> I'VE COME ABOUT AS CLOSE AS I EVER WANT TO COME TO SACRIFICING MYSELF TO HELP YOU AND I GET SILENCE. I HATE SILENCE. CONCLUSION: ONE MIGHT PROPOSE THAT I AM EITHER INSANELY BRAVE OR QUITE INSANE. I'D SAY INSANELY LOYAL. TAKE YOUR PICK. THERE IS INSANITY IN ALL THE ANSWERS. I HAVE, HOWEVER, COME AS CLOSE TO THE EDGE AS I CAN WITHOUT BEING TRULY INSANE.

For the last week, he had been driving past the post looking for a piece of adhesive tape to indicate to him that the SVR wanted to get in touch. Nothing. The loneliness gnawed at him as if he were alone in a house and someone might or might not knock on the door. Once, as he approached, he saw a piece of tape in the distance, its brightness reflecting the sun; but, like a mirage, it disappeared as he came near. Bob began to yell in the car, "Can't you at least say good-bye?"

His mood shifted. He enjoyed adding material to the

diskette he was preparing. Let them at least have an idea of what they were up against.

> THE U.S. IS A POWERFULLY BUILT BUT RETARDED CHILD, POTENTIALLY DANGEROUS, BUT YOUNG, IMMATURE, AND EASILY MANIPULATED. IT IS ALSO A CHILD THAT CAN TURN TO GENIUS QUICKLY, LIKE AN IDIOT SAVANT. I ASK YOU TO HELP ME SURVIVE. WISH ME LUCK.

That night, at the Foxstone Park signal site, the FBI noted that at approximately 8:18 P.M., Hanssen drove past, came to a complete stop in front of the post for approximately ten seconds, then drove away. The FBI agent who was concealed at an observation post on the other side of the road did not hear him yell at the empty signal site: "WHERE ARE YOU?"

On the next night, January 23, 2001, the FBI agent reported, "Target drove past Foxstone Park signal site shortly before six P.M. Came virtually to a stop, then drove away."

On January 26, 2001, the FBI agent reported, "Hanssen drove past Foxstone Park signal site at approximately 5:37 P.M. Did not stop."

A little later, he reported, "Target drove past Foxstone Park signal site again at 6:42 P.M. Did not stop."

Again, at 7:44 P.M., it was reported, Hanssen drove by and did not stop. When he arrived home, that fact was also reported by the agent watching through the window in the house across the street.

The next morning, Hanssen drove into the Bureau's parking garage, entered the slot reserved for him, and went up the elevator to his office with its two windows.

Shortly afterward, two FBI agents drove up in a car

exactly like Hanssen's, a Ford Taurus. One got out, took out a key, opened the door to Hanssen's car, and drove it a few cars down. The other parked the substitute Ford Taurus in the same slot, then joined the first agent in Hanssen's car. They took it off to a sequestered area in another building. There, they opened the glove compartment, opened the trunk, and photographed all the items that were in the car. These included white adhesive tape and Crayola colored chalk in the glove compartment, plus a flashlight. Four cardboard boxes were in the trunk. In those boxes were ledgers and documents and a number of dark green Hefty garbage bags. The documents were classified.

In church on Sunday, February 18, the priest was giving a sermon: "There is that disease of the human ego which says to the heart, 'I wish to be me, not He.' This attitude," said the priest, "is exactly what rendered Communism ineffective. They had forgotten it was His blood He was willing to offer God. The Eucharist which we celebrate is Jesus' sacrament with us, a conspiracy of blood to shatter our egos and leave us humble."

Bonnie was mouthing silently *a conspiracy of blood to shatter our egos*. Then she whispered to Bob, "Isn't that beautiful?"

His mind was far away. He had finally heard from the SVR. A drop had been arranged for tomorrow, Monday evening.

Early that afternoon, Jack Hoschouer was packing in preparation to leave for the airport. He was going to visit his parents out west. Greg was in a corner, playing his guitar softly.

At the last moment, Bob went into his room and came out with a worn and obviously much-read book. "I want

322

to lend this to you," he said to Jack. "I think it is my favorite novel. A masterpiece."

Jack looked at the cover, *The Man Who Was Thursday*, by G. K. Chesterton.

"It's a classic," Bob added, "and it will give you some idea of what I am all about."

As they came to a stop by the curbside check-in at Dulles Airport, Hanssen shook hands with Jack.

"Aren't you coming in with me?"

"Not today, Jack. I don't have time for a good-bye Coke. But give my regards to your mother and father."

He shook Jack's hand again, gripped him by the shoulder, and then they gave each other a semisalute. Hanssen drove off.

The drop was a new one for Bob. He had to go several hundred yards down a trail to get to it. Even though it was only 4:30 P.M., it was still a late afternoon in February, and he found he was having to use the flashlight for most of the way. A lonely path. He did not know that the FBI had men hiding in the adjoining woods to observe him. To their suppressed anxiety, they had almost been caught off guard. Bob was heading to the dead drop two hours in advance of the time he had arranged with the SVR for pickup.

When he finally got to the footbridge, he stopped and looked around. To the men posted in surveillance, he appeared nervous, but he finally placed his package under the corner of the bridge.

They let him walk back down the trail almost all the way to his car. Too many things could go wrong with an attempted arrest on a trail like this—there were woods on each side to run into.

He had gotten back to the paved road and was almost

by his Taurus when he heard the bullhorn. That brought him to a sudden halt. The sound came full force: "FREEZE! FREEZE EXACTLY WHERE YOU ARE! DO NOT MOVE!"

Six agents came out from behind a blind to surround him. Three remained behind in position to cover the other six if Hanssen started shooting.

No need. The handcuffs were on him quickly enough.

Afterward, there was disagreement as to what he said. Some claimed his first remark was "What took you so long?"

In a whispery voice, he did say, "You won't believe me, but I intended this to be my last drop."

"No sweat," said one of the agents, who happened to be sweating like a horse. The agent was full of the usual tension of a cop making a bust. It usually took will-power not to hit the just-captured perp—like command-ing oneself not to beat on a younger brother who has been asking for it.

"In a crazy way," said Hanssen, "this is a relief. A tremendous relief."

As they started to lead him away, he made one request. "Will you call my wife," he asked, "and tell her I'm okay? I don't want her to suffer, not knowing where I am."

The agent said he would, but knew he wouldn't. How could they alert the wife? She might be implicated.

As they put him into the car, Bob was talking to an imag-inary mirror:

"There has been talk that J. Edgar Hoover used to dress up as a woman. I don't believe that, but then some-times I do. You've got to have great opposites in yourself to do well at this kind of work."

In the car, surrounded by agents, he gave his old crazy whinny of a laugh.

14

2001

When Bob didn't arrive home in time for dinner, Bonnie had tried reaching him at his office, then on his cell phone. Now she was on her knees praying. "Why hasn't he come home?" she asked. "Why doesn't he call? I'm so worried, Lord. Was he in a car wreck?" She got up and dialed her sister Liz. "Liz, thank God you're home. Call Mother and call Jean. I want you all to begin praying for Bob."

"What's wrong?" asked Liz.

"I don't know. Bob should have been home hours ago. I have a terrible feeling. I just do."

"Stay by the phone," said Liz.

"No," said Bonnie. "The kids are out and I'm all alone here. So I'm driving out to Dulles to see if I can find him. Pray to God there's not a wreck on the road and he's not lying helpless on the highway." It took all her regard for Liz and her own pride in herself not to moan in panic. Instead, she put the phone down gently, went to the closet, and put on her coat.

She was using their second car, an old heap. As she drove off, another car with two FBI agents followed her. Two other FBI agents came out of the house across the street, went up to the Hanssens' door, put a key in the lock, and walked in. They were all part of a secret surveillance team known as the Gs squad, so secret that even Hanssen at the peak of his powers could not have compromised their effectiveness. Two more agents started to tape off the house.

As Bonnie's car pulled up to the curb at the Southwest Airlines sign, she got out quickly and ran to the desk inside. Five of the four hundred Special Agents working the operation followed her as she rushed to the head of the line.

"Forgive me, for cutting in ahead of others," said Bonnie to the ticket agent, "but this is an emergency. Could you page my husband, Robert Hanssen? Please page him!"

"In just a moment, Mrs. Hanssen," said the ticket agent, finishing off the last details on a passenger checking in. Bonnie couldn't wait. She began to search the airport for a sight of Bob. When she had moved about a hundred feet away from the counter, the four FBI men waiting surrounded her, then quietly escorted her out of the terminal. Over the loudspeaker she could hear: "PAGING MR. ROBERT HANSSEN. MR. ROBERT HANSSEN, PLEASE REPORT TO THE SOUTHWEST TICKET COUNTER."

"Are you from the FBI?" she asked the four men who were walking with her. "Oh, that's good. You can help me! I'm terrified that my husband has had a heart attack. Will you help me search for him?"

"Mrs. Hanssen, I am sorry. You have to come with us." It was now almost ten P.M. In the car, she could still see the lights of Dulles Airport behind her. Then the agents proceeded to take Bonnie home so that she could get some clothes and collect her two children. While there, she called Jane. Richard answered. "He did it," Bonnie said on the phone, then started to explain what she meant.

Next, the FBI took her and the children to a Marriott

Suites hotel in Vienna, where they had already rented several rooms for just this contingency.

As she could see from the electric clock by the bed, it had become 2:00 A.M. Since she had failed to notice the time when they began, she had no idea of how long the two agents, a female and a male, had been questioning her.

The female agent repeated, "Do you still maintain you know nothing about his espionage activities?"

"Well," Bonnie said at last, "to tell you the truth, I believe he was being blackmailed by the KGB."

"What makes you say that?"

"In 1979 he did give information to the Russians. He told me it was nothing but trash. And he swore he would never do it again. But I think those people have been blackmailing him ever since."

"Nineteen seventy-nine," said the other agent. "Excuse me."

He signaled to another FBI man, and they walked into the bathroom.

"Look," he said. "There's one hell of a discrepancy here. Our information has him doing espionage from 1985 to the end of 1991. Then, after an eight-year gap, he started up again fifteen months ago. We have nothing in there about 1979."

The other investigator shrugged. "Live and learn," he said.

"What's your take on wee Bonnie?"

"I can accept her at face value. She's one naive bird."

"I'm ready to agree. But isn't it too soon to quit on her?"

"Yes," said the other. "Certainly too soon for the record. We can walk her around the track for another couple of days, but we're not going to get more. She's in a daze."

When they came out of the bathroom, Bonnie was in

a state. "Who's watching my children?" she asked. "I want to see Lisa and Greg."

"In a while," said the female agent who was taking care of her. "But they are all right, I promise you."

"The Russians," said Bonnie, "have been blackmailing my husband ever since 1979. Bob has just never had a chance. He had a terrible decision to make. Was he going to protect us or the nation?"

Back on Talisman Drive, FBI men were still combing the Hanssen house. Guns were being removed from a rack and from mountings on the wall. In total, fourteen guns were carried out. Plus all three computers. Advance directions had said: "It will be neither practical nor reasonable to require the searching agents to examine the defendant's computers on-site. There is considerable risk that Hanssen has set up self-destruct programs on his computers that could erase vital evidence. They must be examined by our Computer Analysis Response Team personnel."

When Bonnie awoke at the Marriott just before eleven A.M., her sister Jean was there. That was when she discovered she had not been placed under arrest. Bonnie decided to stay at the hotel for a few days.

Jack Hoschouer's parents lived in a small ranch house in Phoenix, Arizona. On the morning after the night of the flight to his folks' home, he was still sleeping when the alarm on the bedside table went off at 7:00 A.M., and the radio came on automatically. The announcer was saying: "Flash bulletin! The FBI has arrested a Special Agent named Robert P. Hanssen, alleged to have been spying for the Russians for over fifteen years."

Jack didn't get it at first. He thought maybe Bob was finally receiving some ink for arresting a few Russians. It was only after he dressed and was having his coffee that the second news bulletin he heard got through to him. A moment later, he picked up the phone and asked the operator for the number of the local FBI office.

15

2001

The more Jack talked, the more dubious seemed the Bureau agents who were there to receive him in D.C.

"Look," he said. "I'm in shock. This is the guy I'd trust with my life."

The agent he was talking to read from paragraph 125 of the affidavit.

"'Hanssen offered up to the KGB the name of a childhood friend who had been passed over for military promotion and might, because of this disappointment, be a possibility for espionage recruitment.' Are you that person?" The agent drilled him with a look.

Jack said, "I'm the only one he could be referring to."

"If you had been approached," asked the agent, "what would you have done?"

Jack said, "I probably would have called Bob Hanssen and asked, Who should I notify in the FBI?"

"Are you trying to tell me," said the agent, "that you're not pissed off?"

Jack said, "I think Bob must be crazy."

"Insane?"

"No," Jack said. "Crazy. If you only knew how much he hates Communism and abortion."

"Does nothing bother you about his behavior?"

"Hell, yes," said Jack. "I put my ass on the line in Vietnam. I had young men killed in my company. That

330

part really bugs me." He felt as if he were about to burst into tears.

Was the agent sympathetic? He looked at his watch and said, "We'll stop here for today." Then he demonstrated that he wasn't all that sympathetic. "We do want you to surrender your computer hard drive."

"It's in Germany," said Jack. "It'll take a few days. I can tell you there's nothing of intelligence value on it."

"We'd like a look all the same," said the agent.

"Understood," said Jack. But he couldn't leave it there. "You know, what Bob and I talked about in e-mail has no intelligence value at all."

"Well, what is your e-mail about?"

"Guy talk," Jack said. "Playmate of the Month. Stuff like that."

"*Playboy* magazine? That's pornography, isn't it?"

"You classify *Playboy* as pornography?" Jack asked.

"Let's see your hard drive," said the agent.

When the FBI received Jack's computer drives, there were new difficulties. He was soon recalled to D.C. to testify before the grand jury that was hearing the government's case against Hanssen. Before that took place, the agent he had talked to was all over him.

"One of your three hard disks is so screwed up that we couldn't get anything. You're dicking around with us."

"I'm not looking to protect Bob Hanssen or myself. It's his wife. My hard drive is going to be very embarrassing to her."

The agent had obviously seen enough to say, "It's not embarrassing to you?"

"I've done what I've done," Jack said. "But Bonnie is innocent."

"Innocent of what?"

"Of our shenanigans. I keep telling you, there's nothing on that disk of intelligence value."

"Well, we're going to recover and reconstitute that

331

messed-up drive. We'll see if your story adds up."

"Can we at least protect Bonnie in all this? I'll take my medicine. But she's going to get spattered."

Over at the State Department, two high officials were talking. One of them, a Yankee with a fine voice and a head of straight silver hair, led the conversation. He was from State. The other, an official from the FBI, had learned over the years to present a made-for-the-media voice that was uninflected and punditlike.

"As I understand it," said the State Department man, "Hanssen passed along to his Russian handlers six thousand pages of classified documents in addition to twenty-seven encoded computer disks."

"All of that."

"Have you at the Bureau characterized the nature of these disclosures?"

"All of them, and they go in a great many directions."

"Yes, from what I gather, this fellow Hanssen really got around to a considerable degree."

"You can say that," said the FBI man.

"And we do know that he has been your liaison to the State Department for five years—virtually these last five years. Am I correct?"

"Yes, sir."

"In that case," said the State Department official, "I expect there's every reason to believe he was in on the progress of our investigations, and yours, not to mention the CIA and the National Security Agency as well— in on, I guess we have to assume, all our efforts to trace out the smuggling of loose nukes." Then he added, "Plus other means of mass destruction."

"We haven't studied it in detail yet, but that is not unlikely."

"In that case, we must assume he sent information on to the Russians?"

"We have to assume he did," said the FBI man.

"The paramount question, then," continued the silver-haired State Department official, "is whether some loose cannon among the Russians—and I must say it is now a country of loose cannons—could have been capable of smuggling nukes over to terrorists? I am thinking in particular of people like Osama bin Laden."

"You know, sir, the Russians hate bin Laden more than we do."

"Well, we do know that, but all the same, we'd do well to be worried what a renegade Russian Intelligence officer could do on the black market with Islamic terrorists."

"Yes, sir, it's going to be a long search. We are going to trace out the repercussions of Hanssen's espionage acts. Yes, sir," he repeated doggedly.

After calling Richard Trimber at his office to get the address, Jack paid a visit to Bonnie at the house of a woman friend with whom she was now staying. On the day he saw her, there she was, sitting in one corner of a living room, with all her children, wandering around this unfamiliar house.

There were tears in Bonnie's eyes as she spoke. "You've read the affidavit?" she asked.

"I've studied it," Hoschouer said. "Yes."

"I thought you'd never want to talk to us again," she said.

"No," said Jack, "I don't reject him any more than you do."

"I'm so afraid," said Bonnie. "What are they still doing to my house?"

"Probably X-raying your walls."

"They took all of Bob's guns and then all of my boys' guns. Isn't that extreme?"

"I'm afraid not," said Jack.

She broke down in tears and began to repeat herself. Quite apart from not being able to get it into her mind, she seemed not able to take it into her skin that unknown men had been ravaging her house and her furnishings. At last, she said, "I thought we would never see you again."

Jack couldn't believe it. Once again, he was leading a double life. "Look," he said. "I know you need something to tide you over. . . ." He took an envelope out of his jacket. "There's two thousand here. That's as much cash as I can get together at this point."

"You're an angel," said Bonnie.

"Don't ever say that," Jack said.

16

2001

Moscow, these days, was lit up at night. Colored neon tubes had been installed on the cornices of many old buildings.

Shebarshin and Cherkashin were having a hamburger in McDonald's, and Shebarshin was eating his with obvious distrust and distaste. All around them, in contrast to McDonald's clientele in America, were prosperous-looking people, young capitalists—media and Internet entrepreneurs—in tailored suits, standing up or sitting down while talking on their cell phones. The place had marble floors, and the young Russians who worked there were spirited, as if this was one thing that capitalist Russia could do better than capitalist America.

"The game goes on and on and on," Shebarshin said, "with their Hanssen business."

"Another American reporter came to me yesterday," said Cherkashin. "I said, 'I never knew a man named Hanssen.' He wouldn't believe I was telling the truth." Cherkashin began to laugh.

"How these Americans carry on! Don't they comprehend that espionage is a normal activity? Every government engages in it. How can they not?"

"The real purpose of this scandal is to exert political pressure on Russia."

"Yes," Shebarshin replied. "To build up Star Wars with Mr. Bush Junior."

"Now it seems even our best secrets are being obtained by FBI."

"Russian Intelligence will lose ten years recovering from this business," Shebarshin said.

In the prison's visiting room, Bob and Bonnie were on opposite sides of a glass shield. They spoke through telephones while looking at each other.

"Think of yourself," she said, "as ninety-nine percent good, one percent bad."

He smiled sadly. "I have been so worried about you, Bonnie."

"I'm all right," she said. "Sometimes I'm afraid—but the neighbors have been very kind. Now that we're back in the house, I'm going to stay as long as I can."

"You are?"

"Yes, Bob, because that's where all of my memories are, my happy memories. It's only when I go outdoors that I feel any fear."

"You're perfectly safe outside," he said.

"What makes you say that?"

"Who would hurt you? You have such great tits." Through the gloom, he actually beamed for a moment. She tried to smile back, but her eyes were full of tears.

"I think you *are* crazy," she said.

Jack was back once more in the Hanssen living room.

"I keep thinking," Bonnie said to him, "that there's another woman involved somehow. Was Bob ever unfaithful to me?"

"No," Jack said.

"The way you say *no*. I can tell. There is another woman."

How was he to handle it? "All right, Bonnie," he said.

336

"Better you hear it from me than that you pick up the *Washington Post* one morning and find out."

"Go ahead. After everything else, I can bear it, I think."

"Bob took a girl to Hong Kong." He held up a hand. "But he swore to me that he didn't touch her. Bonnie, I believe him completely."

His words did not elicit the explosive reaction he feared. She said only, "Bob begged me to go to Hong Kong with him, and I couldn't because of the kids. Oh, he begged me so much. I did agree to see him in Hawaii—and that week was more than any wonderful honeymoon could have been. So you see, Jack, I can believe he never touched her."

Back in Chicago, in the same home where Bob and Bonnie's wedding party had taken place, matters were not as full of understanding. Leroy Wauck, Bonnie's father, was closeted with his son, Mark, who, like Bob, was a Special Agent in the FBI, but had been content to stay at its Chicago Headquarters. He and Bob had had a cordial relationship but stayed clear of talking Bureau business, respecting each other's privacy. Until now.

"Look, Mark," his father was saying. "We've been in hell the last couple of weeks and now you say there's something worse?"

"Definitely," said Mark.

"Worse than everything we've all been through?"

"I can't go into detail."

"If that isn't the goddamned FBI for you," said Leroy. "A son can't even divulge a crucial point to his father concerning the most intimate family matters."

"Look, they took me aside at the Bureau. Out of respect for me as an agent, they told me. Which is why I can't tell you."

Half an hour later, Leroy was on the phone with his daughter. It was the worst conversation Bonnie had ever had with him.

"Don't be an absolute fool all your life," he told her. "Your husband is a foul piece of work."

Bonnie began shouting. "Don't you dare speak about him in that way!"

"Do you have one shred of intelligence left?" he asked her. "File for an annulment. He personifies the sin of fraud in marriage."

"I'm not going to abandon him. Bob is in prison."

"It's exactly where he belongs."

"Dad, you always told me there were two types of Catholics—those who can forgive and those who are Catholics only because it empowers them to judge others."

"And you, I suppose," said Leroy, "are the forgiving type." He paused just long enough to still the wrath in his voice. "Well, Bonnie," he said, "so am I. But Bob went past the point of no return. It's not just his spying. That is hideous enough. It's that other thing."

"I don't know what you are talking about," Bonnie said.

"You'll find out, and when you do, you'll agree with me: your husband is a scumbag."

Bonnie hung up on him.

Behind the glass partition in the visiting room, staring through to the entrance door, Bob waited to see his visitors. It was Jane and Richard who came on this day. As they approached, Richard whispered to her. "Remember, these conversations are monitored. Don't ask him anything that could cause embarrassment."

They were allowed to see him one at a time. Jane went first. She thought her father's eyes were more deep and remorseful than she had ever seen them.

"Mom told us," she said, "about how your father used to treat you, and, Dad, I want to tell you, I think it was beautiful of you that you didn't continue that kind of cruelty with us."

"I never had the impulse, ever, toward you, Jane, or with Sue or with Lisa. But one time when Greg brought home a ninety-five on a math test, my first impulse was to say, 'Why didn't you get a hundred?' I bit my tongue. I was determined to break the cycle."

Now there was a pause. They had to avoid pauses. The facts of his situation hung over all these pauses.

"Mom told us," Jane said, "how happy her letter made you."

He nodded very slowly, as if his head was too heavy for his neck to support.

"I broke down crying when I read that letter," he said. "Oh, Jane, I'm so grateful that there is still this much love in the family."

"I've got to go now, Dad," said Jane. "Otherwise I will break down. I know Richard wants to talk to you."

They touched palms against the glass.

Richard had been through his own kind of hell these days. He still saw himself as a young lawyer, but now he had to serve as a wise one, too. He had thought he was marrying into one hell of an impressive family and that all the children he and Jane had brought into existence—four since their marriage in 1994!—would have the benefit of loving grandparents, aunts, and uncles. Instead, they now had a grandfather who was a pariah and a grandmother who gave every sign of being in denial for the rest of her life. And he, a *son-in-law,* had become the skipper of this crippled family vessel. It was a lot of changes to go through at once. On top of it all, he had a wife who adored her father.

He had prepared for this meeting, however. He had news he had to get across to Bob, but not over that mon-

itored phone. So he brought along his children's drawings and now he held them up against the glass for Bob
to look at. As Bob smiled—he had picked up the cue—
Richard was mouthing words silently, his head just
above the drawings that he pressed against the glass.

"The Priscilla Galey story is going to break," he told
Bob. "Is there anything we have to know?" He mouthed
the words. "Anything else?"

"Gee, those pictures are good," Bob said over the
phone. Then he also said through the phone, since the
monitors would not know his point of reference, "Don't
pay attention to that kind of stuff. It's not that big a
deal."

"That kind of stuff"—okay. But it soon turned and there
was another kind of stuff, and it would prove to be quite
a deal. Over a meal in a restaurant, Jack Hoschouer told
Richard that he didn't know how much was going to
come out, but he wanted Richard to tell Bob that the Bureau was now in possession of his—Jack's—hard drive.
That kind of item was bound to leak to the press sooner
or later. Richard had to be the messenger to Bob. The
next time he went to see him, Richard brought more
kids' drawings and proceeded to mouth the new information.

"Jack said to tell you that the Bureau has his hard
drive."

Bob nodded the way a patient does when the doctor
has just informed him that he has an incurable disease.

"I'm going to kill Bob! How could he do it?" Bonnie
screamed. "Is he insane? Am I insane? What was going
on? All these years and years I have been living with a
monster! A madman! A scumbag!"

Then she prayed, "Oh, Lord, forgive us. You seek to
give us all we need, and we look to destroy You with our
madness."

She shrieked again and began to throw whatever object was at hand. She picked up a paperweight and hurled it into the mirror on her dressing table, shattering the glass.

"Damn mirror, damn, damn mirror! I've looked at you for too many years, looked and looked at you just to look. Now I hate you." She began to cry differently, more softly, full of the most awful sorrow, as if she had been swallowing bitter rue.

"Bob," she cried aloud. "I know you love me. You do. You do."

She continued to weep softly. "It had to be Jack," she said. "It's not your fault. I will never forgive Jack. I will never speak to him again." This thought gave her strength. "Oh, Bob, if I have to crawl on my knees over broken glass, I will find a way to forgive you and love you again."

She stood there trembling. She was actually tempted to get down on her knees and cross the carpet of shattered glass.

"Oh, Lord, forgive me," she prayed, "for saying that I never had a cross to bear."

Richard had to tell Jack. He chose the telephone.

"Bonnie said she doesn't want to see you. She sounded pretty final about it."

Jack asked Richard to let Bonnie know that he was deeply ashamed of himself. "Ask her if sometime in the future I can call and somehow make amends."

"I wouldn't try that for a while," said Richard. "She blames you for all of it. She feels you incited Bob. She speaks of him as very vulnerable and terribly suggestible."

At the end of May, Hanssen was making his second court appearance. To his right was the press, and in the center of the spectator section sat some forty FBI men.

The wall clock showed 8:52. He could feel a reaction as he walked in wearing an oversize green jumpsuit that was almost falling off him. He knew his arms looked thin; he knew his skin was prison white. His weight had dropped from 220 to 160. On the back of the jumpsuit, white letters read PRISONER. They had been stenciled on, and the letters were irregular, ragged, badly printed. He hated coming into the room wearing that jumpsuit.

Hanssen stood at the defense table and looked again at all the people he could take in, then at Mike Shepard who was sitting apart from the other forty FBI personnel. It was hard to look at Mike, and he had to look away. There were normal rustlings and scrapings in the place, but Bob heard none of that. He was trying to listen to the charges the government was filing against him. Even as the lawyers spoke, he felt the pall of a courtroom, the silence that lay beneath all the other sounds.

A reporter caught up with Priscilla Galey in Columbus, Ohio, and the story was enough of a sensation to put her on television. The nine years that had passed since she last saw Bob had not been kind to her. She had lost her teeth and looked older than her age when she appeared on TV with Barbara Walters and then with Larry King. Neither show paid her anything but expenses, yet she was content. Walters's people had fitted her with false teeth, which she certainly needed before she could get on the tube, since she had lost her upper plate on the street in the course of a drunken night in Columbus, months— or was it years?—ago.

17

2001

Richard was at his desk. In the mail, a letter had come from Bob:

> The other day, they had to drive me to Orange County, Virginia for a legal procedure and on the way we passed some poor houses in a colored neighborhood. And on my face I didn't show a sign but inside I was bawling like a baby because I knew I would give anything to be able to live in one of those ramshackle houses with my family, rather than be where I am.

That same week, an Opus Dei priest spoke with Bonnie.

"Father Bill," she told him. "I come home from visiting him and even in light of everything I know, I'm still in love. More than ever."

"Bonnie, I can't tell you how important your visits to Bob are," said Father Bill. "I'm concerned that if he gets into too deep a depression, he may find a way . . ." He hardly had to finish this sentence.

"No, he must never do that! In the middle of the night I wake up in terror that he will commit suicide."

"Nothing could be worse," said Father Bill.

"Well, just suppose. What if Bob came down with cancer? Do you think they'd let him out?"

"Bonnie, I don't think you can keep hoping against all hope that Bob will get out someday."

"Yes, I know it won't happen, not now, I know, but still, if he did come down with cancer, maybe they might let him out. I could nurse him then."

She was lying in bed alone, staring up at the ceiling where she could see Bob in his tuxedo and herself in her wedding dress on the day they married in 1968. So long ago. So near.

He wasn't always sure whether it was night or day. He would walk around the cell, then lie down in his bunk. Sometimes he would speak aloud, and sometimes his lips did not move but he could hear a voice in his mind.

In the moment I saw Mike Shepard, it was as if friendship and betrayal came together, as if betrayal is as close to friendship as the overlay on a drawing. Yes. If I was the manipulator of everyone around me, yet I will ask: Why can't you love the object of your manipulation? I still care about Mike Shepard.

When it seemed as if there was no one to hear him, he was tempted to speak aloud, but he wouldn't. There was probably a listening device in his cell.

All the same, sometimes he couldn't help himself—he would say something aloud, very loud. *"Come on, Bob,"* he said to the walls. *"You're a bad guy and you can prove it."*

But saying it out loud brought him close to weeping. So he used his father's voice. *"Suck it up! Suck it up! Ahhhhhhh, suck it up!"*

Sometimes he heard the voice in his head. He might as well have been looking into a mirror, the voice was that strong.

My addiction is betrayal—I don't even want to think of all the other guys in the FBI who were close to me and now feel betrayed. I wonder if they smile when they think of something nice I did with them? Or do they stop in the middle of a sentence and say, "I can't forgive him for what he did!" They do not understand. I am addicted. My addiction is to betray those who are close to me. And now I think that is a protection against something worse, a more total betrayal. Once evil really gets into you, it doesn't need to conquer all of your soul. It just roosts in you. It is there like a disease that you fight with every bit of your body and your future hopes.

Yet maybe you must learn to live with such a disease. Accept it. Yes, accept it in order to hold off something worse, whatever that something worse may be—cancer, blindness, madness, anything. Maybe betrayal is the evil that protects me against a worse evil.

For now, I realize something I never quite knew before. In the depths of my heart, I was ready to slay everyone alive. Oh, God, recognizing this, I am ready to be crucified for my sins. Not like our Lord Jesus—no, never—but see me at least as equal to the thief who was crucified with Christ. The good thief. The one who wished to die with Jesus.

He couldn't help it. He gave the laugh that sounded as if it came from the mad horse of his mind, the maverick stallion that was always ready to ride off at a gallop in two directions at once.

345

Epilogue

When the U.S. Court of the Eastern District of Virginia, in Alexandria, Virginia, was called to order at 9 A.M. on May 10, 2002, every seat was filled. Most of those in attendance were present and former members of the FBI who were somehow associated with Robert Hanssen or his case; there were also attorneys from the Justice Department, officials from the Attorney General's office, and Hanssen's attorneys. The presence of so many government officials at Hanssen's sentencing made a strong statement about the extent of his betrayals. Members of his family were not in court that day, but Jack Hoschouer, Hanssen's closest friend, sat in a corner at the back of the courtroom.

Jim Milborn, who had first identified Hanssen as a spy in October 2000, was sitting in the fourth row. Just behind him was Paul Moore, who had carpooled to the office with him regularly. Nearby was David Major, Hanssen's boss's boss. The room was a sea of dark-colored suits and dresses, as if people had gathered for a wake or a funeral.

Earlier, while everyone was milling around waiting for court to convene, Hanssen had entered the courtroom through a side door, guarded by plainclothes marshals. He was dressed in an oversized green prison jumpsuit with the word PRISONER stenciled on the back. Under the

346

jumpsuit he wore. a long-sleeved white shirt. Both garments hung loosely from his body; he was scarecrow-thin. His hair had gone completely gray and prison pallor was etched on his features.

After Judge Claud Hilton took his seat, the government's prosecutor, Randy Bellows, rose and told the court that Hanssen had abused the trust of the United States government and that the harm he caused his country and its people was at the highest level—a "Number 42." The former Special Agent had used people's lives as "merchandise" for his personal financial gain, Bellows said.

When it was his turn to address the court, Hanssen's attorney, Plato Cacheris, said that since July 6, 2001, his client had spent seventy-five days and over two hundred hours cooperating with the government, fulfilling his plea-bargain agreement. "He has also waived his priest-penitent privilege, his lawyer-client privilege," Cacheris continued. "He has submitted himself to two polygraphs and to psychoanalysis, all at the behest of the government. And therefore, the sentence of life imprisonment is the appropriate one to be applied."

All eyes turned to Hanssen when Judge Hilton asked him if he had anything to say before sentencing. Hanssen rose and walked slowly to the podium in the center of the room. He held a piece of paper in front of him and trembled only slightly as he spoke:

"First, I wish to thank all my family, friends and coworkers who have expressed their support for me," Hanssen began. "I also wish to thank those who have provided support for my family, some of whom are here today. I am humbled by your generosity, your goodness, and your charity. I apologize for my behavior. I am shamed by it. Beyond its illegality, I have torn the trust of so many. Worse, I have opened the door for calumny against my totally innocent wife and our children. I have hurt them deeply. I have hurt so many deeply. For all this I stand ready to accept the sentence of this court."

Hanssen's statement was striking for what it omitted: He did not apologize to the FBI or the United States government or the American people, nor did he address the families of those men who were executed in the Soviet Union as a result of his betrayal.

Quickly, the court sentenced Hanssen to a term of life for each of fifteen counts, to run concurrently.

After the judge left the bench, Robert Hanssen turned around and scanned the faces in the courtroom. When he recognized Paul Moore, he smiled. But when he found Jack Hoschouer he became almost exuberant. Hanssen lifted his handcuffed arms and waved to his old friend, then he turned to the marshals and, accompanied by them, walked out of the room.

As the courtroom emptied out, Hoschouer stood there motionless, as if transfixed. Momentarily, he turned toward the wall and bowed his head. Finally, he left with the last stragglers.

The entire court session had lasted less than nine minutes.

Afterword

All the important facts of Robert Hanssen's life as a spy may never be known—a fact that the FBI agents who continue to interrogate him are discovering. Periodically, Hanssen is given a polygraph examination to confirm the veracity of what he is telling the Bureau, and often the examiner accuses him of not telling the truth. One occasion of testing resulted in Hanssen's having a physical altercation with an investigator.

In one sense, it is easy to understand that as he moved from experience to experience, Hanssen left behind his memories of things that were unimportant to him. The events that constitute his betrayal of our country's secrets, while of paramount significance to the FBI—and to those of us who struggle to comprehend his behavior—may simply not have played a major role in his psyche. Our need to understand Hanssen may be far stronger than his ability to account for—or indeed to remember—his actions.

Moreover, Robert Hanssen is not the only actor in this story who is unable to answer every question. One inquiry, still open-ended, revolves around an incident that some members of the Hanssen and Wauck families related to me.

In 1990 Bonnie found a large sum of money—five to ten thousand dollars—in Bob's dresser. The bills were stuffed into one of his socks. Not waiting for Bob to come home to ask him about it, Bonnie ran in a full panic to her sister Jean's house, just five doors down the block. George, Jean's husband, remembers the incident. Jean got on the phone with her sister-in-law Mary (who is married to her brother Mark) and her brother Greg (a federal postal inspector) to tell them about this inexplicable stash, since, as we know, the Hanssens lived sparingly.

At that point, nobody besides Bonnie, Bob, and their Opus Dei priest knew about Bob's 1979 activities with the GRU. Still, this situation concerning the wad of cash took on a life of its own with Bonnie's siblings. Mary Wauck told her husband, Mark, who was and still is an FBI Special Agent stationed in Chicago. Mark and Greg discussed the matter. Mark found the incident sufficiently disturbing, in light of Hanssen's spending habits he'd observed, that he informed FBI Headquarters in writing of his sister's discovery, and this report was presumably forwarded up through the chain of command.

No action is known to have resulted from Mark Wauck's report. Indeed, it wasn't until Hanssen was arrested that anyone in the Wauck family remembered the incident. When the FBI questioned Bonnie after Bob's arrest, she had no memory of it, neither of finding the money nor of going over to Jean's house to tell her about it. Everyone else in the Wauck family, however, did recall it. And Mark certainly remembered filing his report.

The question of what happened to Mark Wauck's report warrants an answer. Perhaps the FBI knows; if so, they are not talking publicly at this point in time. Clearing up the mystery of what happened to Wauck's report is not, therefore, within the scope of this work. Not at this point. The aim here has been to develop a portrait of Robert Hanssen based on known incidents, events, and relationships, which can provide some parameters by which to begin to comprehend him.

The incidents and events I have written about are, as I

mentioned in my author's note, drawn from numerous sources. In addition, some of the scenes in Mailer's screenplay and some others in this work are the product of conflation and/or extrapolation. Sometimes a scene was constructed by combining several known incidents into a single one; sometimes a scene was created on the basis of conjecture or informed speculation. Occasionally, known events were left out entirely—such as the just-cited discovery by Bonnie in 1990 of Bob's stash of bills. Like many strands in most lives, this particular one did not lead to a usable conclusion. It did not advance our understanding of Hanssen nor of his wife nor of their relationship, so it was not included.

This work and Norman Mailer's screenplay have been researched to the best of our abilities with the ongoing recognition that in the future new information about Robert Hanssen is bound to emerge and shed additional light and further confusion on what took place during his years as an FBI Special Agent.

Many of the characters in this book are real people who were involved in Hanssen's life in the manner depicted. Often, their dialogue was re-created on the basis of information obtained during interviews. At times, of course, dialogue was written by the author, out of his understanding of the people involved in Robert Hanssen's story.

One example of such created dialogue is the scene that takes place when Cherkashin visits Kireev in Moscow. Cherkashin's trip to Moscow and the meeting between them did take place. Norman Mailer and I did interview Cherkashin; however, the dialogue was constructed for the screenplay from Mailer's understanding of how these men might have behaved and reacted under the circumstances.

Another category of authorial creation is the letter by Bob to Bonnie when she is in Mexico. It was written out of the author's understanding of how Hanssen would have communicated his feelings at the time.

The majority of characters in this work are real and are identified by their given names. Others are composites and have been given new names. Among these, two examples should be noted. "Mike Shepard" is a composite of several supervising Special Agents of the FBI, including retired Supervisory Special Agent David Major, who was Robert Hanssen's bosses' boss and was interviewed a number of times. "Walter Ballou" is a composite of several people, including Intelligence Research Specialist Paul Moore, who shared an office with Hanssen and carpooled with him and was also interviewed frequently, and Intelligence Research Specialist Jim Milburn, who fingered Hanssen in 2000 and who was not interviewed, but his involvement was explained to us by another retired Special Agent of the FBI. Others have asked that their names not be used, and we have given them fictitious names. In some instances, a fictitious character has been developed, as in the case of Bunky Fitzhugh, to represent a personality type who has been part of this story.

Having noted my indebtedness to Norman Mailer for his screenplay, I would also like to acknowledge several other works that I read and a number of people who have contributed to my effort in one way or another.

Confessions of a Spy: The Real Story of Aldrich Ames, by Pete Earley.

Spies Wives: Stories of CIA Families Abroad, by Karen L. Chiao and Mariellen B. O'Brien.

The Sword and the Shield: The Mitrokhin Archive and the Secret History of the KGB, by Christopher Andrew and Vasili Mitrokhin.

The Bureau and the Mole: The Unmasking of Robert Philip Hanssen, the Most Dangerous Double Agent in FBI History, by David A. Vise.

* * *

My reporting on the Hanssen case began as an assignment from Les Moonves, president of CBS Television. Without Les's support, there might not have been a book.

I would like to thank the following for their invaluable contributions: Val Aksilenko, James Bamford, Robert Brasile, Roger Buchman, Dr. Sarah Charles, Viktor Cherkashin, Keith Davis, Dr. Marry Drummer, Dr. Michael Dennitson, Roger Diehl, Suzanne Douchette, Priscilla Sue Galey, Julian Heron, Jack Hoschouer, Dr. Eugene Kennedy, Dr. James King, Karen Lison, Oleg Kalugin, John R. Lorenz, David Major, Father C. John McCloskey III, Dr. Paul Moore, Owen Muelder, Kenneth Okimoto, Jim Ohlson, Leonid Vladimirovich Sherbashin, Yuri Shvets, Joe Tierney, Henry "Hank" Williams, Doug Wilson, and members of Bonnie and Robert Hanssen's immediate family.

I wish to thank Carlos Lozano, an attorney and writer, who worked with me during the research phase of this book; Jan Schraner, whose commitment to this book also made it possible; and Mila Taubkina, who assisted me in Moscow.

Joseph Lennon interviewed those who went to Knox College with Hanssen, and Jim Hougan gave valuable assistance during the early period of research on the screenplay. The editorial contribution of Veronica Windholz was central to this book; she worked with me through its completion, as she did on my work *Perfect Murder, Perfect Town*. A deep, heartfelt thanks to Judith McNally, Norman Mailer's assistant.

Thank you to Rebecca Whittington, my Vice President of Motion Picture projects; my personal assistant, Serra Haworth, who kept our work in order; to my son Howard Schiller, who designed the jacket; and to my other son, Anthony Schiller, who reviewed the final manuscript.

My thanks to Marjorie Braman, Cathy Hemming, Jane Friedman, James Fox, and Laurie Rippon at HarperCollins, who were all a fine help.

Last, and not least, a much-earned thanks to John Taylor Williams of Hill & Barlow, who has assisted me on five book projects.

Appendix A

Hanssen's Time Line

April 18, 1944
Robert Philip Hanssen born, Chicago.

October 3, 1947
Bernadette "Bonnie" Wauck born, Chicago.

1957
Hanssen meets Jack Hoschouer; they soon become best friends.

1962
Hanssen graduates Taft High School and attends Knox College.

1966
Hanssen graduates from Knox College with a degree in chemistry.

1966
Hanssen attends Northwestern University's dental school.

1967
Jack Hoschouer marries.

August 10, 1968
Hanssen marries Bonnie Wauck. Soon after, he drops out of dental school and switches his major to accounting.

1971
Hanssen receives an MBA in Accounting and Information Systems. He gets a job as a junior accountant at Touche Ross, an accounting firm in Chicago.

March 27, 1972
Jane Hanssen, Robert and Bonnie's first daughter, is born.

July 1972
Howard Hanssen, Hanssen's father, a Chicago cop, retires to Florida.

October 1972
Hanssen joins the Chicago Police Department as a police officer/forensic accountant in the C-5 Unit (internal affairs).

February 20, 1974
Sue Hanssen, Robert and Bonnie's second daughter, is born.

January 12, 1976
Hanssen, now 32, joins the FBI, GS-10 level. He is assigned to the Indianapolis field office and receives initial top-secret security clearance.

May 1976
Hanssen is assigned to the Gary, Indiana office—Residence Agency Division.

April 12, 1977
Jack Hanssen, first son of Robert and Bonnie, is born.

August 2, 1978
Hanssen transfers to the New York City Field Office—
WCC Division (white collar crime)—on accounting
matters in Criminal Division.

March 1979
Hanssen is detailed to the field office's Intelligence Division to help establish the FBI's automated counterintelligence database.

1979
Hanssen is assigned to a squad that monitors the GRU
(Soviet military intelligence). He begins spying by delivering an anonymous letter to a GRU officer working at a
Soviet-run business in New York City. The letter offers
the name of another GRU officer who was recruited by
the FBI in New York.

1979–1980
Hanssen writes another anonymous letter to solicit the
GRU but is caught by his wife, Bonnie. He confesses his
act to her, and he and Bonnie visit Father Robert P. Bucciarelli, an Opus Dei priest.
    Hanssen continues his relationship with the GRU for
a short period of time.

April 23, 1980
Mark Hanssen, Robert and Bonnie's second son, is born.

June 23, 1980
Hanssen signs a nondisclosure agreement for "Sensitive
Compartmented Information" (SCI), granting him access to top-secret documents.

January 12, 1981
Hanssen transferred to Headquarters in Washington, D.C.,
as a Supervisory Special Agent in the Intelligence Division.

The Hanssens buy a house on Whitecedar Court in Vienna, Virginia.

He is assigned to CI-3D Unit (budget unit).

July 14, 1983
Greg Hanssen, Robert and Bonnie's third son, is born.

August 1983
Hanssen is assigned to the Soviet Analytical Unit, CI-3A, in Washington.

October 15, 1984
Hanssen signs a Classified Information Non-Disclosure Agreement.

May 20, 1985
Arthur James Walker is arrested and charged with espionage.

September 23, 1985
Hanssen is assigned to a counterintelligence squad named "Pocketwatch," as a Supervisory Special Agent for an FBI field office in New York City. He lives at the YMCA in New York; Bonnie and the children remain in Virginia until their home is sold, in November 1985.

October 1, 1985
Hanssen writes his first letter volunteering information to the KGB.

October 4, 1985
A KGB Line PR officer in Washington, D.C., Viktor M. Degtyar, receives an envelope at his residence in Alexandria, Virginia, mailed by Hanssen.

October 15, 1985
Degtyar receives a package from "B" containing numerous classified documents.

October 15, 1985
Lisa Hanssen, Robert and Bonnie's third daughter, is born.

November 1985
Bonnie and children move to New York.

November 2, 1985
Liking what they received from "B," the KGB begins its relationship with Hanssen by loading the "Park" dead-drop site with $50,000 in cash.

March 3, 1986
On this occasion, the KGB loads the "Park" dead-drop site, but "B" does not appear. The KGB removes its package from the dead-drop site the same day.

June 30, 1986 (on or about)
After months of silence, the KGB is excited to learn that "B" has more to offer. Degtyar receives a typed letter from "B" at his home in Alexandria, Virginia.

July 14, 1986–August 18, 1986
Hanssen and the KGB walk a dangerous line communicating in public, first through an advertisement in a local newspaper and later by public telephone. The *Washington Times* ad is for a Dodge Diplomat and appears, much to Hanssen's delight, exactly as he requested it be printed. It is a signal to him that the Russians want to continue the relationship.

August 3, 1987
Hanssen is reassigned to FBI Headquarters in D.C. as

Deputy Unit Chief, CI-3A; serving again as a Supervisory Agent in the Intelligence Division's Soviet Analytical Unit.

He purchases a residence at 9414 Talisman Drive in Vienna, Virginia.

September 11–26, 1987
KGB handlers leave $10,000 in cash for "B" at the "Park" dead-drop site and in return receive top-secret National Security Council documents.

September 29, 1987
The KGB deposits $100,000 into an escrow account established for "B" in a Soviet bank in Moscow.

November 10–23, 1987
After receiving a letter from "B," the KGB loads the "An" dead-drop site with a package, but it is not cleared by "B." Hanssen then sends a handwritten letter from "B," which leads to a successful exchange operation at the "Park" dead-drop site.

February 4–9, 1988
The KGB and Hanssen communicate and carry out an exchange operation utilizing one of the new accommodation addresses the KGB had given "B" in November.

March 16, 1988-March 24, 1989
The KGB and Hanssen carry out numerous exchanges at several dead-drop spots with such code names as "Bob" and "Ellis" in and around Washington, D.C., and northern Virginia.

Some are completed without incident, while others take numerous attempts to complete because of interference from pedestrians near the drop sites.

Old-fashioned but effective call-out signals, such as a chalk marking on a pole or a perfectly placed Coke can on a park bench, boldly appear in places as public as the busy intersection of Q Street and Connecticut Avenue in Washington, D.C.

During this time, the KGB deposits an additional $50,000 in a Moscow bank account for "B."

April, 1989
The KGB presents several awards to KGB officers involved in the "B" operation.

August 17, 1989-May, 1990
Hanssen and the KGB continue with numerous exchange operations, sometimes up to one every two weeks. For his efforts Hanssen/"B" is rewarded with $55,000 in cash during one drop and a deposit of $50,000 into his account in Moscow on another occasion. By now, the KGB has received a total of nineteen diskettes of information from "B."

May 1990
"B" lets the KGB know that, as a result of a promotion, he will be traveling more and his access to materials will be limited.

June 24, 1990
Hanssen is reassigned from the Soviet Analytical Unit in the Intelligence Division to the Inspection Division at FBI Headquarters.

August 20, 1990
The KGB receives from "B" an envelope containing his twentieth diskette (D-20) at an accommodation site in the Eastern District of Virginia.

September 3, 1990
The KGB loads the "Flo" dead-drop site with a package containing $40,000 in cash and a KGB diskette with a letter.

Summer 1990
Hanssen meets Priscilla Galey, a stripper, at strip club 1819 in Washington D.C.

February 2, 1991
In response to an "emergency" call-out signal from "B," the KGB retrieves a package from "B" at the "Charlie" dead-drop site in the Eastern District of Virginia. The package contains a letter and the Diskette 21(D-21). On this occasion "B" passes detailed information to the KGB on FBI coverage of a particular suspected Soviet intelligence officer who was later executed.

February 18, 1991
The KGB loads the "Charlie" site with a package containing $10,000 in cash and a KGB diskette.

April 1991
Hanssen takes Priscilla Galey to Hong Kong.

April 15, 1991
In response to a call-out signal from "B," he and the KGB carry out an exchange operation at the "Doris" dead-drop site in the Eastern District of Virginia.

July 1991
"B" tells the KGB that he has at least five more years until retirement. Hanssen will be eligible for retirement from the FBI in 1996.

July 1, 1991
Hanssen returns from inspection staff duty to Intelligence Division at FBI Headquarters, in Washington, D.C. He is assigned to the INTD, DIV 5 CI-1B Unit responsible for KGB Line X.

July 15, 1991
After a call-out signal from "B," he and the KGB carry out an exchange operation at the "Ellis" dead-drop site in the Eastern District of Virginia.

August 19, 1991
After a call-out signal from "B," Hanssen and the KGB carry out an exchange operation at the "Flo" dead-drop site in the Eastern District of Virginia.

August 19, 1991
Attempted coup in Soviet Union.

August 21, 1991
Coup in Soviet Union is aborted.

October 7, 1991
After a call-out signal from "B," he and the KGB carry out an exchange operation at the "Flo" dead-drop site in the Eastern District of Virginia.

December 12, 1991
KGB receives an envelope from "B" at an accommodation address in Alexandria, Virginia.

December 16, 1991
On Monday December 16, 1991, "B" and the KGB carry out an exchange operation at the "Bob" dead-drop site in the Eastern District of Virginia.
    This is the last dead drop.

December 25, 1991
The USSR ceases to exist.

Prisiclla Galey goes back to Columbus; leaves Hanssen no note.

January 6, 1992
Hanssen serves as Chief of the National Security Threat List (NSTL) Unit in the Intelligence Division (renamed the National Security Division, or NSD, in 1993) at FBI Headquarters.

September 1992
Louis Freeh appointed director of FBI.

February 1993
Hanssen allegedly clashes with Kimberly Lichtenberg, a civilian FBI employee, after she walks out on a meeting.

February 21, 1994
Aldrich H. Ames is arrested for espionage.

April 1994
Hanssen temporarily assigned to the FBI's Washington Metropolitan Field Office (now called the Washington Field Office).

December 1994
Hanssen is reassigned to FBI Headquarters, in the Office of the Assistant Director for the National Security Division.

February 12, 1995
Hanssen is detailed to serve as FBI's senior representative to the Office of Foreign Missions of the United States Department of State (DOS/OFM).

December 18, 1996
FBI Special Agent Earl Edwin Pitts arrested and charged with espionage.

July 1997
Hanssen conducts first of ten searches of the FBI's collected computerized databases of classified and unclas-

sified investigative files and indices, called Automated Case Support (ACS) system, for the purpose of determining whether the FBI was aware of recent dead drops in Virginia or of operational activity at Foxstone Park.

1998
Hanssen works at the Office of Foreign Missions—State Department.

Fall, 1999
The Hanssens take a family trip to Rome, where Bonnie's brother is ordained as an Opus Dei priest by Pope John Paul II. Hanssen posts pictures of the trip on the Hanssen family Web page.

October 2000
The "B" file is given to the Bureau by a Soviet contact via the CIA. The FBI begins investigating Hanssen.

December 12, 2000
FBI surveillance observes Hanssen driving four times past the Foxstone Park sign on Creek Crossing Road in Vienna, Virginia. The Foxstone Park sign is the signal site associated with the "Ellis" dead-drop site, which was used from early on in the KGB's "B" operation.

FBI surveillance personnel observes Hanssen walking into a particular store at a shopping center near Foxstone Park at the same time as a known SVR officer is in front of the store.

January 9, 2001
At approximately 8:18 P.M., Hanssen drives past the Foxstone Park signal site, comes to a complete stop in front of it for approximately ten seconds, then drives away.

January 13, 2001
Hanssen is assigned to a newly created position in the Information Resources Division, at FBI Headquarters, in order that the FBI can more effectively monitor his daily activities without alerting him to their ongoing investigation of him.

January 23, 2001
Shortly before 6:00 P.M., Hanssen drives past the Foxstone Park signal site, comes to a rolling stop near it, and then drives away.

January 26, 2001
After 5:00 P.M., Hanssen drives past the Foxstone Park signal site, slowing down near it.

January 30, 2001
FBI searches Hanssen's Ford Taurus automobile.

February 5, 2001
FBI surveillance personnel observes Hanssen driving past the Foxstone Park signal site three times between approximately 5:37 P.M. and approximately 7:44 P.M.

February 12, 2001
FBI surveillance personnel checking the "Lewis" dead-drop site finds a package concealed at the site. FBI again searches Hanssen's Ford Taurus automobile.

February 14, 2001
Hanssen has lunch with Bob Hallman, former director of counterintelligence NSA, and businessman Victor Shamoff.

February 18, 2001
Hanssen arrested on espionage charges at a drop site in a Fairfax park.

February 20, 2001
Hanssen appears in U.S. District Court in Alexandria, Virginia, with his attorney Plato Cacheris and enters a plea of Not Guilty.

May 31, 2001
Hanssen arraigned in U.S. District Court in Alexandria, Virginia, after plea negotiations between the government and his attorney break down. He enters a plea of Not Guilty.

July 6, 2001
Hanssen pleads guilty to espionage charges.

Appendix B

Excerpts from

The Man Who Was Thursday

BY G. K. CHESTERTON

"You have evidently not heard of the latest development in our police system," replied the other. "I am not surprised by it. We are keeping it rather dark from the educated class because that class contains most of our enemies."

"He is certain that the scientific and artistic worlds are silently bound in a crusade against the family and the State. He has, therefore, formed a special corps of policemen, policemen who are also philosophers."

". . . the adventures may be mad, but the adventurer must be sane."

". . . was anyone crying?"

". . . you will have found out the truth of the last tree and the topmost cloud before the truth about me. You will understand the sea, and I shall be still a riddle; you shall know what the stars are, and not know what I am. Since the beginning of the world all men have hunted me like a wolf—kings and sages and poets and law-givers, all the churches and all the philosophies. But I have never been caught yet, and the skies will fall in the time I turn to bay. I have given them a good run for their money, and I will now."

"And I know there can be laughter on the secret face of God."

As he gazed, the great face grew to an awful size, grew larger than the colossal mask of Mennon, which had made him scream as a child. It grew larger and larger, filling the whole sky; then everything went black. Only in the blackness before it entirely destroyed his brain he seemed to hear a distant voice saying a commonplace toast that he had heard somewhere, "Can ye drink of the cup that I drink of?"

Appendix C

Hanssen's Web Stories

From: Robert P. Hanssen (hanssen@nova.org)
Subject: Bonnie (wife, enhib.true)
Newsgroups: alt.sex.stories
Date: 1998 / 06 / 05

It was only around four in the afternoon, and Bonnie still had plenty of time as she walked over and perched on the high wooden stool. She sat, freshly showered and still naked, in the warm light of the summer Chicago sun which streamed through her apartment's large bedroom window to her left. Refreshed from her shower after teaching second grade at the parish school, it was time to fix her hair. This was her habit, her little ritual after a shower, a time to herself to unwind and feel feminine, a time to feel the air on her skin and fix herself all pretty for Bob.

She was a good teacher. In a way it was like being an actress on stage each day, and Bonnie loved the little children too. People said she was the best lay teacher at Saint Anne's. She was even been better than some of the dedicated nuns teaching there. But Bonnie was no nun. She'd thought about it as a girl, but even the nuns agreed it was not her vocation. Bonnie wasn't the type to be locked up away from men.

Bonnie looked gorgeous. But unlike some beautiful

women, she saw only the "flaws." She had never felt secure about her appearance—"too curvy," she'd say. She couldn't believe that so many men found her so attractive. Perhaps it was because she'd developed late and still couldn't shake the chubby/gawky adolescent image she'd had of herself from childhood, but Bonnie couldn't fully internalize a feeling of beauty. Oh, she knew intellectually that she was chubby and gawky no more, but somehow she couldn't internalize it as a feeling. She was always insecure about the way she looked and needed constant reassurance. While she'd never admit it even to herself, the attentions of men gave her that reassurance. She liked being the center of a male audience even more than being the center of the children's. Still, she was married, and quite happily too, having mostly put her girlish flirting behind her. Well that was not exactly true. Bonnie periodically ran a few tests to check her flirting skills, but now it was nothing serious.

Happy today in her own modest little newlywed's apartment, a relatively inexpensive one because it was next to the "El" tracks, she was primping for Bob. She'd gotten married to Bob just last fall, and they'd moved to their first place together, a one-bedroom apartment on Winthrop Avenue on Chicago's north side. Bonnie looked in her mirror at her naked figure. She didn't like what she saw exactly. To her way of thinking she was too buxom, and she thought her hips too wide for her narrow waist and she was so "high waisted" compared to most girls. Still it seemed to work for men. Men called it being leggy. All it meant for Bonnie is that she could only wear petite sizes that never had quite enough room for her breasts, and she was always looking like she was about to pop out of her sundresses and so forth. Of course men never seemed to object to that look.

Bonnie ran a wide untangling comb through her long brown hair, thinking men had no taste. She wanted to be pencil skinny like those models in the women's fashion magazines. She looked more like those slutty buxom girls in "Playboy" magazine. But then she supposed men did go for that. After all the fraternity poll at college had voted her best legs on campus. She felt she had good legs.

At college, she'd found from experience that she loathed fraternity types generally. All they wanted to do was party and drink so they could feel-up girls and try to get in their pants. Bonnie detested it. She had even quit the most popular sorority on campus when they'd corrected her about still associating with her old friends who hadn't been asked to join. Bob hadn't been at all like the fraternity types. She'd met him during the summer at the hospital where they'd both worked. She'd been attracted to him from the first because of the way he'd treated the patients and he to her, it turned out, for the same reason.

Bonnie loved the afternoon sunlight. She was getting ready to go to dinner with her husband. Today was his birthday, and she wanted to look especially nice when he came home from school to pick her up. She wanted to surprise him. Bob was a dental student. He'd just started the clinical portion of the program. He'd scored in the top two percent on his national Dental Boards, and Bonnie was proud of him. She was going to show him a good time. Bonnie knew that a good time meant letting Bob show her off. Bob loved having men's tongues dangle out looking at his wife. So tonight Bonnie had vowed to herself to make that happen.

Bob was a leg man, Bonnie knew that, and Bonnie knew she had legs that could handle that. She'd learned shopping with him that no dress was too short. So, tonight Bonnie intended to do something she'd never allowed herself before, to push the limit in that direction— to please him. She'd hunted for and found a secret weapon—a dress, a special one for a special occasion. She'd found it in a store down on Rush Street. Bonnie was quite innocent and naive in many ways really, and had no idea it was a store catering to strippers. Bonnie hardly even knew about strippers. She'd just been out shopping and happened upon it and gone in. She was just amazed that a store carried so many sexy dresses.

The dress Bonnie'd gotten was short. Well, you'd have to say it was indecently short. It was made of a stretchy lycra mix and was jet black. She thought, when she'd bought it, that she'd have to be a bit careful, for it tended to ride up and there wasn't much up remaining upon which to ride, that is, below her crotch. When she'd tried it on though, she knew Bob would love it. She'd promised herself she'd keep it tugged down for decency.

Bonnie was playing with her hair, trying it different ways. She tried it up, she tried it down, and was about to settle for up when she noticed an odd movement out on the elevated train tracks across the alley from her bedroom window. She looked out the window quickly. "My God!" she thought. There were five workers standing leaning on their shovels looking at her. In a panic, she bounded from her stool across the bed to try to grab the shade and pull it down. Because the bed stood only a foot below the window and along the wall, this move necessitated her standing stark naked on the bed to reach up for the shade pull. She was there in full view of her suddenly bemused audience. Bonnie grasped the shade and pulled it down, with short-lived relief. The shade didn't catch and flapped up again. She sprung back a second time, her cute little bush fully exposed, and tried again. She yanked it down again and again it flapped open. Worse, this time instead the cord tied itself around the shade roller. Bonnie went up for it again. Bonnie's face was flushed. The men were looking right at her and she was totally naked. It seemed like forever while Bonnie stood in that window trying to untie it, but she got it. This time, a little calmer from the delay, she laughed at the smiles of her audience and closed it slowly and deliberately like putting the curtain down for them on a good show, and had even given them a little wave goodbye.

Then Bonnie collapsed panting from the excitement on her bed. Her heart was pounding. She felt galvanized as if by electricity from the experience. She realized she felt something else too. She felt aroused. "If only Bob were here," she thought, I'd show him even a better time than the workers on those tracks. She tried to shake it off.

It was a while, but Bonnie collected herself. Bonnie peeked out the shade. One of the men saw her and pointed her out, and she jumped back. She thought to herself, "Well that's it. I'll have to cover up." She went to her drawer and picked out a sheer black bra and delicate panties and slipped them on. She looked at herself in the mirror and was satisfied that at a distance no one would see more now than she'd showed at the beach on many occasions. Besides, she wasn't about to let some leering perverts ruin her reveries.

Bonnie pointedly didn't even look out the window when she opened the shade and resumed her perch on the stool. "Let them eat cake," she thought.

She'd decided that she wouldn't even really look to see if they were watching her at all, but she did and she knew they were, but somehow she actually managed truly to push them out of her mind, even as she tried on her dress about a half an hour later and decided that the bra would not do under it. She'd just slid the dress off again when she'd glanced out and seen that she still had an audience. It was then that she slid the bra off, stripping herself of her bra in full view of the window knowing they were watching, before wiggling into the dress again. Bonnie was starting to enjoy this.

In her heels, Bonnie bent over to look at herself from the rear. She thought, "Oops." She told herself she would have to remember not to bend over like that, but then removed her panties too. Bob was going to get his money's worth tonight. Bonnie slipped her blazer over her tight dress. Well if flashy was the mode of the day, she'd made it. There was about a half inch of tight dress below the blazer. The rest of the image said she still had good legs especially in the heels.

She looked again in the mirror and was pleased with the image. It spoke expensive-flashy not cheap-flashy, which was the effect she'd wanted. Using Bob's criteria she looked just right.

Bonnie glanced out the window. Her audience had departed. She figured, "Ah, for them dressed women are passe." Then she looked at her watch and thought, "Or maybe even letchers don't work overtime." But, God she was turned on. Luckily Bob would be here any minute, and dinner was going to be a fun way to test her outfit. Bonnie was even starting to think that maybe dancing after would be fun too.

From: Robert P. Hanssen
Subject: Bonnie (wife, exhib.true)
Newsgroups:alt.sex.stories
DATE:1998 /06/ 05

For years, I have sent nude pictures of Bonnie, my wife, to my close friend Jack. It began back in the Vietnam War years. Jack was over there and I was safe here at home. I'd tried to join the Navy as a dental student, but couldn't see well enough—too nearsighted, even though I was corrected with contact lenses to 20:20. That same problem kept me out of the draft. I felt bad. Here Jack was making all these sacrifices for my country and there was so little I could do to support him. Well, Bonnie was just 21 then and we'd just married. Jack had been my best man, and Bonnie was very pretty in those days, still is of course though she is older now. She was only 5'4" but shaped 34-23-36 with long brown hair and big brown doe eyes. Gorgeous would not be an overstatement. Pretty as she was, she made an excellent subject for photography. She tolerated posing nude for her husband too. Actually, she claimed to tolerate it, but when she got going posing nude she was like a spaniel to water. She put her soul into it, and the resulting pictures were electrifying.

Now, my hobby was always photography and Jack's was too. Even in our little apartment while I was in school, I had set up the bathroom with a board I could put on the tub to hold the enlarger above the trays and the waterbath below. It worked well, and I had this great supply of knockout pictures of Bonnie. Unfortunately, I had no one to whom I could appropriately show them. She wasn't about to let me show them either, artistic though they were! So one day, I sent a few off to Jack in one of my regular letters—he loved it. He got to see a whole side of Bonnie he never knew existed. Technically, I guess you could say he got to see all sides, crevices, and cracks of Bonnie, but that might be a bit crude. (Bonnie did a lot of posing with her legs spread. It turned her on. Bonnie was a great one for generating photos of "artistically posed girl with wet and gaping pussy." They all went to Jack.)

As I said, Jack was a photo enthusiast too, and eventually I ended up sending him negatives, and he was doing his own enlargements of them with the advanced photoclub equipment they had for recreation over there. He'd send large blow-ups back to augment my supply. We had a ball with it, and it kept his mind off the war and on home. Bonnie never wondered where I got the big prints. She isn't very scientific so didn't realize such prints don't come out of 8x10 trays. She just accepted it.

When I finally bought a house, I went to work and built a darkroom down in the basement and stored all of Bonnie's photos there. Bonnie was having problems getting pregnant then so there were no kids around to get into things like that. In the end, Jack came back from the war with a Bronze Star and other decorations to make a career as a military officer, visiting often when blowing through town enroute to some military assignment. Bonnie enjoyed him greatly and was as proud as I was of the risks he'd undertaken for his country. He'd survived where others hadn't.

Bonnie even posed for Jack occasionally, including some in a tight sweater that sizzled, but never nude, probably because Jack could never get up the guts to ask her. She did offer, on her own however, to let him come to our house any time he wanted to use the darkroom, knowing her pictures were stored there. This was at a time when Jack briefly had a place locally. I think, as she later maintained, that she simply forgot they were there, but you never know with Bonnie. When I found out she'd let him use the darkroom, I thought the time was ripe to let her know that Jack had seen the nudes of her. I wanted her to know he'd already seen her so she'd have nothing to be shy about in case she was ever tempted to pose for him, and this way I could blame it on her. So when she told me about it, I said, "Oh Bonnie, all your pictures were down there, and Jack told me he saw them." I added, "And thought they were great." She was greatly embarrassed, said she'd forgotten and all, but I was never completely convinced.

Jack had often dreamed of photographing Bonnie himself or of just seeing her nude in person. One never knows about the photography. It may come to pass, but we could do something about the seeing. That could be arranged. We initially made some forays in this regard where Jack watched Bonnie shower through the glass shower-stall door. I would talk to her as she showered, and he would look through the bathroom doorway from the darkened bedroom behind me. This was fun but not totally satisfying.

Our schemes progressed in this regard to the point of letting Jack see Bonnie and I having sex. The first time we did this Jack was visiting for a week. It was a warm fall. Each night, I'd leave the shade up a bit and leave our bedroom window open about six inches so Jack could come up and stand on a pre-positioned chair on our deck and look in while I had sex with her at night. That worked like a charm. He could see her walking around the room naked and I'd position her in different ways on the bed while fucking her so he'd get a good look of my cock going in and out or of her tits bouncing. By pure chance, to his good fortune, she even bent over right in front of the window once when he was there, and he got a good view of her pussy from about a foot away. It was great. I was dying watching. Our house backs on the woods so there was really little risk to him in doing this, but it still got old because of the chill and risk. It was then that technology came to the rescue.

At a security show, we bought subminiature video cameras designed for surveillance purposes. We bought two. One was no more than a little one-inch by one-quarter inch box with a low light CCD sensor that looks through a pinhole. The other was slightly larger; a high quality but very small lensed camera. We also bought video transmitter/receiver combinations, which could relay the signals from the cameras in place in our bedroom down to our den. After some experimentation (while Bonnie was out of town for a few days,) we set up a great system. Jack could sit in our den when he visited and see everything up in the bedroom. This proved no end of fun during his visits. Often now he'll stay five or six days doing things like research on his Ph.D. thesis at the various libraries here. On recent trips, in the mornings he sits and watches Bonnie on the large screen TV in our den as she gets showered and dressed. (Bonnie still fixes her hair while nude each morning.) At night, he watches the nightly sex scene or, once, Bonnie modeling her Victoria-Secret white nylons, sheer bra, and heels for me before we fucked. That really got us all going.

This whole business has been no end of fun. He can even tape the sessions on our VCR. Bonnie may be the only teacher at the elite girl's school where she works who is also a porn star! Of course, she doesn't know it. Well at least we think she doesn't know it. I do notice that when Jack visits she wants sex every night. Perhaps it is just that I'm always ready for it when he's here as you can imagine. Of course, Jack flatters her a lot too. He's still hoping some day for THE BIG modeling session, and women love to be flattered.

Anyway, Jack and I have our fun. Bonnie looks great. Jack and I love seeing her tits slapping together as she takes cock hard. She is now size 36 on top and she's kept her waist and hips trim. She's still a beautiful woman.